MW00586921

# CHUGACH STATE PARK

A Naturalist's Guide to
# CHUGACH STATE PARK

Jenny Zimmerman

To my parents -

Whose continual faith and support in their daughter, let her believe she could do anything.

©1993 by Jenny Zimmerman.

All rights reserved. No part of this book may be reproduced or transmitted in any form or by any means, electronic or mechanical, including photocopying, recording or by any information storage or retreival system, without the written permission of the publisher.

First Printing, 1993.

Cover photo:
View of Eklutna Lake and Bold Peak from the Twin Peaks area by Tom Soucek.

ISBN 0-9637309-0-8

Printed in Alaska at
A.T. Publishing and Printing, Inc.
8600 Hartzell Road
Anchorage, Alaska 99507

# Acknowledgments

One name may appear as author of a book, but there are so many others who assist in its creation.

First and foremost, I wish to thank the people at the Alaska Department of Natural Resources, Division of Parks & Recreation, and Chugach State Park for their continued support and encouragement in making this a reality. Many, many thanks to Jill Johnson, park ranger, for her support and suggestions; to Al Meiners, Superintendent of Chugach State Park; to Rolf Buzzell for the mining information; to Doug Reger for information and suggestions on the chapter on natives in Chugach; to Jo Antonson for assistance on park history; and thanks to Neil Johanson, Director, Division of Parks & Outdoor Recreation, Department of Natural Resources, State of Alaska, who understood the need for this book.

Many people and friends went out of their way to keep me headed in the right direction. A special thanks to Joe Kurtak, U.S. Bureau of Mines, without his support and direction, I could not have written the geology chapter, and would still be banging my head against a rock; to Lois Bettini, U.S. Forest Service, whose enthusiasm and support turned me into a budding entomologist; to Dan Fleming and Bruce Merrill at the Z. J. Loussac Library, Alaska Collection, who found information in places I would never have guessed existed; to Doug Fesler, who shared anecdotes of his days as a park ranger in Chugach; and to Jill Fredston, who salvaged a very difficult chapter — among other things — much thanks.

Then there are the behind the scene characters, those whose efforts turned an idea into reality. Words cannot express my gratitude to Mei Mei Evans who edited the text, doing all those things editors do to make things flow smoothly; many, many thanks to Joanna Mergler Mayer, for her undaunting work on the supplementary drawings while awaiting the imminent arrival of her baby boy; my gratitude to Dave Thorp, whose magic fingers on the computer gave this book life; and thanks to Ron Engstrom for his map-making genius. To anyone I might have missed, my thanks for your help on this book.

No undertaking of this length and magnitude can be done without the support of one's immediate family. My husband, John Bauman, has endured every draft, every word change, and my fluctuating state of high anxiety as the book neared completion, all with his usual patience and warm assurances — for that I am eternally grateful.

It was not possible to include all the information available in a book of this size; I leave that for others to do. As for the errors — many eyes have travelled the pages of this book looking for errors and making corrections, any of the remaining mistakes are strictly my own.

Jenny Zimmerman

# Picture Credits

Most of the illustrations in this book have come from other publications, and are reprinted with permission. When several drawings come from a single source, a set of initials corresponding to the citation will be used, and, if applicable, a photo identification number. When one or two pictures are used, then they will be credited individually.

Alaska State Library, Juneau, Alaska. Key: ASL

Anchorage Museum of History and Art, Archives, 121 West 7th Ave., Anchorage, Alaska, 99501. Key: AMHA

Columbia University Press: permission to reprint drawings of lichens from *American Arctic Lichens 1. Macrolichens* by John W. Thomson. Key: CUP

Cynthia Cassell, supplementary drawings. KEY: CC

Doubleday & Company: reprinted illustrations of birds from *Illustrated Encyclopedia of American Birds* by Leon A. Hausman from original copyright 1947. Key: AMB

HarperCollins Publishers Inc.: permission to reproduce drawings from *Complete Guide to North American Wildlife* by Jay Ellis Ransom. Illustrations copyrighted 1981 by Harper & Row, Publishers, Inc. Key: HCP

Holt, Rinehart & Winston: permission to reprint insect drawings from *An Introduction to the Study of Insects* by Donald R. Borror and Dwight M. DeLong. KEY: HRW

Houghton Mifflin Company: permission to reprint drawings of fishes from *A Guide to Pacific Coast Fishes of North America from the Gulf of Alaska to Baja California* by William N. Eschmeyer et al. KEY: HMC

Joanna Mergler Mayer, supplementary drawings. Key: JMM

Little Brown & Company: permission to reprint drawings from *A Guide to Observing Insect Lives* by Donald W. Stokes. KEY: LBC

McGraw-Hill Publishing Company: permission to reprint drawings from *Introduction to Bryology* by W.B. Schofield. Key: MCP

Random House Incorporated: permission to reprint insect drawings from *The Audobon Society Field Guide to North American Insects and Spiders* by Lorus and Margery Milne. KEY: RHI

Simon & Schuster: permission to reprint drawings of mushrooms from *Collecting & Studying Mushrooms, Toadstools, and Fungi* by Alan Major. Key: SIM

Stanford University Press: permission to reprint drawings of plants from *Flora of Alaska and Neighboring Territories*, by Eric Hulten. Key: SUP

United States Department of Agriculture: drawings from *Alaska Trees & Shrubs* by Leslie A. Viereck & Elbert L. Little (reprinted by University of Alaska Press). KEY: USDA

University of Alaska Fairbanks, Archives, Alaska and Polar Regions Dept., Elmer E. Rasmuson Library, John M Brooks Collection Key: UAF

University of Toronto Press: permission to reprint the drawing of a woodfrog from *Introduction to Canadian Amphibians and Reptiles* by Francis R. Cook. Key: UTP

U.S. Geological Survey. Key: USGS

John Wiley & Sons, Inc.: permission to reprint mammal drawings from *Mammals of North America*, volumes 1 & 2, by Raymond E. Hall. Key: JWS

# Table of Contents

**Part Three**
**Natural History of Chugach State Park**

We need another and a wiser and perhaps a more mystical concept of animals. Remote from universal nature, and living by complicated artifice, man in civilization surveys the creature through the glass of his knowledge and sees thereby a feather magnified and the whole image in distortion. We patronize them for their incompleteness, for their tragic fate of having taken form so far below ourselves. And there in we err, and err greatly. For the animal shall not be measured by man. In a world older and more complete than ours they move finished and complete, gifted with extensions of the senses we have lost or never attained, living by voices we shall never hear. They are not brethren, they are not underlings; they are other nations, caught with ourselves in the net of life and time, fellow prisoners of the splendor and travail of the earth.

Henry Beston  *The Outermost House* (1928)


The wilderness has never been thought of as a museum in which the treasures of the natural world are preserved, against which man can measure himself and see how human habitation alters his environment.

Ann Zwinger  *Land Above the Trees* (1972)


Touch the earth, love the earth, honour the earth, her plains, her valleys, her hills, and her seas; rest your spirit in her solitary places. For the gifts of life are the earth's and they are given to all.

Henry Beston  *The Outermost House* (1928)


The beauty and genius of a work of art may be reconceived, though its first material expression be destroyed; a vanished harmony may yet again inspire the composer; but when the last individual of a race of living things breathes no more, another heaven and another earth must pass before such a one can be again.

William Beebe  *The Bird: Its Form and Function* (1906)


Ability to see the cultural value of wilderness boils down, in the last analysis, to a question of intellectual humility.

Aldo Leopold  *A Sand County Almanac* (1949)

Part One

# CHUGACH STATE PARK

**an introduction**

# CHAPTER ONE

# THE SETTING

Stretching almost three hundred miles east toward Canada, the Chugach Mountains are bordered on the on the north by the Matanuska River and the Copper Basin plateau, on the east by the St. Elias Mountains, on the south by Prince William Sound and Turnagain Arm, and on the west — nestled in the crook of the Alaska Range — by Cook Inlet. The mountains influence weather in southcentral Alaska by blocking the intense storms that blow in from the North Pacific. Their snow and ice provide a clean and abundant source of water, and they are an ever-present reminder of a wilderness heritage. These mountains also form the core of one of the largest state parks in the nation — the half million acre Chugach State Park.

A vast wilderness of rugged mountains and deep U-shaped valleys, Chugach State Park lies only seven miles from downtown Anchorage, Alaska's largest metropolitan area. Tidal flats and forests, rivers and lakes, alpine tundra and glaciated peaks form the warp and woof of the park's wild tapestry.

The Chugach Mountains are the second highest mountain range in the state, and the highest coastal range in the world. Mount Marcus Baker at 13,176 feet is the highest peak in the entire Chugach Mountain range. The single most striking visual feature of Chugach State Park is its vertical relief from sea level.

Along Turnagain Arm the mountains plunge a precipitous 5000 feet to the tidal currents below. On the west and north, the mountains rise up from the glacial moraine along Knik Arm and Knik River to the summit of striking Pioneer Peak, whose face almost equals the relief of the Grand Teton in Wyoming.

Glaciers are one of the most dynamic features of the park. Thousands of years ago during the Pleistocene, what is now the park was completely glaciated; today, approximately 10% of Chugach State Park is still covered by glaciers. Although now in retreat, these ancient ice masses continue to play a significant role in the character of the park.

Facing page: The Chugach Mountains rise above Anchorage — Alaska's largest city
(John W. Warden)

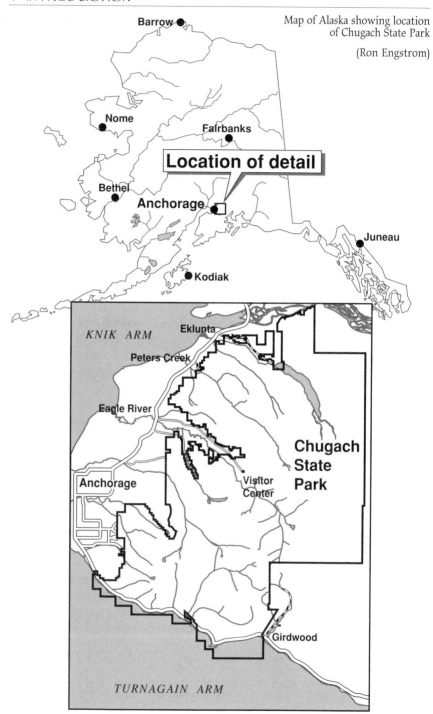

Map of Alaska showing location
of Chugach State Park

(Ron Engstrom)

The history of human interaction with this land, as well as a rich diversity of plant and animal life, with all their seasonal variations, contribute to a unique wilderness ecosystem. And there is more, much more, awaiting both the casual and the long-term visitor. This book is intended to aquaint you with some of the fascinating features of Chugach State Park.

**What's in a name?**
**Chugatz, or is it Chugatch? No, maybe it's Chugaz. No, no, the Russians said, Tchougatskoi.**

**Chugach is the tribal name for the Eskimos who once inhabited the Upper Cook Inlet region. The name was first recorded by the Russians as "Chugatz" and "Tchougatskoi." It was later spelled "chugatz" or "chugaz" according to the European interpretation of the Eskimo pronunciation. In 1898, Admiral W.R. Abercrombie gave it the spelling "chugatch," which he also applied to the mountains. At some point the "t" was dropped and the current spelling of "Chugach" was retained.**

**BORETIDE**
The Cook Inlet estuary has tidal fluxes which are second only to those of the Bay of Fundy in Nova Scotia, Canada. Chugach State Park is embraced by two arms of the giant Cook Inlet tidal estuary - Turnagain Arm to the southeast, and Knik Arm to the north. Extending 43 miles east from Anchorage, Turnagain Arm is much narrower than the broad 45-mile long Knik Arm. Turnagain is so long and narrow that water continues flowing out even after the tide has reversed direction.

Turnagain's tidal flux is the most pronounced in Cook Inlet,which has a large tidal range of 35 foot + tides. The incoming tide often becomes a churning wall of water as it advances up the Arm. This is the only location in the United States where tidal bores regularly occur, and it is the most visible bore anywhere in the Western Hemisphere.

**WHY A BORE TIDE IN TURNAGAIN ARM?**
Turnagain Arm is uniquely suited for the formation of bore tides as it was once a glacially-gouged fjord with a depth in excess of 1,000 feet. Today sediments have almost completely filled the Arm, creating a shallow basin. By comparison to the rest of Cook Inlet, Turnagain Arm is narrow and shallow with a gentle slope. This forces the incoming tide to form a tidal flood with an abrupt edge that overrides the outgoing flood.

At low tide Turnagain Arm appears to be a network of braided rivers. Bores running up these river channels constantly change depending on the depth and width of the channel. The more shallow or narrow a channel, the more pronounced the bore. If a particular channel widens or deepens, a bore may disappear altogether. The size and speed of the tidal bores in Turnagain Arm has diminished since the 1964 earthquake, when the bottom subsided — creating deeper channels and thus, smaller bores.

Bore tides are often thought to be a single wall of water moving up a basin, but this is not the case. A tidal bore usually appears as an undulating swell, continually changing character depending upon the configuration of the basin bottom. It becomes most dramatic when the incoming wave overrides the outgoing stream. Winds blowing from Portage toward Anchorage, in the direction of the incoming tide, can enhance the size of the wall.

Bores along Turnagain Arm range from six inches to six feet high, and travel at speeds of 10 to 15 miles per hour. Large bores can be heard rumbling up the Arm like a distant train. Tidal bores occur just after low tide and can be seen almost every day in Turnagain Arm. The size will depend on the range of tide; the most dramatic tidal bores occur during times of extreme minus tides (between -2.0 to -5.5 feet) and a full or new moon. Tide charts can assist in planning the best time to see a tidal bore.

Bore tides can usually be viewed from the Seward Highway between McHugh Creek and Indian, approximately two hours after the predicted low tide in Anchorage. As the bottom configuration changes, the time it takes the bore to pass a specific area will also change. Knik Arm also has bore tides, but they are smaller, less dramatic, and more difficult to observe. Check with Chugach State Park rangers for summer programs on tidal bores.

Facing page: View of a boretide from Bird Ridge (Todd Frankiewicz)

# CHAPTER TWO

# CLIMATE AND WEATHER

Alaska's climate is as wild as the country. Situated north of the tempestuous Gulf of Alaska, Chugach State Park is in a transition zone between the cold, dry continental climate of the Alaskan interior and the warm, wet maritime climate of southeast Alaska. Weather here tends to oscillate between the two extremes.

## Latitude and Slope Angle

Chugach State Park sits at about 61° N latitude. The tilt in the earth's axis causes drastic changes in day length from winter to summer. The longest day of the year is June 21$^{st}$, summer solstice, which has 19 hours, 21 minutes of sunlight. The shortest day is December 21$^{st}$, with only 5 hours, 28 minutes of sunlight.

Unlike more equatorial latitudes, the northern sun does not suddenly drop down below the horizon enveloping the world in darkness. Rather the earth's tilt causes the sun to move across the sky at a very low angle, providing long periods of dawn and dusk both in summer and winter, giving the illusion of longer periods of daylight than we actually receive.

In this northern mountain range the sun hits the ground at an oblique, or low, angle even in summer, resulting in less heating by the sun than at more southerly latitudes. With the low angle of the sun, slope angle is extremely important. The south-facing slopes are warmer, drier and usually have different flora than the colder, darker north-facing slopes. Occasionally, south-facing inclines are snow-free in winter, exposing vegetation for Dall sheep to browse.

## Annual Weather Patterns

The park's northern latitude and mountainous terrain interact to produce local weather patterns. The mountains affect patterns of precipitation around the park. They act as barriers to air flow by creating different conditions on the windward and leeward sides. Moist, warm air blowing northwest off the Gulf of Alaska is forced up the south side of the Chugach Mountains, slowing the movement of fronts. As a result clouds condense and a majority of the precipitation is deposited on the southeast portion of the park along Turnagain Arm, near Girdwood. The leeward side, to the north near Eklutna, sits in a

Facing page: High Cirrus clouds over Cook Inlet (Doug Fesler)

rainshadow.   It receives considerably less precipitation since most of the moisture has already been squeezed out.

Annual precipitation in the park varies depending on locale.   The southeast corner near Girdwood receives about 160 inches annually, averaging 5 inches of rain per month during the summer.   West and north, the weather becomes drier.   The rainshadow effect of the Chugach Mountains reduces rainfall around the Eklutna area to about 1.4 inches per month in summer; Eklutna may receive as little as 12 inches of precipitation annually, the majority of which falls in July, August, and September.   June is the driest month throughout the park, although March, April, and May have the clearest skies.

Snow can fall during any month of the year, although most snowfall occurs between November and February.   Snowfall varies from about 70 inches at Anchorage, to 39 inches at Eklutna Lake.   Girdwood receives the greatest snowfall with approximately 150 inches a winter.   Snow begins falling in earnest  in the park by September, and finally leaves the higher elevations by June.

Cumulus clouds up Powerline Pass (Doug Fesler)

## Air Temperature

Temperatures in the park vary from highs in the summer of 85°F to lows of - 50°F. The Southeast portion of the park is the warmest, with a mean annual temperature of 45° F. The Anchorage-Peters Creek-Eklutna periphery has a mean annual temperature of 42°F.

Frost may occur at any time of the year, but freeze-up doesn't occur until mid-October. Snow can begin to disappear as early mid-March at lower elevations. In years of heavy snow and extreme cold, snow may remain on the ground as late as June in areas at or above treeline. The Chugach mountains are generally free of permafrost.

The mountains often experience inversions, especially in winter, when dense, cold air sinks into the valleys and the Anchorage bowl. A warm front pushing in off the Gulf may override the colder air creating a distinct temperature difference. A visitor getting out at Glen Alps may enter a balmy, above-freezing world, a far cry from the frozen city below.

**Table 1**          **Air Temperature**

| Daily Temperature in Degrees F | Alyeska (el. 250') | Glen Alps (el. 2260') | Eagle River VC (el. 630') | Eklutna (el. 40') |
|---|---|---|---|---|
| January Max. | 25.0° | 29.3° | 23.6° | 17.6° |
| January Min. | 13.6 | 16.6 | 9.2 | 0.9 |
| March Max. | 34.8 | 31.9 | 40.9 | 33.8 |
| March Min. | 19.3 | 16.8 | 19.9 | 11.7 |
| May Max. | 51.9 | 46.5 | 58.1 | 58.9 |
| May Min. | 35.0 | 33.5 | 36.0 | 35.5 |
| July Max. | 64.3 | 58.0 | 68.0 | 68.9 |
| July Min. | 47.2 | 44.5 | 47.4 | 47.0 |
| September Max. | 54.0 | 49.1 | 57.9 | 55.7 |
| September Min. | 38.3 | 36.0 | 36.3 | 36.9 |
| November Max. | 31.0 | 29.8 | 28.3 | 26.3 |
| November Min. | 18.6 | 16.3 | 12.6 | 11.3 |
| **Temperature Extremes in F** | | | | |
| Record High | 88.0 | 76.0 | 83.0 | 92.0 |
| Month/Year | 7/72 | 6/86 | 6/90 | 6/53 |
| Record Low | -30.0 | -37.0 | -27.0 | -44.0 |
| Month/Year | 1/89 | 1/89 | 1/82 | 1/75 |

(Data from Arctic Environmental Information and Data Center, University of Alaska: *Climatological Summary* for period 1963-87, and Climatological Updates for 1988-90.)

## Winds

Hurricane-force winds occasionally blow through the mountains of Chugach State Park, hitting Anchorage with devastating effects. The most severe winds occur annually during the winter months, when the water in the Gulf is warmer than the snow-covered land — an effect caused by the Chugach Mountains, which protrude up into the atmosphere, diverting and obstructing air flow. Air pushing against the windward side of a mountain gets compressed; following the path of least resistance, it then pours over passes and down mountain valleys. The low-lying foliage of the alpine tundra produces little drag on the wind, which can reach high speeds only a few feet above ground.

Winds come from the southeast and travel across the Chugach mountains down through the passes and valleys. Usually, a surface layer of cold air will act as a buffer for these southeast winds, deflecting them away from Anchorage. However, if the cold air layer is absent, the fierce winds will scour the valleys of Rabbit Creek, Ship Creek, Eagle River, Peters Creek, and the North and South Forks of Campbell Creek. The winds increase speed as they are constricted into the valleys. A windspeed of 30 mph can easily intensify to over 100 mph depending on the configuration of the valley. As the winds flow down the open forested slopes of the park they begin to dissipate. Winds of 100 mph in the mountains may be clocked at only 40 mph by the time they hit Anchorage.

Part TWO

# THE PARK IN TIME

# CHAPTER THREE

# ORIGIN OF THE ROCKS

**SETTING THE STAGE**

Contrary to appearances, Alaska is not a solid block of land. It is the geologic dumping ground for a rock conveyor belt running thousands of miles up the west coast of North America. As many as 50 separate rock masses make up the state of Alaska, most of which originated hundreds or thousands of miles to the south. Over millions of years these landmasses travelled north, colliding with what is now the northwestern corner of North America. The mountains of Chugach State Park are a recent chapter of this geologic odyssey.

**Continents Adrift**

The earth is a dynamic, ever-changing sphere. Throughout geologic time our planet's surface has undergone dramatic and often violent changes. Land-masses have collided and pulled apart. Continents once in the lush tropics have slowly moved toward higher latitudes. Seas have appeared and disappeared. Mountains were formed, and then crumbled away. Glaciers continually advanced and retreated.

The theory of continental drift, or plate tectonics, has been around for almost 90 years, yet the idea has gained acceptance only within the past two decades. A diversity of disciplines including marine geology, paleobotany, physics, and geography have helped bring together evidence of the earth's mobile crust. Scientists have studied the geometric matchup of continents, the magnetic orientation of rock crystals, localized fossil evidence on distant continents, and seafloor spreading to better understand how and why plates move.

Most continents are now thought to have been part of an ancient supercontinent called Pangea - Greek for all Earth - formed by the collision of continental landmasses some 260 million years ago. The North American landmass began to pull away from Europe, Asia and Africa in fits and starts, eventually colliding with the Pacific plate. The entire western coast, from Baja to Alaska, was assembled piece by piece from the Pacific plate. It has taken the last 200 million years to build the present-day mountainous west coast of North America.

Facing page: Siltstone of the McHugh Complex along the Seward Highway (Jenny Zimmerman)

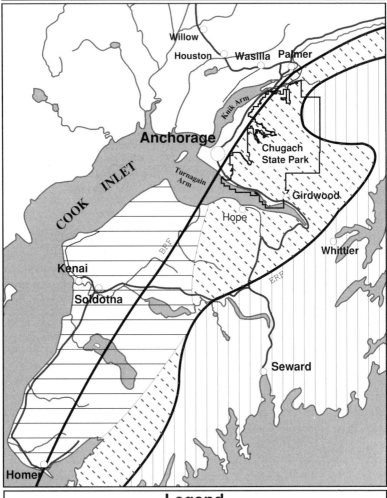

# Distribution and geologic framework of Chugach terrane

**Legend**

Shallow marine deposits (Neogene)

Melange subterrane of the Chugach terrane (Cretaceous)

Flysch subterrane of the Chugach terrane (Late Cretaceous)

BRF   BORDER RANGES FAULT    ERF   EAGLE RIVER FAULT

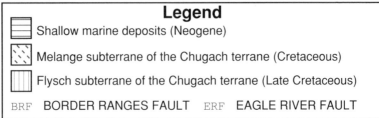

Distribution and geologic framework of the Chugach Terrane (Ron Engstrom)

Rock is continually being added to the North American continent through upwelling of molten rock and the subduction of continental plates. The frequent shaking and rumbling of earthquakes from California to Alaska are the result of the Pacific plate slowly sliding its way northward. The plate grinds endlessly into the crook of southcentral Alaska, where it dives under the American plate, forming the 5-mile deep Aleutian Trench.

## Alaska and Plate Tectonics

Alaska is made up of blocks of foreign rock, or *terranes,* shoved against each other by the northward movement of the Pacific plate. Terranes are structurally and geologically distinct blocks of seamounts, island arcs, oceanic ridges, and oceanic crust. This process of adding new material to continental edges is called *accretion.* Both fossils and magnetic information in the rock provide clues which scientists use to determine a rock's origin prior to its arrival in Alaska. Most continents are built up as sediments which are scraped off the top of a plate as it is sucked beneath the continent. In Alaska, however, blocks have piled up next to each other row after row, due, in part, to the relatively shallow angle of the Aleutian trench.

## THE STORY OF THE CHUGACH TERRANE

Compared to the 4.6 billion year history of the earth, the Chugach Mountains are a geologically young jumble of rock whose story has not been easy to decipher. Understanding the story of the rocks is like piecing together clues in a detective story. Scientists can only speculate as to what our earth was like 100 or 300 million, or even 12,000 years ago, but fossil evidence and magnetism provide important clues. What follows is a scenario based on current knowledge of the earth's geology.

The Chugach Mountains are part of a 1,000-mile belt of rock called the Chugach Terrane. The Chugach Terrane arcs from Kodiak Island south of Cook Inlet, up through the Kenai Mountains across Turnagain Arm, curving past Palmer then eastward toward the Wrangell Mountains. This broad band, almost 65 miles across at its widest point, is composed of oceanic crust, volcanics, and sediments. The terrane is composed of two rock units - the McHugh Complex and the Valdez Group.

## Carboniferous Beginnings

In the early Carboniferous some 300 million years ago, there was no Alaskan landmass. The earth's landmasses were creeping on a collision course to form the single continent of Pangea. The worldwide climate was warm and tropical, and the low-lying land was surrounded by shallow seas.

The end of the Carboniferous saw the beginnings of the McHugh Complex. During this time life began in the ancient tropical seas. Fusilinids, a unicellular plankton swimming the shallow seas around Pangea, were deposited by the billions. Their calcium carbonate skeletons drifted down onto the seafloor. They are now found as fossils scattered in the limestone deposits and marble blocks of the McHugh Complex.

## The Triassic and Jurassic Periods

The Valdez Group formed when sub-marine runoff from rivers and streams was swept away by deep ocean currents. Flowing down off continental shelves, the sediments came to rest on the deep-sea basin floor as layered sediments, or turbidites.

Dinosaurs dominated the earth as layers of the siliceous skeletons of minute marine organisms called radiolarians, along with silt and mud of the McHugh Complex, were deposited on the floor of shallow Jurassic seas.

## The Violent Cretaceous

In the early Cretaceous Period approximately 130 million years ago, there was a period of intense mountain building. The Border Ranges Trench formed close to 40° North latitude when the Superterrane composed of the Wrangellia, Peninsular, and Alexander terranes collided with North America. A warm global climate raised the sea level to an all-time high with little or no polar ice

Most of the west coast of North America had still not arrived at its present location, but accretion was slowly proceeding. From 100 to 65 million years ago, as the Chugach Terrane rode northward on the Pacific plate, the rocks from the Valdez Group were subducted into the Border Ranges Trench. The heat and pressure squeezed out gold-carrying silica-rich fluids, injecting them into fractures in the rock to form quartz veins. The two components of the Chugach Terrane - the Valdez Group and the McHugh Complex - united in the late Cretaceous under the ocean as they slowly moved northward from around 40° N latitude near present-day Oregon. The end of the Cretaceous saw the end of intensive mountain building.

## Tertiary Period

At the beginning of the Tertiary, the Pacific plate began to slowly rotate counterclockwise from its northerly direction. This created more side-slipping along the west coast of North America and an increase in velocity as the plate rotated to its present direction, moving northwest into the developing Aleutian Trench.

About 65 million years ago, the bulk of the Chugach Terrane collided with the Peninsular and Wrangellia Terranes. As the terranes moved northward they occasionally left pieces clinging to the continent. The Chugach Terrane continued to accrete along the Border Ranges Trench. As it moved imperceptibly northward, a chunk of Chugach Terrane remained on Vancouver Island in British Columbia, as well as near Sitka, Alaska. Slowly, the terrane stretched and bent into its current configuration.

About 40 million years ago, the Chugach Terrane emerged as it collided with the continental blocks. The McHugh Complex was pushed up and onto the Valdez Group. As subduction continued, there was a rapid uplifting of the mountains. This uplift continued, producing the metamorphic rock of the Valdez Group.

## QUATERNARY PERIOD

### Pleistocene Glaciation
The Quaternary Period, in which we now live, was ushered in about 2 million years ago with extremely cool temperatures and high precipitation. About 600,000 years ago, the first of several major periods of glaciation marked the beginning of the Pleistocene Epoch. Over 80% of Pleistocene glaciation occurred in the Northern Hemisphere where glaciers expanded and advanced down the mountains into the lowlands of Europe and North America. It was the beginning of the Ice Age.

Each glaciation was named for its southernmost North American advance. There is little evidence of the early major glaciations - the Nebraska, the Kansas, or the Illinois - other than remnants of their terminal moraines.  Only the Wisconsin Ice Age left obvious evidence of its passage in the Chugach area, while obliterating most traces of previous ice ages. Short intervening warm phases caused the glaciers to retreat before yet another ice age began; each succeeding glaciation was less extensive than the last.

Glaciation in Alaska has been primarily alpine, with glaciers originating in the mountains and flowing down into the valleys and lowlands. With continued cold and snow, glaciers expanded downward until they reached a climatic equilibrium - where melting equaled accumulation. Glaciation was more intense on the coastal side of the mountains than in the interior of Alaska. During the height of Pleistocene glaciation, over half of Alaska was covered with glaciers. Today, only about 5 % of the state is glaciated.

Moraine deposits indicate there may have been as many as six glacial advances within the Cook Inlet basin. Local climatic patterns fluctuated, creating variances from global weather patterns. Geologists understand the sequence, but have difficulty aging the early advances.

The earliest pre-Wisconsin glacial advance, the *Mount Susitna*, filled Cook Inlet basin with over 4,000 feet of ice. The massive glacier system, originating in the Alaska Range, extended down the Susitna river basin and on down Cook Inlet. Smaller tributary lobes from the Knik and Matanuska glaciers, and Turnagain Arm converged over Anchorage where they coalesced with the massive Susitna lobe before receding back into the mountains. Evidence of the glacier's passing is round-shouldered Mount Susitna across Cook Inlet from Anchorage.

The *Caribou Hills* glacial advance followed the Susitna, again covering the floor of the Cook Inlet basin. This glaciation is named for a series of hills at the southern end of the Kenai Peninsula. Lateral moraines, which were formed about 200,000 years ago to an elevation of around 3,000 feet, are lower than those from the *Susitna* glaciation.

During the *Eklutna* glacial advance there was considerable glaciation of ridges and spurs at the 2,000 to 2,800 foot level along the front of the Chugach Mountains. The rounded knob of Near Point was formed as glacial ice covered Cook Inlet. Distinctive lateral moraines occur along the west end of the Chugach Mountains, extending - with elevations 2350 and 2700 feet - from the Eklutna River valley to Turnagain Arm. This glacial advance formed the current drainage system in Chugach State Park and ended about 130,000 years ago.

The Wisconsin Ice Age, the last major North American glaciation, began 70,000 years ago. Ice appears to have persisted in the Chugach Mountains throughout most of this period. The more recent *Knik* glacial advance extended into the Cook Inlet Basin, coalescing one final time. Ice reached heights of 700 to 2400 feet in the lowlands. Ice in the Rabbit Creek Valley was over 800 feet thick before a brief nonglacial period began about 52,000 years ago.

The *Naptowne* glacial advance produced the most conspicuous and most continuous glacial sculpting in Cook Inlet. The Naptowne, named for a small community on the Kenai Peninsula, began 47,000 years ago, reaching its maximum 14,000 years ago. During the Naptowne, the Knik-Matanuska glacial lobe produced the Elmendorf moraine complex which overlies the Bootlegger Cove Formation. The Bootlegger Cove Formation resulted from the layering of glacial silt, sand, and clay first laid down over 40,000 years ago. Fluctuating sea levels and deposition of freshwater alluvial fans from glacial streams, respectively covered the Anchorage bowl on a number of occasions during the Pleistocene.

A series of lateral moraines along the front of the Chugach Mountains east of Anchorage were exposed 11,000 to 14,000 years ago. These moraines were formed over tens of thousands of years as glaciers retreated and advanced with changes in climate. The poorly developed Ski Bowl lateral moraine, named for the ski area up Arctic Valley, is the highest lateral moraine on the east side of the basin. The *Naptowne* advance ended 9,500 years ago and was followed by rapid glacial retreat.

## Moraines Today

Turnagain Arm produced several lobes which feathered out west of its mouth onto the Kenai Peninsula. The Bird Creek lateral moraine is close to the water's edge near Indian, Bird, and Penguin Creeks but rises as it approaches Girdwood. Evidence of the moraine can be viewed from Bird Ridge, looking down into Bird and Penguin valleys. The moraine paralleling the Seward Highway is not penetrated by Penguin Creek, but instead forces the creek to take a sharp 90° turn north until it joins with Bird Creek.

Potter Creek moraine extends in a series of lateral moraines along the north side of the mouth of Turnagain Arm above Potter Section House. It arcs north along the front of the Chugach Mountains above Anchorage, where it runs into the Fort Richardson moraine near Hillside Drive at Rabbit Creek. O'Malley Road crosses several lateral moraines on its way up to the Park.

Aerial view of the Twin Peaks area of Chugach State Park showing the highest levels of Eklutna, Knik, and Naptowne glaciations. (R.G. Updike)

The highest lateral moraines of three major glaciations are visible on the slopes of Pioneer and Twin Peaks. Eklutna, Knik, and Naptowne glaciations form prominent benches as seen in the photograph on page 21. The Border Ranges Fault cuts below Twin Peaks which are composed of Chugach Terrane and the downslope rocks of the Peninsular Terrane.

Glacial erratics, large boulders left by receding glaciers, are reminders of the glaciers' passage. A couple hundred yards up the Falls Creek trail, a large six-foot erratic boulder sits off on the right hand side of the trail. On the glaciated slopes of Near Point, erratics lie scattered in disarray.

**The Holocene Epoch, or Recent Times**
Although climatic fluctuations have occurred right up to the present, they have lacked the intensity and duration of the preceding 60,000 years. With a general warming of the global climate, the Ice Age came to a close about 12,000 to 14,000 years ago. The melting glacial ice again raised sea levels, inundating the Turnagain Arm area as far as Bird Point. This resulted in another layer on the Bootlegger Cove Formation. Then the climate cooled briefly and the Turnagain Arm ice lobe advanced to within a mile of Resurrection Creek on the south shore of the Arm. Around 10,000 years ago, the Turnagain Arm ice retreated once again, this time to the Girdwood area, establishing the near-modern sea level.

A "thermal maximum" occurred around 6,000-7,000 years ago when glaciers retreated to their present size or smaller. Several Little Ice Ages, known as the Alaskan glacial advance, have occurred over the past 6,000 years. The last Little Ice Age, between 1500 and 1920, sent glaciers advancing yet again. When Europeans first arrived in Alaska in the 1700's, glaciers had expanded well beyond their present limits. Then around the early nineteenth century, the climate warmed and glaciers once again retreated - as they continue to do to this day.

Raven Glacier (Steve Johnson)

# CHAPTER FOUR

# SHAPING THE CHUGACH LANDSCAPE

## Bedrock Geology

An ability to read the story of the rocks creates an intimate familiarity with a place. With some knowledge and a little practice, even an untrained observer can identify the principal bedrock formations of Chugach State Park. The rock type, the geographic location within the park, and its structure aid in identification.

The Valdez Group and the McHugh Complex are the two rock groups of the Chugach Terrane. The **Valdez Group** is composed of weakly metamorphosed sediments called flysch which eroded from ancient mountain ranges.

Above: Inoceramus fossils in rock of the Valdez Group, Late Cretaceous (Jenny Zimmerman)
Facing page: Overlooking Raven Glacier near Crow Pass — Eagle River Trail (Steve Johnson)

Worm Burrows in sedimentary rock of the Valdez Group, Late Cretaceous (Jenny Zimmerman)

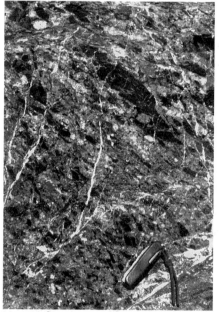

Metaconglomerate sandstone of the McHugh Complex (Jenny Zimmerman)

Flysch consists primarily of graywacke and argillite deposited in seawater. Turbidites are a common form of sediment deposition. Larger particles settled out first with finer sediments slowly settling afterwards. Turbidites can be seen at Mile 105.5 of the Seward Highway .5 miles before Falls Creek. [Caution: No parking available.]

Studies suggest these rocks were deposited about 25° south of their present location before they crashed into North America in the late Cretaceous. The age of the rocks is determined by rare occurrences of a late Cretaceous mollusk-like fossil of the genus **Inoceramus**. The rarity of fossils is probably due to deepwater deposition of the sediments. There are deformed examples of this rare fossil embedded in slate approximately one mile beyond Bird Creek, around Mile 100 of the Seward Highway. The rocks along the shoreline occasionally reveal fossil shells and worm burrows preserved in the ancient sediments.

The **McHugh Complex** is composed of a melange of discontinuous, weakly metamorphosed blocks and pieces of rock mixed with fine grained sediments. This melange has been metamorphosed and sheared while it was being subducted. Lack of continuity in deposition and deformation suggests a melange of 2 different groups forming a chaotic mixed block. Volcanic rocks of the McHugh Complex are mostly basaltic greenstones associated with chert, and argillite. The clastic sequence formed when rock such as graywacke, siltstone, conglomerate sandstone, as well as some marble, was transported by crustal movement to its present location. A fine example of metaconglomerate sandstone is at Mile 107.4 of the Seward Highway where sandstone boulders with chunks of granite, marble, and siltite are found in a roadcut on the east side of the highway. At Mile 103, siltstone (light) and mudstone (dark) are layered. Occasionally rippled siltstone from ancient water currents is visible in the layers.

## Faults

The *Eagle River Thrust Fault* separates the Valdez Group from the McHugh Complex where the two rock masses slide past each other. This is a complex fault zone with the McHugh complex consistently overlaying the rocks of the Valdez Group. Originating by Skilak Lake on the Kenai Peninsula, the Eagle River Thrust Fault wiggles its way through the Chugach Mountains, crossing the Matanuska River near Pioneer Peak where it continues eastward, stopping just south of the town of Glennallen. At Mile 105.5 (before Falls Creek trailhead)the fault zone is barely visible at an elevation of about 300 feet above the roadway. It curves back up Indian valley and snakes its way north across the Chugach Mountains.

The *Border Ranges Fault System* began life as a subduction trench during the mid-Cretaceous. It runs north-south along the front of the Chugach Mountains above Anchorage, extending past Pioneer Peak, where it curves eastward, stopping abruptly at the Copper River. The Glenn Highway between Palmer and Glennallen parallels the fault. The Border Ranges fault separates the Chugach Terrane from the Peninsular Terrane in the west, and from the Wrangellia Terrane to the north and east. It is considered an active fault although no earthquake activity has taken place in the last 300 years. It splits the upper Hillside from the Anchorage bowl and is most visible at Hillside Ski Area off Abbott Road.

## Mineral Deposits

Gold occurs in veins, or lodes, in the Cretaceous rocks of the Valdez Group. A lode deposit is commonly a gold-bearing quartz vein which intruded as hot fluids into argillite, sandstone, or conglomerate rock under high temperatures and pressure. Placer deposits are the most common occurrence of gold in Chugach State Park, the result of veins which eroded through weathering, glacial activity, avalanches, and runoff. Gold, a heavy metal, washes downstream and sinks to the bottom. The gold filters through the rock and sand, filling in stream bottoms where it settles out on the bedrock surface beneath. Gold may combine with silver to form a natural alloy - electrum.

Silver, often a native or uncombined element, forms at medium or greater depths in the earth under high heat, and occurs in lode deposits in greenstone basalt or quartz veins. It is often found with gold or mercury.

In the 1880s, prospectors on their way to the Klondike gold fields discovered gold in the Turnagain Arm area. In 1895, three men from the Hope-Sunrise Mining District crossed to the north side of the Arm in the vicinity of Girdwood, where they found gold in California Creek. The next year gold was found in Crow Creek, as well as up Indian and Bird creeks. A single silver lode deposit was staked near Eagle River glacier in Chugach State Park. [See Chapter 7 - *Prospecting For Gold*]

## PROCESSES OF FORMATION

Once the blocks of the Chugach Terrane had welded onto North America, the real shaping began. Mountains are continually undergoing a slow transformation from young jagged blocks through the vigorous stage of peaks and valleys to the final stooped, round-shouldered hulks of ancient ranges. The Chugach Mountains may have once been low hills when they first emerged from the ocean; continued uplifting forced them into their present shape. There are many other processes at work, as well.

Degradation of the rock surface is the most fundamental factor involved in forming the Chugach mountains, as it changes the face of a mountain through decay of sediments, or weathering and erosion. This process provides material for surface deposits elsewhere on the mountain or in valleys: talus, alluvium, landslides, and stream braiding. In northern latitudes, glaciers play an important role in shaping the landscape. The deep u-shaped valleys and serrated ridges of Chugach State Park are the imprint of ongoing glacial sculpting.

### Chemical Weathering

Chemical weathering is due to the susceptibility of rock to the chemical decomposition of its minerals. Water, oxygen, and carbon dioxide are important agents in weathering. The effectiveness of weathering depends on rock composition, particle size, and ability of solution to move through rock. Quartz, for example, is almost insoluble; therefore, it decomposes slowly.

### Mechanical Weathering/Freeze & Thaw

Mechanical weathering, such as frost action, is the result of the freeze/thaw cycle of water. This breaks rocks because water expands 9% by volume when it freezes. This causes ice crystals to wedge into rock and soil, causing expansion and contraction to break apart rock and churn the soil on an annual basis.

## Solifluction

Solifluction is caused by the freeze/thaw cycle of moist soil at high altitudes or latitudes. The upper soil warms, but the frozen subsurface layer prevents water absorption, causing the heavily saturated soil to sag downslope. This process causes the soil and rocks to build up into sheets, or lobes, as they move forward. The football field below O'Malley Peak has wonderful examples of solifluction lobes.

## Rock Glaciers

Rock glaciers may be hundreds of feet thick. They occur in valleys formerly occupied by snow glaciers. Ice mixes with coarse rock fragments and assists in the imperceptibly slow creep downslope. Excellent examples of rock glaciers are far up Peter's Creek valley and North Fork Campbell Creek.

## Glaciation

Glaciation scrapes away rock debris from the bedrock and sides of valleys; this in turn is carried to the terminus of the glacier where it is deposited or washed away.

## Avalanches

Avalanches carry down rock and soil which are torn loose by the sliding snow.

Rock Glacier on North Fork Campbell Creek (Joe Kurtak)

## Rivers and Streams/ Running Water

Rivers and streams are important factors in sculpting landforms. The running water wears away sediments, rock formations, and bedrock, displacing tons of rock debris downstream. In Chugach State Park, rivers and streams are associated with the remnant glaciers far up the valleys. They continue to wash down glacial debris which is deposited downstream. Running water from rainfall and snowmelt washes over rock and soil, removing particles and minerals.

## Flooding

Flooding occurs when the rate of discharge exceeds the amount of water a stream channel can handle. Overflowing channels carry away vast amounts of rock. The main causes of flooding are excess rainfall, rapid snowmelt, and the damming of drainages which then overflow releasing a torrent of water.

Since the Pleistocene, Lake George, on the north side of the park, flooded annually when Knik Glacier advanced against the side of Mt. Palmer (6,940 feet). An ice dam almost 300 feet high blocked the meltwater from the Lake George, Colony and Knik glaciers from flowing into the Knik River. The water overflowed the ice dam each summer, increasing the river's flow almost thirty times its normal rate for nearly two weeks. No flooding has occurred since 1966, when the Knik Glacier retreated beyond the reach of the canyon wall. In 1980 the channel between Knik Glacier and Mt. Palmer was only 300 feet wide. A minor advance could once again create Lake George.

## Biological Action

This is a small, but important aspect of sculpting, and includes everything from root expansion and biochemical breakdown of the soil, to the digging and burrowing of animals, as well as the compacting of trails by hooves and boots.

## Earthquakes

Chugach State Park is on an active earthquake belt where one plate dives under another. Earthquake activity has caused the mountains to subside and be uplifted. Quakes cause rocks and soil to get displaced. Earthquakes are a constant reminder that these mountains are still forming.

Earthquakes occur when there is vibration from the release of a pressure built up along a strained section of a fault. It may occur as an irregular grating along a fault due to frictional drag, or the sudden break and release at one point along a fault with stress increasing sharply elsewhere along the same fault. Abundant earthquake activity occurs along spreading plates, subduction zones where plates are being consumed and sink into the mantle, fault zones where plates move against each other, and when there is uplift.

## THE 1964 GOOD FRIDAY EARTHQUAKE

On March 27, 1964 at 5:36 pm, southcentral Alaska was jarred by the most violent quake to shake North America in the 20th Century. The ground shook for a duration of one to seven minutes. The earth rippled in undulating waves and cracked into gaping fissures; landslides occurred where the ground was unconsolidated. By the time the earth stopped rocking one of the most active earthquake belts in the world had released twice as much energy as the 1906 San Francisco earthquake.

The 1964 earthquake was a notable quake. Its magnitude of 8.7 on the Richter scale was unusually high. The epicenter was only 90 miles from Anchorage in a mountainous region in northern Prince William Sound (Unakwik Inlet), and was estimated at 12-31 miles below the surface. Aftershocks followed the continental margin from Prince William Sound to Kodiak Island along the Aleutian Trench. There were 28 aftershocks of a magnitude greater than 6 within the first 24 hours of the main quake. There were 12,000 minor shakes of a magnitude 3.5 within 70 days of the main quake. These were primarily concentrated along the landward side of the Aleutian Trench.

Although 114 people were killed, destruction was considered minimal. Destruction was due primarily to tsunamis, a Japanese word meaning "tidal wave", which resulted from quake-induced underwater landslides. Waves swept into the coastal towns of Valdez, Seward, Whittier, and Kodiak. In Anchorage, destruction occurred where homes rested on the unstable Bootlegger Cove Formation. Shaking from the earthquake liquified the clay, allowing it to flow like mud. The Turnagain area of Anchorage sitting atop this formation collapsed and slid into Cook Inlet. The land deformation caused by the 1964 earthquake can best be viewed at Earthquake Park in Anchorage.

The most interesting aspect of the 1964 quake was the vast area—over 100,000 square miles of the earth's crust — deformed either by uplift, subsidence, or horizontal slip. Uplift was as great as 38 feet on Montague Island, but averaged only six feet around Prince William Sound. Subsidence averaged 2.5 feet with a maximum drop of 7.5 feet to the north-northwest in the Kenai-Chugach Mountain region. The area around Portage and Girdwood dropped about 4 feet. Sea water partially flooded the valleys, killing many trees. The Chugach Mountains subsided over two feet in the west near Anchorage to barely six inches in the east, near the Copper River.

## GLACIERS: Sculpting the Landscape

Glaciers are responsible for creating some of the most dramatic scenery in the world. Humans have always stood in awe of glaciers and snow-capped mountains. As early as the 1700's scientists began to accept the idea that mountain ice moved. In the early 1800's Louis Agassiz, a young Swiss-American naturalist, identified glacial deposits in Europe and North America. Agassiz in 1837 published his Glacial Theory of massive "ice ages." His basic theory has withstood the test of time.

During most of the earth's 4.6 billion year history, the earth has been ice-free. Glaciers have only existed during a flash in geologic time. Today, about 10% of the earth's land area is covered by ice as compared to 30% during glacial maxima.

In Chugach State Park, glaciers are a major feature and remain an important aspect of its formation. Glaciers cover approximately 73 square miles of park land. Without glaciers, the beauty and grandeur of Chugach State Park would not exist. To understand their inner workings is to understand their impact on the land.

### Formation of a Glacier

To form a glacier, two criteria must be met - consistently cool temperatures and snow. The climate must remain cool even in summer. Over time, this reduces melting and allows snow to accumulate. The moderately cold winter temperatures of North America, just below freezing, can hold more moisture than the extreme dry cold of Antarctica.

Temperature is a crucial factor in the rate at which glacial ice melts or accumulates. *Snowline* is the highest point above which snow remains from year to year and accumulates over time. *Accumulation* occurs on roughly the top two-thirds of a glacier's surface. *Ablation* is the wasting process where snow is lost through melting or calving on the lower third of a glacier.

Snow, the lifeblood of a glacier, is of course a crystalline form of water. Snowflakes occur in an infinite variety of shapes, from hexagonal crystals to capped columns. After snow has fallen the extremities of the flakes begin to melt. Water moves toward the center of the flake where it recrystallizes and merges with other flakes. This partially consolidated granular snow is called *firn*. Firn becomes glacier ice when it is no longer permeable to air or water. Glacial ice is made up of large interlocking ice crystals interspersed with trapped air. Snow decreases nine times in volume by the time it becomes glacier ice.

## TRANSFORMATION OF SNOW CRYSTALS TO GLACIER ICE.

### Equitemperature (Destructive) Metamorphism

| Original crystal forms | Original forms distinguishable with difficulty. | Original forms fragmented and no longer recognizable; fine-grained, old snow. | Rounded ice grains. |
|---|---|---|---|
| | | | |

### Firnification

| Melt-freeze metamorphism; grains bonded by freezing. | Pressure metamorphism; grains bonded by compression and recrystallization. | Glacier ice — non-communicating pores. |
|---|---|---|
| | | |

Illustrations by Joanna Mergler Mayer

The *firn limit* is the uneven line between accumulation and ablation. The firn limit is higher on the colder, drier north side of the Chugach Mountains than on the warmer, wetter south side. Snow in this region may become firn after only a single summer of melt. As snow accumulates and pressure builds, the ice grains are compacted together, forming ever-expanding ice crystals. Ice crystals grow under the weight of overlying snow until the firn compacts into a solid mass of ice. Glacier ice requires only a few years to develop in the warm moist climate of southcentral Alaska; in Antarctica, it requires centuries.

### Movement of Glacial Ice

The surface of glacier ice has a brittle elasticity. Movement between the layers of ice is partly due to the weak molecular bonds that connect the crystals, allowing the ice to flow under its own weight. The size of the crystals tends to increase with age, distance travelled, and rises in temperature. As the ice thickens, the weight causes the lower layers to act like fluid plastic near the bottom of the ice sheet. Ice then slowly spreads out over the irregular land surface, driven by its own weight and gravity.

Movement of a glacier varies according to the climate, ice thickness, type of bedrock, the shape and slope of the channel, and the environment at the terminus, as well as the direction of flow, or aspect. Snow fields, which form in the mountains, follow the path of least resistance as the ice begins to flow. The length and speed of the glacier depends on the rate of snow accumulation, thickness of the ice, and rate of ice loss at the terminus.

## Speed of Movement

Glacier movement is usually slow, but measurable. The prime mover is gravity. Glaciers tend to follow old drainage patterns down the mountains. Movement is so slow that the debris scraped off rock builds up on the surface of the ice. Along the sides and at the terminus debris is often so thick that it permits vegetation to grow on the glacier.

## Features of a Glacier

Glaciers appear either as expansive icefields, or more commonly tongues of ice flowing down mountain valleys. A snow field at the head of a glacier resembles an unbroken expanse of white. The snow is still unconsolidated. Moving down the glacier, deep irregular cracks appear on the surface of the ice. At points along the way, the ice forms gigantic blocks as it cascades over a drop in the bedrock.

Movement down and over landforms causes crevasses, or fractures, to appear on the glacier's surface. Crevasses occur when the slope steepens, or when a glacier meets resistance along valley walls, or at the terminus when a glacier fans out. Crevasses open and close depending on extension of the lower glacier, shearing, and compression. Icefalls occur when a glacier pours over a steep drop or bench, forming a jumble of ice blocks.

As glaciers scrape and scour the land, they pile up material in their path like a bulldozer. Rocks and debris can be seen along the middle, sides and top of the glaciers. Rock is also transported in the ice, or dragged underneath, smoothing and scouring the bedrock. This leaves telltale striations and grooves on the underlying rock, visible once a glacier has retreated. The exposed rocks near McHugh Creek are excellent examples of glacially polished rock.

There are several debris features which are evident as the ice begins to melt and a glacier retreats. A *moraine* is a ridge of drift, or debris, deposited along the edges of a glacier. A *terminal moraine* is formed when drift is pushed up in front of a glacier, or as meltwater deposits material when it drains from beneath. A *lateral moraine* forms along the sides of a glacier as a result of shearing downslope movement. A *medial moraine* is a ridge of debris visible down the middle of a glacier formed when two glacial lobes meet and continue to move along side each other.

# GLACIAL FEATURES

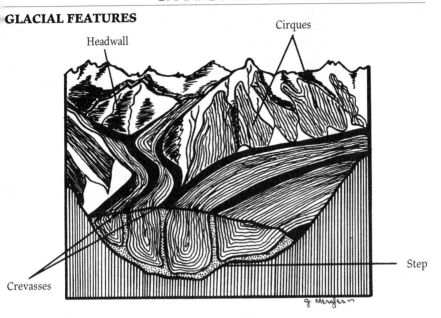

Headwall

Cirques

Crevasses

Step

# THE SAME AREA AFTER DEGLACIATION

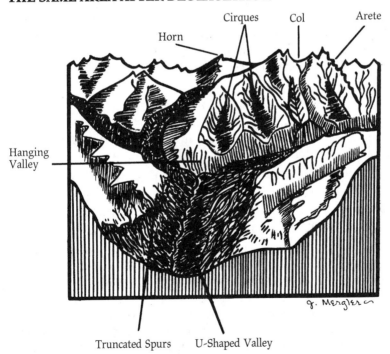

Horn

Cirques    Col    Arete

Hanging
Valley

Truncated Spurs    U-Shaped Valley

Illustrations by Joanna Mergler Mayer

*Kettle lakes* are the last remnant of a retreating glacier. They form when a stagnant block of ice remains behind the retreating glacier in a depression in the ground. The block of ice is protected from rapid melting by a covering of debris, but eventually melts and fills the kettle hole with water, forming a lake. Mirror Lake, between Eagle River and Eklutna, is an example of a kettle pond.

Valley glaciers produced a number of distinctive features in the mountains of Chugach State Park. As snow accumulated and advanced, gouging the valleys, the sculpting was hidden under a blanket of ice. Once the glacier retreated, the drama unfolded.

The head of a glacier where snow accumulates is often encircled by precipitous headwalls called *cirques*. Once a glacier has disappeared, a gouged-out depression is all that remains. The melting ice leaves a small lake, or *tarn*, such as the lakes seen below O'Malley Peak or Suicide Peaks. A pass, formed where two cirques converge cutting into the wall, is known as a col; a col is visible at Powerline Pass.

As a glacier recedes, it smooths and rounds out a valley leaving blunt ridges called *truncated spurs*, as can be seen at the junction of Hidden valley and South Fork of Campbell Creek. A receding glacier also exposes tributary glacial valleys called *hanging valleys*. The narrow, steep serrated ridges of glaciated mountains are called *aretes*, form along the crests of mountain ranges and ridges that separate valleys. Good examples are ridges on O'Malley and Tikishla peaks. Shaped by glacial erosion and formed late in glaciation from isolated preglacial peaks, *horns* are sharp peaks that project above the surrounding area. O'Malley, Ptarmigan and Suicide peaks are examples of horns.

## Glaciers of Chugach State Park

Chugach State Park was once completely covered by ice and snow. Today, only 10% of the park is covered by glaciers, most of which are now hidden deep within the park. Those that remain are in active retreat, leaving behind sculpted valleys and alpine lakes.

A rugged 4-mile trek up to Crow Pass (3500 feet) leads to the most accessible glaciers in the park. From there one can see Raven and Clear glaciers which drain into Raven Creek, a tributary of Eagle River. Bird Creek also has several small glaciers far up at its head, just to the west of Crow Pass.

Drainages along the front range of Chugach State Park have a few residual glaciers, and evidence of recent glaciation in the upper valleys is obvious. Several cirques contain ice fields, the residual ice of ancient glaciers. At the head of the North Fork of Campbell Creek is a glacial remnant complete with bergshrund, a crevasse at the head of a glacier which separates moving ice from stationary ice. The Suicide Peaks are the result of ancient glacial gouging. The peaks are horns and the lake is a tarn. Ship Creek has only one small glacier up the North Fork near Moraine Pass.

The most active glacier in Chugach State Park is Eagle River Glacier, which is retreating at an average of 100 feet per year. The firn limit has slowly climbed in elevation, from 3300 feet in 1938 to over 5000 feet by 1964. Although the level has fluctuated throughout the years there has been an upward trend in the snowline. Nunataks, the summits of glacially-buried mountains, become exposed, as well as increased exposure of older nunataks. Eklutna Glacier is the second most active in the park, retreating at a rate of 72 feet per year.

View up Eagle Glacier, Anchorage District, Cook Inlet Region, Alaska. Circa 1915 (S.R. Capps 732)

View up Eagle Glacier, 1982. Notice glacier has receded to the knob on the right in upper photo (Dave Albert)

# CHAPTER FIVE

# EARLY MAN IN CHUGACH STATE PARK

"Discovery" of the Americas occurred thousands of years before Columbus set sail. Paleolithic people from Asia wandered into Alaska by crossing a broad steppe-tundra plain called Beringia This vast land bridge between Alaska and Siberia, emerged several times during the Pleistocene Ice Age when water, alternately locked up and released from glaciers, raised and lowered the sea level by as much as 400 feet. The Bering land bridge appeared at least three times - 70,000, 40,000, and 25,000 years ago - before the rising sea level broke through Beringia for the last time about 14,000 years ago.

What was the ancient environment like when humans first arrived in upper Cook Inlet?  What attracted them to this cold and hostile landscape?  For thousands of years the Cook Inlet region was covered with a thick sheet of ice, not readily accessible to man by land or sea. As the climate warmed, glaciers receded up into the Alaska Range and Chugach Mountains, exposing bedrock to the rising ocean.  Over the eons two major cultural groups — maritime Eskimos and interior Athapaskan Indians — came together at the area known today as Chugach State Park.

Most of the research on early man in the Cook Inlet basin has been conducted around Kachemak Bay and at Beluga Point on Turnagain Arm.  Archaeological sites are scarce in Cook Inlet, requiring comparisons with concurrent sites elsewhere around Alaska.  Tectonic movement of coastal areas in southern Alaska, and a fluctuating sea level may have destroyed sites, leaving gaps in our knowledge.  However, based on contemporary data, archaeological studies, and pollen analysis used to reconstruct a prehistoric climate, 10,000 years of sporadic human habitation can be pieced together.

Facing page: Pacific Eskimos at Beluga Point (Joanna Mergler Mayer)

---

**BERINGIA: the Bering Land Bridge**

During the Pleistocene, more and more of the earth's water became trapped in glacial snow and ice. The removal of water from the oceans caused the sea level to drop by as much as 400 feet. With the onset of the Wisconsin Ice Age 70,000 years ago, a land bridge appeared, exposing the area between Alaska and Siberia — now referred to as Beringia. The cool, dry climate produced a grassy treeless steppe-tundra. That first land bridge lasted only a few thousand years, when a period of interglacial warming melted glacial ice and again raised the sea level. A second glacial period began about 40,000 years ago and the "bridge" reappeared.

The Wisconsin glacial maxima was reached around 18,000 years ago, when 29% of the Northern Hemisphere was covered by a thick sheet of ice. The sea level fell to its Wisconsin Ice Age minimum during the same period. The central and western parts of Alaska were left uncovered by ice, creating a refuge for plants, animals, and man. Once again a vast expansive steppe-tundra formed, providing abundant food for large numbers of herbivores such as woolly mammoths, camels, giant elk, giant beaver, saiga antelope, horses, muskox, and man. The land bridge was finally inundated by the sea about 14,000 years ago.

---

**THE FIRST ALASKANS**

It is not known how the first people arrived in the upper Cook Inlet region, but artifacts show they entered this new territory about 10,000 years ago. Glaciers retreated about the same time as the climate grew warmer and wetter. The Turnagain Arm ice lobe withdrew to the present townsite of Girdwood, and the sea was almost to its modern level. Turnagain Arm, a 1000-foot deep fiord, accelerated the retreat by permitting excessive calving of its tidewater glacier.

Beluga Point Archaeological Site, 17 miles south of Anchorage in Chugach State Park, has been repeatedly inhabited by man for almost 10,000 years. The site offered one of the few sheltered locations for early man along the rocky shores of Turnagain Arm. A beach between two large rock promontories gave access to the uplands as well as protection from the prevailing east winds. The icy waters were rich in marine life. In synchrony with their environment, the first Alaskans may have followed the newly-opened expanses left by the retreating ice into a new land.

People of the American Paleo-Arctic tool tradition left core and blade material, as well as projectile points at Beluga Point. These correspond to interior Alaskan archaeological sites between 8,000 and 10,000 years old. They are associated with a nomadic culture which once hunted large herd animals. Dall sheep, mountain goat, and caribou were attracted to the tundra plants which dominated the newly deglaciated land around upper Cook Inlet. Dwarf birch, sedges, and grasses carpeted the treeless landscape, as well as mosses and lichens.

Approximately 8000 years ago the climate began to cool and precipitation increased, changing the character of the plants and animals in the Cook Inlet basin. The complex vegetation of the Pleistocene steppe tundra gave way to a simpler plant community of aspen, alder, and spruce which invaded Cook Inlet. Moose and snowshoe hare adapted to the woody browse and the increased winter snowfall. Dall sheep and mountain goats withdrew to the windswept mountains along with the retreating tundra. Dall sheep, hunted along the slopes above Beluga Point, were prized by early man for their meat and skins.

**A MARITIME CULTURE AT BELUGA POINT**
There is a 4,000 year gap in human occupation at Beluga Point, thought to be due to destruction of portions of the site from road and railroad development, and the loss of a sizable chunk of the Point from the 1964 earthquake. During this period of time the local environment changed. Between 6,000 and 7,000 years ago the climate reached its warmest. Tree line extended north beyond its present range, glaciers receded above their present extent, and sea levels were at their highest. Caribou, which may have once populated the Chugach Mountains, were forced out of their former range as the vegetation changed; the caribou began to move out of the upper Cook Inlet region about 6000 to 7000 years ago.

Around 4000 years ago a proto-Eskimo-Aleut maritime people of the Denbigh Flint Culture stopped at Beluga Point. Archaeological evidence suggests they followed an oceanic route direct from Asia. Successfully exploiting the marine environment, they found the Bering Sea a rich stepping stone for migration to Alaska since whales, seals, sea otters, and Steller's sea cows thrived in the cold waters off Beringia. Living in temporary camps while following game, they left little trace of their passage - only small, finely chipped stone blades used for tools and weapons.

Early man had to continually manufacture tools. Chert, siltstone, and slate were common materials used for spearheads, knife blades, scapers, adze blades, and ulus. During early habitation of Beluga Point, blades and projectiles were flaked into shape, but approximately 4000 years ago tools began to be ground into their desired shape on whetstones or grinding slabs.

A few hearths have been found at Beluga Point. Some hearths were gouged into the ground with a fire built directly on top. Others have rocks placed around in a ring with gravel spread on the bottom and a fire built on top. The oldest hearth at Beluga Point dates from approximately 4000 years ago; the most recent is from 1300 AD. The scarcity of hearths suggests the site received use as a stop-off camp rather than more constant use as a seasonal summer camp.

## PACIFIC ESKIMOS

Around 2500 years ago, Pacific Eskimos suddenly arrived from the Bering Sea into southern Alaska, displacing earlier arrivals. They were completely adapted to life on the sea. Two groups collectively considered Pacific Eskimo exploited the upper Cook Inlet basin. The Chugach Eskimo settled in Prince William Sound, and may have crossed into Cook Inlet over Portage Pass after the glacier receded. The Unegkurmiut, a lesser known group, inhabited the Kachemak Bay region. The two groups probably shared a common language, interacted socially, yet remained politically independent.

Eskimos of Cook Inlet preferred the more hospitable region around Kachemak Bay for their semi-permanent winter villages. Villages were located close to shore in protected areas adjacent to rugged headlands, which provided both fortification and an observation point.

As spring lengthened into summer it brought excitement in the villages. Families prepared to move to summer camps, and men set out to hunt. Excursions into upper Cook Inlet in search of game brought hunters to the shores of Turnagain Arm. In passing they left behind ground stone spear heads, ulu blades, grinding pestles, adze blades, and scrapers.

These maritime people had adapted their mode of transportation for life on the sea. Kayaks, a narrow, skin-covered boat which held one or two people, were used mainly for hunting. Umiaks were larger, open skin boats used for hauling heavy loads and people to and from camps.

The most important foods - primarily marine mammals and fish - came from the ocean. Seals were an important source of meat, oil, winter clothing, and boat building materials. Seals, following salmon and eulachon (known locally as hooligan), probably brought Eskimo hunters into upper Cook Inlet. Seal hunters commonly hunted alone. A hunter in a kayak would approach a sleeping seal on an ice floe, harpooning the animal with a detachable spear head attached to an inflated seal stomach float. The wounded animal would then be killed with a lance or a club.

Fall was the last time the Eskimos could amass food stores before winter. Hunting upland animals required more effort since land transportation was on foot. They probably hunted with snares, and bow and arrows. Black bear were hunted throughout the year, but especially in the fall when they fed on berries. Although moose were never common, they became part of the Eskimo diet in the Cook Inlet basin about 2800 years ago. Medium-sized animals such as wolves, fox, beaver, and wolverine may have been trapped using snares and deadfalls. Marmots were prized for clothing. Both terrestrial birds and waterfowl were hunted or trapped in nets or snares.

The Eskimos' mobility allowed them to trade with neighbors for food and tools. A small fragment of native copper from the Copper River area was left by its owner at Beluga Point about 700 years ago. But something happened. Around 1000 years ago, the Eskimos of Cook Inlet were displaced by the Tanaina Athapaskan Indians; no one knows exactly what happened. Increased sedimentation of the salt water may have reduced the food resources of this once-rich marine environment, causing the Eskimos to abandon Cook Inlet for the outer Pacific coast. Borrowing from their Eskimo neighbors, the Tanaina adapted to both inland and marine subsistence activities. Perhaps the Tanaina's success in adapting to such a wide array of food sources forced the Eskimos out of an impoverished Cook Inlet.

# CHAPTER SIX

# DENA'INA: THE PEOPLE

They call themselves Dena'ina — The People. The Tanaina, as they are also called, are a mountain people originating west of the Alaska Range, in the area between Lake Clark and Stony River. Despite rugged terrain and long distances, they established transportation routes across the Alaska Range into the Cook Inlet basin. The Tanaina are, as a consequence, the only Northern Athapaskan Indians with substantial territory on saltwater.

Little is known of the traditional subsistence patterns of the Upper Inlet Tanaina prior to European contact. Archaeological evidence shows that Pacific Eskimos still paddled the waters off Chugach State Park as late as 1700. At Beluga Point, the most recent Eskimo hearths date back to 1300. Sometime between 1650 and 1780 the Tanaina finally supplanted the Eskimo and spread over most of Cook Inlet.

Why the Eskimo population in Cook Inlet moved out to the coast is still a mystery. Lack of marine mammals may have forced them out, with the Tanaina filling in the void left behind. Whatever the cause, the Tanaina had settled into upper Cook Inlet by 1700. In the late 1700s the Tanaina were the only natives encountered by Captain Cook and other European explorers in upper Cook Inlet region. What little is known about the Tanaina traditional subsistence lifestyle is intertwined with information recorded by early explorers and contemporary archaeological research.

At the time of contact, three societies of Tanaina occupied the Cook Inlet basin. The Interior people lived west of Cook Inlet around Lake Clark and Iliamna Lake. The Kenai people occupied the Kenai Peninsula from Seldovia and Kachemak Bay north to Point Possession. The Susitna people of upper Cook Inlet travelled the area from Tyonek, Susitna River, and Knik and Turnagain Arms.

Facing page: Russian Orthodox Church at Tanaina village of Eklutna (AMHA)

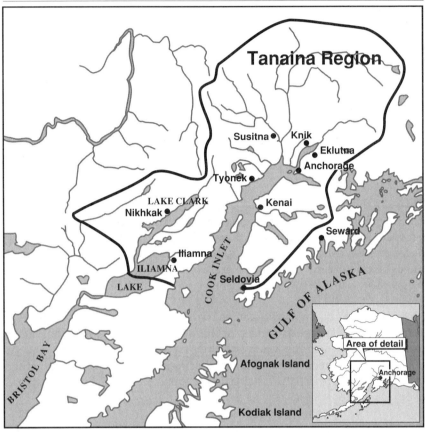

Map of Tanaina Territory at time of Eugopean contact (Ron Engstrom)

The Knik Arm group of Susitna people used the area in and around Chugach State Park. They fished from Point Woronzof in Anchorage north to the Matanuska River. They hunted in the Talkeetna and Chugach mountains as well as into the Copper River basin. Where once there had been many settlements, today the only active Tanaina village on Knik Arm is Eklutna.

Unlike their nomadic relatives, the Tanaina settled into semi-permanent villages. A plentiful supply of salmon and other abundant fish and wildlife provided the Tanaina with food throughout the year. Although there were lean winters, the Tanaina thrived in the rich environment of Cook Inlet. Prior to the arrival of the Europeans, the forest and sea provided "The People" with all their needs. Their lives were closely attuned to the natural cycles of the land.

## TRADITIONAL SUBSISTENCE CYCLE

### Geese Month:

By spring, supplies from winter caches would be disappearing with the melting snow. The Tanaina looked forward to the coming abundance. Geese-month (April) brought a flurry of activity. Geese and ducks migrating north provided a welcomed change in diet. Women snared waterfowl and collected eggs for the village. Women and children gathered the Hedysarum root, or "Indian potato", from Eklutna Flats. Men would harpoon beaver as the ice melted from ponds; the meat would be smoked for later use. Preparations for leaving the winter villages began. In Baby-month (May), families headed for their fish camps along the shores of the Eklutna and Eagle rivers, Ship and Campbell creeks, and Fire Island. Eulachon, an oily marine fish, was one of the first fish caught in late spring from the waters of upper Cook Inlet. It was preserved for use in lamps during the dark winter months.

### King Salmon Month:

Once settled in their summer fish camps, the Tanaina began the serious work of catching and preserving their winter supply of salmon. During King-salmon-month (June) they caught their preferred fish, but red and silver salmon were also added to the stores. Men caught the fish in underwater basket traps and fish weirs. During the long days of summer women split the salmon with ulus, boys washed the fish, and old men hung the meat to dry. Salmon were either dried, smoked, or pounded into meal for later storage in elevated log caches. The fish would be shared with the entire village during the winter months.

Transportation was easiest in summer. Birchbark canoes with spruce frames were used to ply the lakes and rivers around Cook Inlet. Larger moose skin boats were used to carry heavier loads. Lower Inlet Tanaina also adopted the Eskimo kayak and umiak, which were occasionally used by Upper Inlet Tanaina for hunting harbor seals and beluga whales that followed the salmon and eulachon up Cook Inlet.

### Ripe Berries Month:

Hunting season began in Ripe-berries-month (August), when the Tanaina moved up into the Chugach Mountains. The Eklutna and Peters Creek valleys provided abundant resources and were the most accessible from the winter village on Eklutna Flats. The Tanaina had hunting trails criss-crossing the Chugach from Eklutna Lake down Indian and Bird creeks on the north side of Turnagain Arm. While the women and children and old ones picked berries, the men moved up onto the high ridges with their dogs to hunt mountain sheep and goats. Bear and occasionally moose were hunted in It-turns-yellow-month (September). Tanaina elders say that moose were a recent arrival to this area and were not around in the late 1800s when they were young. The Upper Inlet Tanaina may have hunted caribou in the Talkeetna or Kenai mountains, or the Copper River basin, to provide skins for clothing.

Tanaina at summer fish camp (Joanna Mergler Mayer)

**Snow Month:**

By **Snow-month** (November), the Tanaina were back in their winter villages of subterranean log cabins. To break the monotony of an all-salmon diet the men occasionally hunted bear and moose during the winter months, or went ice-fishing in local lakes for trout. They would also hunt porcupine, hare, and ptarmigan with bow and arrow, snares, or a deadfall in the area around the village. Following an extensive network of trails, the Tanaina travelled in winter on foot or on snowshoes of birch and babiche (rawhide). Dogs were used for packing, but were not put into harness to pull sleds until the early 1800s during Russian occupation.

## TANAINA IN THE RUSSIAN PERIOD: 1741 - 1867

The Russians arrived in Alaska in 1741. By 1784 the first Russian settlement was established on Kodiak Island. The Russians entered Tanaina territory in the late 1700s, placing outposts at Iliamna Lake and Tyonek in the hope of subjugating the Tanaina to obtain furs, but they were not the first Europeans to come in contact with the Tanaina. The Tanaina retaliated against the Russian excesses and destroyed both outposts in 1797.

Berry-picking in the Chugach Mountains (Joanna Mergler Mayer)

Although the Russians had already been in Alaska for almost four decades Captain James Cook in 1778 was the first European known to have contac with the Upper Inlet Tanaina. The Tanaina were also the first group of interio. Athapaskans to come in contact with Europeans. Cook encountered a camp a Point Possesion, on the south side of Turnagain Arm, where he traded with the Natives.

By 1799 an organization called the Russian-American Company (RAC) wa: given exclusive rights by the Russian government to their Alaskan territory on this remote corner of the North American continent. Their goal was to obtain furs; the sea otter was the primary objective. The main trading station. were located on the Kenai and Kasilof rivers.

For many years the Upper Inlet Tanaina had escaped the repressive acts o Russian occupation that had befallen the Aleuts and Pacific Eskimo on the coast. The Tanaina preferred to barter rather than pay tribute to the Russians By 1800 the sea otter population in southern Alaska was on the brink o extinction. As furs grew scarce the Tanaina tried to act as middle men b acquiring furs from the Interior people for the Russians.

In 1836 a smallpox epidemic broke out in Sitka, spreading north over the nex four years. The pre-contact Tanaina population has been estimated at abou 5000 throughout Cook Inlet. By the time the epidemic ended in 1840, half th Tanaina were dead. In this fragile state missionary activities among th Tanaina intensified; Russian Orthodox churches sprang up in winter villages The epidemic drastically disrupted subsistence activities, thus ending th independence of the Upper Inlet Tanaina. Guns became available by the 1840: furthering the transition from an exclusively subsistence lifestyle. For th next two decades, the Tanaina struggled to regain their former strength, bu by the 1860s their population had dropped to 1500 people.

The Russian Period ended in 1867, when the United States purchased Alask Although the Russian Period lasted 126 years, its impact on the Tanaina wa: not as great as the American occupation that followed. The Russian legacy ir Tanaina culture was the Russian Orthodox church which continues to play ar important role in their culture today.

## THE EARLY AMERICAN PERIOD: 1867 TO 1918

The Upper Inlet Tanaina had survived Russian occupation with much of thei. traditional culture intact. They maintained some semblance of the old way into the first few decades of the American period. The monopoly of th Russian-American Company had kept settlements and exploration to a mini mum, but the American free-enterprise system was on the move.

In 1868 the Alaska Commercial Company (ACC) bought out the Russian-American Company, and by 1875 had set up a trading station in Tanaina territory at Tyonek. Initially, only light trading for furs occurred with the Tanaina, but the Indian's desire for manufactured goods grew. Not until the Americans arrived did the Tanaina use ready-made clothes. To obtain guns, steel traps, and wool clothes, the Tanaina began trapping even when prices were low, in order to acquire items only the ACC could provide. Times were rapidly changing. By the1880s Tanaina men began to cut their hair and preferred manufactured, not skin, clothing.

Americans also established commercial fishing ventures and canneries up and down the Kenai Peninsula, thus preventing access to the most productive streams and traditional fish camps. Not only did the Americans usurp fish from Native sources, they purchased salmon from the Tanaina out of their winter supplies. The Tanaina exchanged fur and fish for flour, sugar, beans, and clothing, creating an adverse affect on their traditional subsistence patterns.

By the 1890s the Upper Inlet Tanaina had lost their relative isolation. Supplies of salmon and fur-bearing mammals had been drastically reduced. In 1897 the Alaska Commercial Company reduced fur prices and halted the practice of extending credit to the Tanaina. The ACC turned from fur trading to outfitting, as prospectors moved into Tanaina territory. A rush for gold up Turnagain Arm brought an influx of people into upper Cook Inlet.

The need for goods supplied by the ACC and the location of the Russian Orthodox churches caused many outlying villages to be abandoned - except "Old Knik," or Eklutna. By 1917 most Tanaina had moved to the new settlements of Anchorage and Wasilla, along the newly-constructed Alaska Railroad line.

In 1918 an influenza epidemic struck, killing many of the Tanaina elders. Whole villages vanished as people moved to larger settlements to be with relatives. The traditional lifestyle, which had been on the decline, was now almost lost with the deaths of so many who knew of the old ways. The coming of the Alaska Railroad now provided a wage-economy for the Tanaina, further reducing their need for a subsistence economy.

This was the beginning of the end for Tanaina culture. Many continued to cling to traditional ways in the outlying settlements up to the 1930s, but changes in transportation and the allure of growing communities attracted the Tanaina to more urban areas. The traditional subsistence lifestyle survived in the memories of Tanaina elders well into this century, but most are now gone having taken their wisdom with them.

## Dena'ina Place Names in Chugach State Park

- Pioneer Peak ~ Denal'iy, or one that watches us. It was claimed that the mountain had the face of a bear which gazed down on them.
- Lake George ~ Diltisi, or freezes up lake.
- Eklutna village ~ Eydluytnu, or by several objects river. The objects are believed to be the hills around the village.
- Thunderbird Creek ~ Tsiskatnu, or big ochre creek.
- Bold Peak ~ Nudzi Qeneh, or sheep house.
- East fork Creek ~ Niltanikda Betnu, or leaning creek. Located at the south end of Eklutna Lake.
- Mount Eklutna ~ Snutnadzeni, or stand off steep.
- Peters Creek ~ Htestighitun Betnu, or pass trail creek
- Eagle River ~ Nuk'elehitnu, or spawn again creek. The Tanaina word was corrupted by Captain Glenn of U.S. Army in 1898, to Yuklahitna, a name given to both the river and a mountain up the valley.
- Mount Magnificent ~ K'ults'ey, or winds against it.
- Tanaina Peak ~ Qin Tseghi, or ridge crying.
- Rabbit Creek ~ Ggeh Betnu, or rabbit creek.
- Potter Creek ~ Hkayditali, or lumber. Tanaina used to walk the beach around Potter area in search of driftwood for lumber.
- Turnagain Arm ~ Tutl'uh, or backwater.
- Bird Creek ~ Esbaytnu, or mountain goat creek. Bird Creek was accessible by trails from Eklutna.
- Indian Creek ~ Nuti Editenti, or saltwater it flows into. Indian Creek was approached by trails from Eklutna.

From James Kari, 1978.

Woman with basket (Joanna Mergler Mayer)

# CHAPTER SEVEN

# PROSPECTING FOR GOLD

Was the Turnagain Arm gold rush a boom or a bust? The 1880 discovery of gold near Juneau served as the springboard for gold seekers into Alaska and the Yukon. It began as a restless northward migration of California gold seekers into the remote mountains and streams of the north in search of the next Eldorado. Enduring extreme hardships, men wandered through the unexplored territory panning for gold.

Struck by gold fever, Robert Michaelsen and Neil McCush discovered gold in 1888 on Sixmile Creek on the south side of Turnagain Arm. For the first few years there was little activity. Yet men still came, and searched surrounding creeks for "color." The town of Hope was founded in 1895, and Sunrise City just a short distance away, the following year. Both towns provided supplies for the growing number of gold seekers.

The early mining techniques were simple and crude. To check a stream for color men would initially pan for gold. If color was found, then the pick and shovel technique was used. Placer mining was done by hand as men worked the gravel to extract the eroded minerals deposited in the stream beds. They shoveled the gold-bearing rock into sluice boxes, where water from the creeks would wash off the gravel. The heavier gold flakes and nuggets would be trapped by the riffles, or slats, along the bottom of the box.

The year 1896 brought a flurry of activity to Turnagain Arm. As many as 3000 men were reported to have landed at Tyonek that year, enroute to Turnagain Arm and Susitna River in search of gold. Prospectors F.J. Perry, Christopher Spillum, and Fred Crew crossed to the north side of Turnagain from the Hope-Sunrise mining district in search of gold. While prospecting, they found high grade gold ore in California Creek, a tributary of Glacier Creek, in the vicinity of present-day Girdwood. Gold was also discovered in Crow, Winner, and Glacier creeks that season. In 1898 there was a second, larger gold rush of 7,000 to 10,000 people into Turnagain Arm. These two gold rushes would be short-lived as prospectors moved on to the richer gold fields of the Yukon and Nome.

Facing page: Two prospectors sluicing for gold, 1898 (James Wickersham Collection PCA 277-12-53 ASL)

Village of Tyonek, Cook Inlet, Alaska, 1898 (W. C. Mendenhall 15 USGS)

Hopeful of boosting business, in 1898 the Alaska Commercial Company began advertising in Seattle to attract prospectors to the Cook Inlet gold strike. They claimed the region differed favorably from the Klondike. It had "rich gravel deposits, active volcanos, and a balmy climate," making it more appealing than the remote and frigid Yukon. The Alaska Commercial Company provided transportation and supplies for the newcomers. Among those lured north by the dream of gold were farmers, shoemakers, architects, steamfitters, tanners, lawyers, and blacksmiths.

Two who were drawn by this rosy picture of prospecting in Cook Inlet were the young James Herdman, and his father, who set sail from Seattle aboard the "Dora" for the gold fields of Turnagain Arm. Their fellow passengers ranged from a steamboat captain to a "little Russian priest with a long black beard and a long black gown," as well as a "dancehall girl going to Sunrise to entertain the boys," young Herdman would write in his memoirs. After a long, cramped voyage they anchored at Tyonek to change to the smaller flat-bottomed schooner, the *F.J Perry*, which provided regular service between Tyonek and Sunrise. At this time Herdman and his father received dispiriting news from Austin Lathrop, the *Perry's* captain. According to Lathrop "everything was staked from hell to breakfast." The Herdmans agreed that a man would have to be at rockbottom to swing a pick or shovel for wages. Instead, they decided to try their luck up the Susitna River valley.

A well-prepared prospector, 1898 (James Wickersham Collection PCA 277-12-56 ASL)

Schooner, *L. J. Perry,* at Sunrise City, Alaska, 1898 (John M. Brooks Collection VA68-32-566 UAF)

Alaska Commercial Company Store, Sunrise City, Alaska, 1898, with dog teams heading to gold fields (H.M. Wetherbee Collection 866-146 UAF)

As more of the gold was extracted from the creeks around Turnagain Arm, greater volumes of gravel had to be processed. Experienced miners from California, with money and equipment, brought the new technique of hydraulic mining to Cook Inlet. This method required larger volumes of water under pressure to blast away the gravelly hillsides. The gravel was then run through long lines of sluice boxes, thus processing more gravel than the old hand-mining method.

A few lode deposits were found along Turnagain Arm. These were hard rock deposits where gold was still located in solid rock. The principal lode mines were the Monarch-Jewell Mine up Crow Creek, and the Indian Valley Mine on Indian Creek.

By 1908 most of the gold-bearing streams were mined out. The thousands of men and women drawn to this gold strike moved on. The boom towns of Hope and Sunrise saw their populations dwindle rapidly. Within 10 years, Sunrise City became a ghost town reclaimed by nature. Hope retained a small population of several dozen over the years. Today, it is a small, but active community. The supply center of Girdwood thrived in the years to come, due to the construction of a major transportation route along the north side of Turnagain Arm.

The legacy left by the early gold seekers was the permanent settlement of the Cook Inlet region by Americans. Although many were just passing through on their way to somewhere else, others chose to stay. As the US government struggled to open the vast Alaskan territory, opportunities for the new settlers grew.

## CROW CREEK

Crow Creek, above Girdwood, became the largest placer gold-producing stream in southcentral Alaska. Discovered in 1896, the first claims were filed in 1897. Crow Creek produced 600 to 4400 ounces of high grade gold each year from 1898 to 1904. Mining of the rich stream gravel was done by pick-and-shovel method, or placer mining.

In 1904, eight partners called the "Crow Boys" established the Crow Creek Consolidated Mining Company. As the gold was mined out of the stream gravel, hydraulic mining became the more common method of extraction between 1904 to 1940. The Crow Boys operated only a couple years before they sold out to the Nutter-Dawson Company in 1907. In 1914 Nutter-Dawson reorganized into the Alaska Crow Creek Mining Company, with a total of 16 claims.

In 1924, Harry Staser bought the Crow Creek Mining Company's Monarch mine. The Monarch was one of only two lode gold mines on the north side of Turnagain Arm. He got the Monarch back into production by 1933. During its first year it produced $80,000 in gold, but in the succeeding years production dwindled. It closed for good upon Harry's death in 1940.

The Crow Creek Mining Company is now a tourist attraction just outside the town of Girdwood, 7.5 miles north off Milepost 90 of the Seward Highway.

Bird Creek and Bird Point were first mined in 1898. Two quartz veins were discovered along Turnagain Arm west of Bird Point in 1911, but the veins were below the extreme high tide line. A shaft was started, but was destroyed by an extreme high tide. In 1915 two men were hired to drive a tunnel into the east side of Bird Creek, 8 miles up from the mouth. By August 1915 the tunnel was 144 feet long. Work was difficult and the gold was a poor grade, so mining ceased within a couple of years, never to resume.

Two prospectors preparing to overwinter on their claim (James Wickersham Collection PCA 277-12-54 ASL)

Peters Creek received active prospecting on a group of claims near its headwaters. In the early 1900s two cabins were built near the claims. One cabin was erected in the main valley where it emerges from the glacier; the second cabin, 2,000 feet higher, was located near the edge of the glacier. A tunnel about 37 feet long was excavated 1100 feet above the valley cabin. By 1915 these claims were no longer being mined.

Ship Creek was prospected by one man in the early 1900s. He sluiced a small tributary of Ship Creek near the Chugach Mountains, finding small amounts of gold, but not enough to mine commercially. By 1915, Ship Creek was no longer being mined .

Upper Eagle River produced the only lode deposit discovery which wasn't gold. Silver was discovered on June 1, 1911 by J.P. Frisbie, William Murray, and M.S. McMelan. The site of the Mayflower Lode is on the south bank of Eagle River just below the lake at the glacier's terminus. It was restaked in 1930, but little work was ever done after 1911.

# INDIAN VALLEY MINE -
# NATIONAL REGISTER OF HISTORIC PLACES

Peter Strong of East Rutland, Vermont, arrived in Alaska in 1898 after hearing news of gold discoveries up north. He landed in Valdez and travelled west through Prince William Sound, crossing Portage Glacier enroute to Tyonek. For ten years he mined Clear Creek, a tributary of the Talkeetna River. At age 51 Strong began prospecting the north side of Turnagain Arm, where he discovered a quartz deposit three-quarters of a mile west of Indian Creek in November, 1909. His mine was one of two successful lode mines on the north side of Turnagain Arm.

Strong was a self-reliant Vermonter. He had a complete blacksmith shop and made all his own tools. Each summer he worked the soil to grow his own vegetables. In 1915 Strong switched to placer mining to extract the gold. He had to construct a 1 1/2 mile-long ditch from Indian Creek to his mine site to run water through his sluice boxes. In 1916 a fire and the government railroad forced Strong to build a new cabin on the hillside overlooking Turnagain Arm. During the 1920s and 1930s, Strong switched from placer back to lode mining.

By the late 1930s Strong was in his mid-eighties. He leased his operation to two men who extracted some gold but found it was not high-grade ore. When all mining activity ceased in World War II, Strong ended his mining operation, never to resume. He lived at the mine site until 1949, when at the age of 95 he moved to the Pioneer's Home in Sitka. He died the following year.

Located at Mile 154.2 of the Seward Highway.

Indian Valley Mine (Jenny Zimmerman)

Walter C. Mendenhall sporting geologist's field attire, Alaska, 1898 (USGS)

## MENDENHALL IN THE VALLEY OF THE YUKLA:

### The First Recorded Crossing of the Western Chugach Mountains

In 1898 Captain Edwin Forbes Glenn of the US Army led an expedition into Alaska. He was assigned to explore and to report on potential transportation routes, military base sites, and natural resources in the recently acquired territory. Among the men accompanying the expedition was 27 year-old Walter Curran Mendenhall, a civilian geologist.

Walter Mendenhall and his assistant, Luther "Yellowstone" Kelly, were assigned to traverse the western end of the Chugach mountains to determine a route from Portage to Knik Arm. The U.S. government wanted to establish a winter route overland from Prince William Sound to the settlement of Knik. Earlier forays around the Portage and Twentymile valleys led Captain Glenn to suspect the short, but steep route up Crow Creek to be the most feasible.

On June 21, 1898, Mendenhall and Kelly left Ladd's Station on the Susitna River aboard the steamer, *L.J.Perry,* bound for Sunrise City. Upon their arrival, Luther Kelly hired C.C. Smith to help haul gear and to serve as a guide from Glacier Creek to Crow Creek. At 5 am the following morning they attempted to cross the Arm, but the seas were too rough. By evening they were finally able to cross in a small skiff. The men spent the night at Dr. Freeman's prospecting camp on Glacier Creek. Here they had their first unpleasant experience with the "mosquito pest." Mendenhall observed that the mountains were green about half way up, with snow at higher elevations.

Luther "Yellowstone" Kelly, Mendenhall's assistant, at Portage, Alaska, 1898 (W. C. Mendenhall 9 USGS)

On June 23rd, the men were slowly making their way up Crow Creek. They encountered Mr. Davidson working his claim just below treeline. Neither Mr. Davidson, nor his men, were able to provide any information as to what lay beyond the pass. Just below the pass the three men "camped that night above timber line, and it proved above the mosquito line also, much to our relief," wrote Kelly in his journal.

On the morning of June 24th, the men reached the pass and proceeded down the other side. After several stream crossings, they stopped for lunch and to dry out in the sun. Prospectors nearby told them they called the stream Raven Creek. Mendenhall took notes on the surrounding geology of the upper valley, writing, "I am sure that I have never before seen such slopes maintained to such heights." Mountain sheep were seen in abundance on the upper slopes. Later that evening they camped on one of the gravel bars of the Yuklahitna (Eagle River).

The next morning, June 25, Smith headed back over Crow Pass, having come farther than he had intended. Mendenhall and Kelly hiked on in awe of this spectacular glaciated valley. Mendenhall found the upper Yukla "a miniature Yosemite." Kelly observed, "This valley is one of great beauty, well timbered and walled at its upper extremeity by bold, and precipitous mountains." The valley began to widen as they meandered and bushwacked down river. Occasionally, they located an old trail but lost it again in thick brush. Finally, they made camp on a river bar as far from shore as possible to escape the mosquitoes. Headnets and gloves were standard attire.

On June 26, they "entered a region of forest fires, whose smoke obscured everything until [they] reached the coast, and at times was so close and heavy as to be stifling, but which never seemed to affect in any way the activity of the insect pests," Mendenhall lamented. They passed several Indian hunting shacks with remains of moose and mountain sheep. Mendenhall was overcome by the heat for a time as they hiked with heavy packs, gloves, and headnets.

The following day they continued their trudge down the valley of the Yukla, crossing and recrossing the river, and hacking through brush. Smoke still obscured the valley. Mendenhall continued to suffer from the heat and broke out in a rash. At 9 pm they finally emerged on to the mud flats and could see the opposite shore near Knik. Kelly killed a grouse for dinner - a welcome change of pace. The mosquitoes were the worst yet, and neither man was able to eat much of his meal.

It had taken them a week to reach the coast. Bogs, fallen timber, and the winding Yukla all worked against them. They were also burdened with heavy packs. Indian and game trails appeared and then vanished. Kelly wrote later in a report for the US Army that it was the "heat and mosquito pest in all its fury" that slowed them down. At the coast they hired an Indian to take them across Knik Arm, where they rejoined the expedition at Tyonek.

Knik, Alaska (U.S. Alaska Engineering Commission PCA 131-167 ASL)

# CHAPTER EIGHT

# THE IDITAROD TRAIL

With its origins deeply rooted in wild days of the Gold Rush, the Iditarod Trail Sled Dog Race has grown into a world-famous event  Originally, it began as a network of trails connecting Indian villages and trading posts. Then the Klondike gold rush of the 1890s created an overflow of prospectors who poured through Alaska. Prospectors set their sights on the new discoveries at Nome, Fairbanks, and Iditarod. During the winter months gold seekers arrived in the port towns of Valdez and Seward in need of access to the Interior gold fields. Those once-faint trails developed into major access routes to the gold.

In 1898, the same year thousands arrived at the Cook Inlet gold fields, "three lucky Swedes" struck gold at Anvil Creek near Nome. Word reached Seattle the following year, and another gold rush began. By 1900, a tent city of 30,000 gold seekers was encamped on the beach at Nome. Like all gold strikes, boom turned to bust as the gold was mined out. In five years Nome's population dwindled to about 5,000, yet it remained the center for transportation for northwestern Alaska.

When land and sea froze solid during the long, dark winter months government officials realized the need to develop transportation routes to the Interior towns of Nome and Fairbanks. The port of Valdez provided access to Fairbanks with connections to Nome, but members of the Alaska Road Commission were interested in shortening the distance to Nome.

On January 31, 1908, an Alaska Road Commission reconnaissance party left the port town of Seward to locate a sled road to Nome. Following the route over Crow Pass, the men  arrived in Nome on April 5, 1908. George Pulham, who was in charge of the party, and Walter L. Goodwin, the commission superintendent for the Nome district, favored this route. It was nearly 400 miles shorter than the Valdez-Fairbanks-Yukon River route.

On Christmas Day, 1908, William A. Dikeman and John Beaton discovered gold on Otter Creek, a tributary of the Iditarod River. It was only 60 miles south of the Alaska Road Commission's newly established trail. Iditarod was the last major gold strike in Alaska.

Dog teams at Bird Creek outbound on the Iditarod Trail (U.S. Alaska Engineering Commission PCA 131-167 ASL)

## CROW PASS TRAIL VS. INDIAN PASS TRAIL

The Crow Pass Trail, traversed by Walter Mendenhall and Luther Kelly in 1898 during their US Army geological survey, was used for many years as a winter route to Knik and points north. In the fall of 1908, a trail was completed by the Alaska Road Commission between Girdwood and Indian providing access to the longer, but less severe Indian Pass route. Goodwin, nevertheless, felt one mile of tough going through Crow Pass was better than the five miles over Indian Pass. He provided funding in 1909 to improve the Crow Pass Trail. In the succeeding years, although Crow Pass was graded, Indian Pass remained the more popular route. The avalanche-prone Crow Pass Trail fell into disuse until the 1970s, when Girl Scouts of America, Susitna Council, rebuilt the trail for recreational use.

In two years the town of Iditarod was booming. It became the center of the "Inland Empire" with two banks, 12 saloons, two wholesale liquor houses, a hospital, two sawmills, machine shops, cold storage plant for meats, and a bottling plant. It was the hub for a vast gold field which boasted its own telephone system.

The *Iditarod Pioneer* and the *Iditarod Nugget* kept news-hungry prospectors satiated with a constant supply of information. Iditarod businesses advertised in the popular *Alaska-Yukon Gazeteer* published in Seattle, Washington. More and more prospectors traveled over the Iditarod Trail each day, forcing the Alaska Road Commission to improve the trail from Seward to Iditarod and Nome.

Valdez, with the blessing of Major Wilds Richardson of the US Army Engineers, began a promotional campaign in 1909 which advocated the Valdez-Fairbanks-Iditarod route to the interior gold fields. Not to be outdone, the citizens of Seward organized the Seward Commercial Club to publicize their town as **the** port of entry to the Iditarod - "Seward, the Gateway to the Iditarod." At the same time, the US Congress appropriated funds for the construction of "roads" in Alaska. The Seward route was still considered secondary, and initially received less funding than the Richardson Highway out of Valdez, but things would change.

Pressure on the federal government to develop better roads in Alaska finally prevailed. Walter L. Goodwin of the Alaska Road Commission led a party of eight men and six dog teams of seven dogs each out of Nome on November 9, 1910. Their purpose was to clear and mark the trail, construct bridges, and grade where necessary. Three and a half months later the party arrived in

Seward. The trail from Seward to Nome via Iditarod was measured by a cyclometer to be 958 miles long; it is actually over 1100 miles.

No sooner had Goodwin's party arrived when gold seekers just off ships from Seattle began the long haul north. Initially, few men mushed, as dogs were scarce and fairly expensive. What dogs could be found were trained daily on the streets of Seward for the long haul to the Interior. Most men walked or snowshoed 10 to 60 miles a day. Soon more and more cheechakos, or Alaskan green-horns, would arrive in Seward for a life of adventure and riches. What follows is a chronological sampling of early trail-users (see next page).

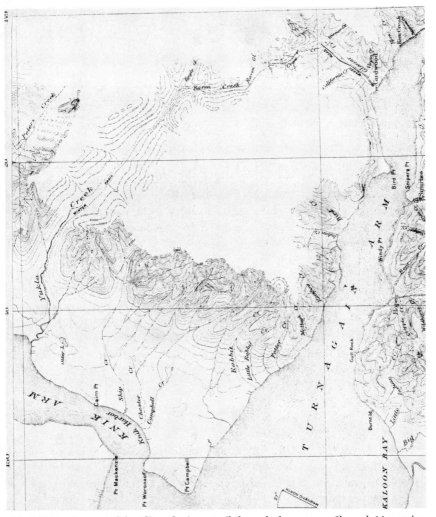

Alfred H. Brooks map of the Iditarod winter trail through the western Chugach Mountains, 1915 (USGS Bulletin 642)

Dog teams waiting in Seward for loads to haul north on the Iditarod Trail (AMHA)

- The Wells Fargo Express Company opened offices in Seward and Iditarod in 1911. A gold shipment, under contract with Wells Fargo left Iditarod on December 14, 1911, for Seward. Under the guidance of expert dog mushers Bob Griffiths and Gus Norton, 11 mushers drove four dog teams pulling one ton of gold dust. The teams reached Girdwood on January 5, 1912, following the route over Crow Pass. The mushers drove down Fourth Avenue in Seward on January 27, 1912.

- In March 1912, Belmore Browne, Herschel Parker, and photographer, Merl Lavoy, departed Seward by dogteam for Mt. McKinley. Browne and Parker had been members of Fredrick Cook's 1906 expedition to circumnavigate Mt. Mckinley, but left before Cook's infamous claim to have climbed the highest peak in North America. Later, hearing Cook's claim, the two men were skeptical; they were determined to prove once and for all that Fredrick Cook had not climbed Mt. McKinley. It would be many years before their discovery was confirmed.

- Browne, Parker and Lavoy accompanied Bob Griffiths, on his return trip from the Wells Fargo delivery, up the Crow Pass Trail to Knik. After a rough crossing over the pass, they spent the night at the Raven Creek roadhouse at the head of Eagle River valley. The following day they rose at the crack of dawn for the 20-mile mush to the Eagle River roadhouse. Since Eagle River was open in many places, they had to pull the sleds through the icy water. The next day they arrived in Knik for the long journey inland.

Knik, Alaska (AMHA)

* Weekly mail service to Iditarod and Nome began 1914 . Mail was run in relays. It usually took 25 days one-way to get mail from Seward to Iditarod. With improvements to the trail the run was cut to 14 days. Mail service over the Iditarod Trail continued through the winter of 1918-19, when rail service from Seward to Wasilla brought an end to use of this section of the Iditarod Trail.

* In the spring of 1915, Kenneth Gideon and his friend, Art, arrived by steamer in Seward to seek their fortunes. Trudging their way on foot toward Turnagain Arm, they hauled sleds over the snow-covered trail. Instead of

U.S. Mail team going up Indian Creek Pass, 1917, with Carl Deupree, dog driver (AMHA)

crossing the mountains over Crow Pass, they decided to follow the more popular trail over Indian Creek Pass. This new trail had one serious drawback - the winds along Turnagain Arm. The two men encountered long stretches of the trail blown clear of snow.

- Hauling their gear up and over Indian Creek Pass, Gideon and Art stayed at Fat's roadhouse. Gideon wrote in his memoirs, *Wandering Boy*, that "a chap known only as 'Fat' went up to timber line on the Anchorage side of the pass and built a 'roadhouse'... a cottonwood pole structure which no self-respecting farmer would use for a stable. But Fat was smart. He knew what those blizzards were like on the Pass and he knew they were frequent. Therefore he reasoned that if he should build a shelter at timber line a goodly percentage of those traveling from Anchorage would be compelled to stop."

With the completion of the railroad between Seward and Anchorage in 1915, the Iditarod Trail through Chugach State Park fell into disuse. By the 1930s the use of dog teams to haul mail and supplies would diminish with the advent of the airplane. By the 1950s, even dog teams were becoming a thing of the past as snowmachine use increased rapidly throughout Alaska. The trails over Crow and Indian passes disappeared under a dense cover of alder and willow thickets. It would be many years before these trails again became popular thoroughfares — this time for recreation.

**JUJIRO WADA: AN UNUSUAL MUSHING ENTREPENUER**
On a trip through Seward in early 1909, the Seward Commercial Club (SCC) asked dog musher, Jujiro Wada, if he could mush from Seward to Iditarod and back in less than 50 days. The SCC would pay his expenses. Wada proposed an additional $500 bonus if he could get 1,000 mushers over the route (either way) by the end of April, 1910. The SCC accepted Wada's proposal and hired Alfred Lowell of Seward to accompany him for $5.00 a day. Who was Jujiro Wada? Why did the Seward Commercial Company seek his help in promoting Seward ?

Jujiro Wada arrived in Alaska in 1890 aboard a whaling ship. He was reported to have jumped ship at Icy Cape to live among the Eskimos. By 1900 he was in Barrow, carrying mail by dog team and trading furs. Wada was a well-known dog musher in the Tanana District when Felix Pedro, in 1902, made his gold strike near Fairbanks. For a time Wada worked as a cook on E.T. Barnette's steamer. In 1907 Wada began a year-long odyssey: travelling by dog team from the head of the Chandalar River to the Arctic Ocean, Wada spent several months on Herschel Island near the mouth of the McKenzie River in the Yukon Territory. He subsequently travelled up the McKenzie to the Rat River, where he crossed over to the headwaters of the Porcupine.

Wada and his dogs survived on seals he killed along the coast and game he shot inland. While crossing to the Porcupine River he lost his goggles and became snowblind. Unable to hunt for food, he boiled the rawhide from his snowshoes for himself and his dogs. As the dogs weakened, they enviously sniffed and licked at his oil-soaked clothing. Still miles above Fort Yukon, he began feeding his dogs strips of the seal-skin clothing he wore. Finally, one year after he had set out, Jujiro Wada and his dog team arrived in Fort Yukon.

Two years later, in December, 1909, Wada and Lowell, the most experienced mushers in Alaska, set out from Seward. They were the first mushers over Rainy Pass that winter. By late January, the first stampeders headed back with Wada, who carefully blazed and flagged the entire trail on the return journey. Once in Seward, Wada headed to Seattle to pick up the mushers he would guide to Iditarod. The Seward Commercial Company paid Wada his $500 bonus.

In 1913 Wada was once again in Seattle, putting together a large outfit to take to a new gold field near Aniak on the Kuskokwim River. Ever the businessman, he approached the tabasco millionaire, E.A. McIlhenny, whom he had met years earlier in Barrow, for financial support. McIlhenny gave Wada $15,000 for the venture. The following year Wada paid his philanthropic backer a visit in Louisiana to report on the mine.

Dog teams leaving Seward, Alaska, enroute to the gold fields, circa 1904-06 (Wheatley Collection, AMHA)

His mushing exploits and prospecting ventures continued in Canada. In 1923 Wada left Herschel Island in the Canadian Arctic for a 130-day dog sled trip to Winnepeg, Manitoba, "to consult with Winnepeg businessmen." In 1937 Wada was in California visiting friends from Fairbanks on yet another venture when he contracted pneumonia. He died in San Diego on 5 March 1937 at the age of 65.

---

**IDITAROD TRAIL SLED DOG RACE**

In 1966 dog musher, Joe Redington, Sr. met  history-buff, Dorothy Page. Page was appointed president of the Wasilla-Knik Centennial Committee, organized to help celebrate the 100th anniversary of the purchase of Alaska from the Russians. She proposed a sled dog race to Joe Redington. Their fortuitous meeting gave birth to an idea of celebrating Alaska's 1967 centennial with a tribute to the contribution mushers had made to Alaska. The first race was two heats of 25 miles each along a segment of the old Iditarod Trail.

Over the following years Redington kept alive the dream of a race to Nome. Finally, in March, 1973, the Iditarod Trail Sled Dog Race became a reality. Thirty-four teams signed up to run the 1,049 miles from Anchorage to Nome for a purse of $51,000. It took Dick Wilmarth 20 days to claim his first-place prize.

In the early days, the Iditarod race was a long camping trip - the trail vague and support was minimal. Over the years, dog care and gear improved dramatically, increasing speed and efficiency along the trail. The fastest teams now traverse the 1,049 miles in as few as ten days.

Yet the Iditarod Trail remains a piece of history. Not much has changed in almost a hundred years. Mushers and their dogs must still endure the hardships of the trail - the cold, the snow, the rugged terrain, and the moose. Every March, business booms again for the settlements along the Iditarod Trail as mushers seek out warmth and hospitality. And a little gold and silver await those who dare to traverse this rugged trail through wild Alaska.

# BROWN & HAWKINS

Every Stetson bears the Stetson Name

If you select a

## Stetson

you are bound to get the popular style, as well as the hat which is well proportioned and becoming.

We have the Stetson Soft and Derby Hats in all the latest styles.

**The Store With the Goods**

# Iditarod Stage Line

PAT KEYS AND PHIL MAYHAN, PROPS.

Telephone Main 61.          Office at Ophir House, Willow St.

TRIPS EVERY DAY EXCEPT SUNDAY

Leaves Flat Creek ........................ 9:00 a. m.
Leaves Flat for Discovery Otter at ........ 5:00 p. m.
Leaves Discovery Otter at ......... . .......8.00 p. m.
Leaves Ophir House, Iditarod ........... . 2:00 p. m.
Round trip to Flat, $6 ; round trip to Discovery Otter, $8.

**PASSENGERS, EXPRESS and FREIGHT**

# Clark Lumber Co.

Phone 10—IDITAROD— Phone 10

## Rough and Dressed Lumber

ALL KINDS OF FREIGHTING DONE. PROMPT DELIVERY GUARANTEED.

# Alaska Commercial Co.

Have Established a Station at Susitna, at the forks of the Susitna and Yentna rivers, and will carry a full line of miners' supplies

OTHER STATIONS AT

UNALASKA, KODIAK, KARLUK, KAGUYAK, AFOGNAK, TYONICK AND SUNRISE

## WE SATISFY THE HUNGRY

# The Royal

## TODAY---SPECIAL SUNDAY DINNER---TODAY

Everything in Season

WILLOW STREET          T. L. McGRATH, PROP.

Advertisements (*Iditarod Pioneer* and *Iditarod Nugget* Newspapers, 1911)

# CHAPTER NINE

# THE ALASKA RAILROAD

Early prospectors wanted the American government to provide better access and transportation to the gold fields of Alaska. Trails were being built, but they were less reliable than railroads. Access overland during the winter was worse than travelling by boat in the summer. With all the gold being shipped out, they argued, the government should do something. The federal government, on the other hand, assumed private capital should pay for railroads as it had in the crossing of the Great Plains, over 50 years before.

Finally, inspired by public comment and the large gold strikes in Alaska, Congress passed a railroad act on May 14, 1898. The Act granted railroad companies, organized under the land law, to obtain rights of way, terminals, and any raw materials needed for construction. In the two years following the Act, 11 companies filed for railroad routes in Alaska. Few were successful.

## ALASKA CENTRAL RAILROAD (1902-1909)

In 1902, a group of Seattle businessmen formed the privately-financed Alaska Central Railroad Company (ACR). C. W. Dickinson was president and general manager; John F. Ballaine was secretary and auditor.

In 1903, surveyors arrived in Seward and by mid-summer began surveying the right-of-way to Turnagain Arm. Ballaine acquired a homestead belonging to Mrs. Alfred Lowell, widow of the famous dog musher, and with his brother, Frank Ballaine, laid out the new city of Seward. On August 23, 1903, Seward was officially founded.

Ballaine formed the Tanana Construction Company with himself as president and manager. The Alaska Central Railroad then contracted the Tanana Company to build the railroad; in the deal Ballaine retained a majority of the railroad's stock.

On April 16, 1904, construction began. Beginning wages were $2.00 a day. Backed by the Sovereign Bank of Canada, two financiers, A.C. Frost from Chicago, and H.C. Osborne from Toronto, invested heavily in the Tanana Construction Company and the Alaska Central Railroad.

Facing page: Engine with nine foot rotary snowplow at Potter Section House, Chugach State Park Headquarters (Al Meiners)

Fearing Alaska's natural resources would be gobbled up by large companies, President Theodore Roosevelt issued an executive order in 1906 prohibiting coal mining on public lands in Alaska. The action was compounded by the financial panic of 1907, and the failure of the Sovereign Bank of Canada. The Alaska Central Railroad, its rails extending only 51 miles from Seward, 13 miles short of Portage, went bankrupt the following year.

## ALASKA NORTHERN RAILROAD (1909-1915)

The Alaska Northern Railroad (ANR) was chartered in 1909 in Washington State, following the foreclosure of the Alaska Central Railroad. The majority stockholder was a Canadian, F.C. Jemmett of Toronto. They took over three steam locomotives, two baggage cars, 33 freight cars, and one service car from the Alaska Central Railroad. The Alaska Northern immediately repaired the rails and completed construction to Mile 71 at Kern Creek near Girdwood. Transportation continued from Kern via the Iditarod Trail, over either Crow or Indian passes.

No sooner had the Alaska Northern started trains running again when they ran out of money and halted construction. Receiving no financial support or tax relief from the federal government, the Alaska Northern Railroad was

Dinkey No. 20, narrow gauge, 0-4-0ST, Davenport Locomotive Works, 1908. Panama Canal Surplus. (Alaska Railroad Collection, AMHA, Alaska Engineering Commission G 443)

buried under an avalanche of operating costs. They begged the federal government to intervene.

In 1911, the Secretary of Interior, Walt Fisher, visited Alaska. He concluded that Alaska's sluggish economy was due to its poor transportation system and he recommended to President Taft that the federal government purchase the ANR and complete construction to the Yukon River. Taft signed the Alaska Railroad Organic Act in February, 1912. Congress, however, was skeptical and promptly halted the funding of construction until further study.

**ALASKA RAILROAD (1915 to present)**
Finally, in 1915, President Woodrow Wilson, by executive order, purchased the ANR and its 71 miles of track and equipment for $1.5 million. Wilson placed the new government railroad under the auspices of the Department of Interior. The Alaskan Engineering Commission was appointed to oversee construction of the "government railroad," which remained nameless until 1923.

It took two years to repair the original 71 miles of track and to begin regular train service. Meanwhile, construction camps were established to work on other sections of railway as well. In 1915 a construction camp was built at Ship Creek, four miles off the main route of the railroad. Within a few weeks, close to 2,000 people crowded the expanding tent city. Men arrived daily, attracted by the prospect of jobs. Pay was 37.5 cents an hour for manual labor.

The tent city lasted only a few weeks. The railroad needed the land along Ship Creek for facilities, and feared the overcrowded conditions might contribute

The short-lived tent city of Anchorage, 1915 (Alberta Pyatt, photographer, AMHA)

to water contamination. A townsite was selected on the bluff south of the creek, with homesites for sale. Citizens of the new settlement voted to call the town Anchorage. There was to be no alcohol or gambling.

To complete the 471 miles of track from Seward to Fairbanks, the Alaska Railroad required additional machinery. The completion of the Panama Canal in 1914 left a vast surplus of equipment, so the federal government transferred steam shovels, derricks, locomotives, and shop machinery from the equator for construction of a railroad almost 6000 miles to the north. No sooner had the equipment arrived than World War I began.

World War I delayed construction of the Alaska Railroad. By 1919 the Seward - Anchorage line was greatly improved, but still not complete. Trains could get through to Mile 47, where passengers would transfer to dog team or horse sled for 15 miles, at which point they would again embark on a train to Mile 71 at Kern. For six miles past Kern they would again go by dog or horse transport, and finally take the train the remainder of the way to Anchorage. Impassable terrain was the main obstacle.

On February 5, 1922, an inaugural run from Seward to Nenana celebrated the newly completed line. The total cost of construction was $65 million. President Harding arrived in Seward in 1923 for a train trip to Nenana and on

Railroad construction camp at Bird Point, 1917 (P.S. Hunt, photographer, Alaska Railroad Collection AEC G 608, AMHA)

July 15, 1923 in an atmosphere of sweltering heat and mosquitoes, he drove a gold spike commemorating the completion of the Alaska Railroad.

The year 1938 was a landmark. It was the first year since this railroad line was constructed that the Alaska Railroad made money. During World War II, there was a rise in profits when the railroad began hauling military and civilian supplies. Following World War II, there was fear that Alaska's small population could not sustain a multi-million dollar railroad, but the Railbelt grew. Although passenger service between Seward and Anchorage was suspended in 1954 with the completion of the Seward Highway and regular airplane service to the Outside, the railroad remained an important link to the Interior.

The railroad has provided passenger service, and delivery of mail and goods to landlocked communities of Interior Alaska. In 1966, Congress established the Department of Transportation with the new Federal Railroad Commission taking over jurisdiction of the Alaska Railroad. In January, 1985, the Alaska Railroad was sold to the State of Alaska for $22.3 million. The Alaska Railroad was the only railroad ever owned by the United States government.

---

**ALASKA RAILROAD MILEPOST**
**from Seward to Potter Section House**

Mile 0 — Seward, Alaska - the southern terminus and primary port of entry for the Alaska Railroad.

Mile 64 — Portage, Alaska - the community was destroyed in the 1964 earthquake, when the ground dropped as much as 12 feet.

Mile 71 — Kern Creek - the track was completed to this point when the Alaska Northern Railroad was purchased by the federal government in 1915.

Mile 74.8 — Girdwood, two miles up valley, was settled in 1896 by prospectors looking for gold. The road to Crow Creek Mine and the Iditarod Trail follows the valley north.

Mile 78 — Last rail, between Seward and Anchorage, laid on September 11, 1918.

Mile 86.6 — Bird Creek served as a major construction camp for the railroad

Mile 88.7 — Indian Creek -provided access to Indian Creek Pass, the alternative to the Crow Pass/Iditarod Trail, through the Chugach Mountains.

Mile 93.5 — Rainbow served as a construction camp for the railroad

Mile 100.6 — Potter Section House State Historic Site was built in 1929 by the Alaska Railroad. The section house currently houses the headquarters for Chugach State Park and a visitor center in summer. There is an example of a snowblower engine on the tracks next to the building.

# CHAPTER TEN

# A GRASSROOTS TRIUMPH:

## CREATION OF CHUGACH STATE PARK

After purchasing the Alaska territory from Russia, the federal government retained loose control over vast tracts of land. The mountainous backdrop above Anchorage was one of those parcels. Following World War II, Anchorage grew rapidly; the burgeoning population slowly moved up into the mountains to live and to recreate - hunting, hiking, or driving. The situation was starting to get out of hand.

There was a growing fear among a myriad of recreationists that access to the mountains had become more and more restrictive as the populations of Anchorage and Eagle River increased. Private land encircling the mountains already threatened to cut road access, forcing confrontations between property owners and recreationists with occasionally hair raising results. It was feared that further growth might cut road access altogether forcing people to trespass. There was also the problem of numerous trails spreading out in a haphazard network of troughs through the alpine tundra. There was little or no maintenance of trails and footpaths. Hunting was allowed throughout the Chugach Mountains, and by the mid-1960s hunting pressure from a growing human population began to take its toll on wildlife.

People were beginning to react. Vern Haik and his wife, homesteaded 40 acres in Chugiak in the early 1940s. Vern saw firsthand how quickly the communities of Chugiak and Eagle River were growing and threading their way up Eagle River valley. When Alaska was still a territory Haik told a meeting of the Isaak Walton League, a conservation organization of sport fishermen, that some of the land up in the mountains around the housing developments should be preserved as a park.

The Alaska Sportsmen's Game Preservation Association, a group of sportsmen from Eagle River, felt Dall sheep were disappearing from the front range of the Chugach Mountains. They felt that this was a direct result of development and increased hunting pressure from a growing human population. They had done some footwork prior to 1970 in the direction of protection. According to Dale

Mount Rumble from Peter's Creek Valley (Steve Johnson)

Bondurant, an activist in the fight to preserve the Chugach, their main concern was loss of habitat. The group was willing to accept restrictions on hunting in the mountains if habitat was to be preserved. As Bondurant said, "Without habitat, there's no game."

In 1969 logging sales in Bird and Indian valleys threatened to disrupt a rugged, forested retreat enjoyed by many local residents. A group of private citizens filed suit against the State of Alaska to prevent private logging operations from destroying this beautiful paradise. Claiming "grandfather" rights, they won their suit to preserve this area for quieter pursuits.

For a handful of people who dared speak of preserving wilderness, Alaska in the 1960s was a hostile place. In August, 1969, a small group of Alaskans met to discuss their concerns over the threats they perceived to the mountains above Anchorage. With a population of only 126,000, Anchorage's growth was already pushing its way up into the foothills. As new communities sprang up around the Chugach Mountains, people took a personal interest in the vast landscape above them. Concern for human growth, for destruction of habitat, and for loss of wildlife brought together a diverse group in an attempt to protect their own backyard.

Those who savored a sojourn in these mountains were sick of fighting political brushfires, and decided it would be better to protect the entire area once and for all. Why not a state park? someone asked. A state park that would

Eklutna Lake at sunset (Steve Johnson)

encompass as much of the western end of the Chugach Mountains as possible. This August meeting was the genesis for the Chugach State Park Ad Hoc Committee, which sought to stop the twin threats of development and destruction. There were a number of events which precipitated the park's creation and laid the groundwork for swift passage of a bill. It would take an immense grassroots effort to save the "land beyond the trees."

Local men and women worked quietly through the winter months to garner support for the idea of a state park just outside of Anchorage. Their work was made easier by the blossoming environmental movement. They presented talks and slide shows explaining the need for protection. Over and over they told their audiences that these mountains belonged to the people. Development should not cut off access to recreational areas.

They spoke with one voice. There was broad support and endorsement from such diverse organizations as the Issac Walton League, Anchorage Motor Mushers, Alaska Conservation Society, Alaska Chapter of Sierra Club, Friends of the Earth, Nordic Ski Club, Mountaineering Club of Alaska, City of Anchorage Parks and Recreation Commission, the City Water Utility, Borough Planning Commission, and the Alaska Sportsmen's Game Preservation Association. It was a synergistic effort which produced remarkable results.

What land was available for a park? The federal government over the past decade had slowly released lands to the state as part of the Alaska Statehood Act. Alaska was eligible to "select" some 103,500,000 acres from vacant, unappropriated public lands around the state over a twenty-five year period. A vast 490,866 acre chunk of land above Anchorage, under the jurisdiction of the Department of Interior's Bureau of Land Management (BLM), was about to be granted to the state through this selection process. The Chugach State Park Ad Hoc Committee decided to go for the whole chunk hoping to get a large part. According to Sharon Cissna, chairperson of the committee from 1969-70, with so much land being turned over to the state, they decided to ask for every acre. And they got every acre.

The proposal was not without opposition. There was the question of "locking up" such a large area. Opponents hollered they would be locked out of their favorite stomping grounds. Objections came primarily from the motor sport groups and hunters who feared restrictions on their favorite pursuits, and at the worst, being locked out altogether. For years snowmachines, dirt bikes, and cars had ranged freely through the mountains above Anchorage. Hunters roamed the ridges in pursuit of their quarry. Some people suggested that further study was needed to determine the best possible uses for the land. All of these concerns were addressed in the final bill.

Dedication ceremony for the new Chugach State Park, 1970 (Chugach State Park Archives)

Conflicts were resolved by zoning areas for specific activities. The eastern, more mountainous section would be designated wilderness, the central area would be a scenic area, and the western periphery would be for recreational activities. The bill stated that the establishment of the park was "to protect and supply a satisfactory water supply for the use of the people, to provide recreational opportunities for the people by providing areas for specified uses, to protect areas of unique and exceptional scenic value, to provide for the public display of local wildlife where it shall be protected from hunting except as otherwise required to preserve habitat on the advice of the Department of Fish and Game, and to protect existing wilderness characteristics of the easterly interior." The bill was now ready to be presented to the Alaska State Legislature.

Finally in January, 1970, the Chugach State Park Ad Hoc Committee sent Art Davidson of Indian to Juneau to present the bill to Senator Lowell Thomas, Jr. Thomas was an excellent choice to introduce a bill creating Chugach State Park. A few years earlier he and Charles Lindbergh, the famous aviator, had discussed the concept of setting aside some of Alaska's unique wilderness. Thomas invited Lindbergh to speak before a joint session of the Alaska State Legislature in 1968, to promote the idea of setting aside some of Alaska's treasures. The seed had been sown.

Once in Juneau the bill gained bi-partisan support. A similar bill was introduced in the House by Representative Helen Beirne of Anchorage. The Senate bill passed through committee first, so action was taken on that bill. It passed both Senate and House in May, 1970, and was signed onto law on August 6, 1970 by Governor Keith Miller.

It is, in hindsight, a remarkable piece of legislation. Through citizen involvement and grassroots organization this park was brought to fruition. The juxtaposition of a wilderness and a growing metropolis is unique in this country. The rugged mountains which rise above our city form a daily reminder of the frontier spirit which compelled a group of Alaskans to set aside a part of wild Alaska. Future generations will now be able to experience a wilderness kept "unlocked" for all time.

Part Three

# Natural History of Chugach State Park

# CHAPTER ELEVEN

# NATURE IN CHUGACH STATE PARK

Interest in nature is not the private reserve of scientists. Amateur naturalists have always sought out wild places for pristine beauty, for wildlife, for colorful wildflowers, and for meditation. Naturalists such as Henry David Thoreau and John Muir, Barry Lopez and Edward Abbey, Terry Tempest Williams and Ann Zwinger, cultivate others interest in the wonders of nature. Their writings demonstrate our kinship with the natural world, encouraging us to take a closer look.

At a casual glance the landscape of Chugach State Park appears as a mosaic of rock, water, and vegetation, an inanimate place devoid of living things. Upon closer examination we may see a moose, a ptarmigan, or a spruce tree, yet plants and animals are not randomly distributed. Plant distribution is determined by soil, topography, temperature, and water. Animals, in turn, rely on specific plants for food and shelter. All of these facets are intertwined to form a whole functioning ecosystem.

How does the natural world function? Why does an animal live where it does? How can plants survive sub-zero temperatures? How have animals adapted to living in northern latitudes? How can we appreciate the nature and beauty of Chugach State Park unless we understand how the pieces fit together? What follows, I hope, will provide new insight into this special place.

**Plant Communities**
Nature is a vast community, or ecosystem, made up of living and nonliving components. Plants and animals together form the biotic (living) component; materials, such as water, soil, and rocks, make up the abiotic (nonliving) segment. Over the years various classification systems have been used for describing communities, or groupings, within an ecosystem. The most widely used method is to identify dominant plant species and their associated animals. Although plant communities may merge into one another, each community is bound together by similar nutrient requirements and climatic conditions.

Facing page: View of Mount Rumble from Peter's Creek (Steve Johnson)

Plant communities are complex. They are influenced by various factors such as microclimate, slope, aspect, water, and soil found at a certain altitude or latitude. Plant communities do not follow the contour lines up a mountain side, but meander down drainages on northern exposures, and edge upward on southern exposures. There is a gradual transition from one community into another as one ascends up a mountain. The most abrupt border between communities is **treeline,** the boundary beyond which trees no longer grow.

Although communities can be dissected into finer and finer categories based on such factors as percent of canopy cover, height of vegetation, moisture, and species composition, for the purposes of this book the community classifications will remain broad. There are nine such major biotic communities within Chugach State Park (Table 2).

---

**TREELINE**

From a distance a ragged line of trees is visible part way up the slopes of the Chugach Mountains. A dark carpet of spruce ascends the mountain's folds until this vanguard finds resistance to its upward momentum. Treeline - one of the dominant features of the park - is the biological boundary beyond which trees cannot grow. A feature of elevation and latitude, it is the limit of tree growth on mountains and in polar regions.

Two main factors influence treeline - climate and topography. As one travels up into the mountains, there is an increase in total precipitation - especially snowfall. Although snow falls in large quantities in the mountains, it is deposited by the wind at varying depths. In excessive amounts, snow can limit tree growth by limiting the growing season. Topography varies widely resulting in an irregular treeline along mountain slopes. South-facing slopes receive more solar heat, therefore spring arrives earlier than on north-facing slopes. As a result, timberline occurs several hundred feet higher on southern exposures than on northern ones.

Many environmental factors act in concert to influence treeline by inhibiting tree growth. Cold-hardy conifers, the dominant treeline species, are able to tolerate extremes in temperature down to -80° F. in North America. Cold winter temperatures are not a limiting factor to tree growth. Even the hardiest conifer requires a two-month growing season with little or no frost. During the summer months, new needle growth is extremely sensitive to freezing temperatures.

Wind is a major cause of tree damage above treeline. There are two primary ways that wind damages trees above treeline - abrasion and desiccation. Abrasion occurs when the wind scours bark and needles with blowing ice and snow, occasionally breaking branches or the top of the tree, or crown. Desiccation results when warm, dry chinook winds evaporate the protective layer of snow or rime, exposing the tops of stunted trees and dehydrating the branches. Spring reveals dwarfed trees topped by a belt of dead, rust-colored foliage.

For all the extreme harshness of the alpine environment, a few trees may survive above treeline. In this windswept alpine domain, they live as scattered islands of shrubs hundreds of years old. Krummholz, a German word meaning "elfin timber", or "crooked wood," are the bonsai trees of the alpine world. They are formed as a result of severe wind exposure and desiccation of new growth. These dense tree islands often develop from a single tree which has been forced to grow horizontal along the ground. Since Krummholz rarely produce seeds, a second generation begins where upper branches pressed against the soil take root, producing erect stems. Growth spreads leeward under the protection of a rock, or a depression, or the tree's own branches. (continued on next page)

Krummholz spruce tree hugging the ground above treeline (Jenny Zimmerman)

Chugach State Park is truly a "land above the trees." Over 75% of the park is above treeline, making alpine tundra the largest biotic community. Treeline generally follows the 1,500 foot contour up Turnagain Arm, but zig-zags up and down drainages along the front range as it passes above Anchorage. On the north side of the park treeline rises to almost 3,000 feet spreading up the valleys deep into the mountains. Although the land seems barren, there is an abundance of life in the alpine tundra. Crouching down to examine the myriad of miniature plants, a new world lies outstretched at our feet.

## Competion and Selection

Biotic (living) communities are not static, but dynamic and ever-changing. Organisms must compete for resources such as light, water, minerals, food, and shelter. Mammals and birds select a "preferred" habitat within a community to meet their specific needs. A variety of birds and animals can share a habitat by selecting different parts of a community - such as the forest canopy, low shrubs, or forest floor. Partitioning of a community allows a greater number of creatures to share resources.

The open alpine tundra of Chugach State Park, for example, can accommodate a variety of birds because of differences in feeding behavior. Snow Buntings spend the summer slowly searching the steeper, rockier areas for insects and seeds. Horned Larks and Water Pipits actively hunt out insects on short-grass tundra. Northern Wheatears hop from rock to ground on open slopes in pursuit of flying insects.

In a plant community, competition results in a prolonged sequence of changes called **succession**. Succession occurs under a variety of conditions and, in most communities, each change not only affects the plant community, but the animals which depend on the plant communities resources. Moose, for example, prefer willow, birch, and alder ranging from 3 to 25 feet in height. A tall-shrub community usually indicates a disturbed site, one that has been burned or cleared, and thus is subject to changes in successional growth. Leaves dropped by the shrubs prepare a rich medium for growth by spruce seedlings. As a forest matures, the shade-intolerant shrubs can no longer compete. Moose must then move to a more favorable site for food.

**Three types of succession that may be encountered in Chugach.**

First is forest succession on a dry site, following a major disturbance such as an avalanche

— Fireweed/grass community

    — Alder/willow shrubs

        — Aspen

           — Spruce climax forest

Succession on unvegetated sites following glacial retreat occur on bedrock and glacial moraine. This may take hundreds of year to reach a climax community.

— Lichens/mosses

    — Heath/grass community

        — Shrubs

           — Black cottonwood

                — Spruce forest

Ponds or old stream channels slowly begin to silt in, creating a new environment. Bogs and muskeg are the result of succession that begins with an aquatic environment.

— Aquatic plants

    — Sedge mat

        — Shrub/ sphagnum

           — Bog Forest (black spruce)

                — Climax Forest (white spruce)

**Table 2**                    **Biotic Communities of Chugach State Park**

**Hemlock-Spruce Forest**
(dominates SE Alaska with its most northerly extension in Turnagain Arm)

**Dominant plants:** western hemlock, Sitka spruce, rose, alder, willow, devil's club, huckleberry, blueberry.

**Common animals:** moose, black & brown bear, porcupine, red & northern flying squirrels, marten, spruce grouse, Steller's jay, rufous hummingbird, saw-whet owl, winter wren, white-winged crossbill, pine Siskins, Townsend's warbler.

**Spruce-Hardwood Forest**
(white spruce dominates drier, south-facing slope; black spruce dominates north-facing)

**Dominant plants:** white & black spruce, aspen, birch, balsam poplar, willow, crowberry, cranberry, dwarf dogwood, lichen.

**Common animals:** moose, black & brown bear, red fox, snowshoe hare, short-tailed weasel, porcupine, red & northern flying squirrels, squirrels, marten, gray jays, common redpolls, varied thrush, yellow & blackpoll warblers, boreal chickadee, 3-toed woodpecker, great horned owl, ruby-crowned kinglet.

**Tall-shrub thicket**
(coastal, riparian, & timberline zones)

**Dominant plants:** alder, willow, birch, ferns, grasses.

**Common animals:** moose, snowshoe hare, Iynx, wolverine, red fox, brown & black bear, coyotes, red-backed vole, singing vole, willow ptarmigan, hermit & gray-cheeked thrush; Townsend's solitaire; sparrows: white-crowned, golden-crowned, American tree, & fox; alder flycatcher; warblers: orange-crowned, yellow, & Wilson's; Say's phoebe; common redpolls.

**Muskeg**
(in former river bottoms, basins, old sloughs, & other poorly drained depressions)

**Dominant plants:** Sphagnum mosses, sedges, lichens, bog rosemary, Labrador tea, willow, cranberry, blueberry, black spruce, alder.

**Muskeg (continued)**

**Common animals:** muskrat, tundra vole, meadow vole, northern bog lemming, little brown bat, short-tailed & least weasel, mink, common shrew, northern flying squirrel, meadow jumping mouse, red-backed vole, Bohemian waxwing, Lincoln's sparrow, merlin, short-eared owl, rusty blackbird, common snipe, darkeyed junco, greater yellowlegs, great blue heron.

**Alpine Tundra**
**(above timberline)**

**Dominant plants:** mountain avens, heather, moss campion, blueberry, cranberry, crowberry, birch, Labrador tea, lichens, sedges, grasses.

**Common animals:** Dall sheep, mountain goats, hoary marmots, singing voles, brown bear, wolves, wolverine, coyotes, ermine, least weasel, dusky & tundra shrew, white-tailed & rock ptarmigan, water pipits, horned larks, rosy finches, northern wheatears, wandering tattlers, surfbirds, golden eagle, Wilson's warbler, golden-crowned sparrow.

**Riparian Habitat**
**(lakes, rivers, streams)**

**Dominant plants:** willow, alder, poplar, cottonwood, rushes, sedges, grasses, pondlily, common marestail.

**Common animals:** moose, beaver, muskrat, mink, river otter, brown & black bear, little brown bat, water shrew, wolverine, belted kingfisher, rusty blackbird, northern waterthrush, semipalmated plover, bald eagle, great blue heron, common & Barrow's goldeneye, harlequin ducks

**Table 2., continued**    **Biotic Communities of Chugach State Park**

| Coastal wetlands<br>(salt marshes, mudflats) | **Dominant plants:** sweetgale, dwarf birch, willow, bluejoint, beach rye, & cotton grass, sedges, rushes, blue-green algae. |
|---|---|
| | **Common animals:** river otters, muskrat, meadow voles, coyotes, red fox, mink, brown bear, glaucous-winged & mew gulls, Arctic terns; Savannah, Lincoln's, and song sparrows; spotted sandpiper, greater yellowlegs, lesser golden plover, red-necked grebe, northern harrier, Hudsonian godwit, northern shoveler, Canada geese, mallard. |
| **Rocky Intertidal**<br>Alga | **Dominant plants:** rockweed (Fucus); Irish Moss (Chondrus); Red (Gigartina); Lichens (Verrucaria, Caloplaca) |
| | **Dominant Animals:** barnacles; mussels; limpets; Glaucous-winged, mew, herring, & Bonaparte's gulls; spotted sandpiper; river otter |
| **Marine Waters**<br>(Cook Inlet) | **Dominant plants:** Plankton (diatoms) |
| | **Common Animals:** zooplankton, salmon, hooligan, beluga & Minke whales, sea lions, northern fur seals, harbor seal; glaucous-winged, mew, herring, & Bonaparte's gulls; Arctic terns, Canada geese, mallard, common merganser, greater scaup. |

Heritage Falls, Mile 4, Eagle River Trail (Dave Albert)

# CHAPTER TWELVE

# PLANTS OF CHUGACH STATE PARK

Chugach State Park is a land of vast alpine tundra fringed with boreal forests. Climate, latitude, and geology all interact to create the characteristic northern coniferous forests and low treeline which stretch across the subarctic regions of North America and Eurasia. This subarctic landscape is characterized by long, dark winters and persistent snow cover.

## PLANT ADAPTATIONS FOR A LONG, DARK WINTER

During the long, dark winter, most plants of Chugach are safely hidden away under a deep blanket of snow. Yet conditions vary. A late snow or an early freeze may kill plants which ordinarily would survive even the harshest winter. A mid-winter thaw followed by a deep freeze can kill even a winter-hardened tree.

Plants, like animals, are susceptible to the forces of winter - snow, cold, heat loss, and wind. The energy consumption factor does not have an effect on plants. They cannot add to their energy reserves during the winter months, so they do not generate heat in winter. Since they cannot resist freezing, they must acquire adaptations which allow them to tolerate its effects or else they will perish.

As days grow shorter and temperatures begin to drop, a plant has two options for survival. Fireweed, for example, dies off at the end of the growing season, only its seeds remaining (annuals) through the winter; whereas a birch tree goes dormant (perennials). Perennial plants store reserves over winter to begin growth immediately with the longer, warmer days of spring. Those plants that go dormant must **harden,** or acclimate, to the growing cold. Fluids in plant cells change chemically, resulting in a lower freezing point. As a result plants in the north can photosynthesize at lower temperatures than their more southerly relatives. This is not a rapid process, but a slow cooling of the plant's growth.

Facing page: Boreal forest to alpine tundra with Mount Rumble in background (Steve Johnson)

A serious winter threat to dormant trees is **desiccation,** a lethal loss of moisture or drying, at a time when there is no water absorption from the frozen soil. Inadequate snowfall, or wind scouring snow away from vegetation can expose the plant to desiccation. Winter desiccation can be identified in the spring, especially at timberline, when melting snow reveals the dead orange-brown foliage atop the stunted trees.

For the purpose of this book, plants will be listed from the most obvious down to the macroscopic. There are approximately 430 vascular plants known to occur in the park, and the most common are described below.

## TREES: the Tall Woody Plants

There are six needle-leaved, cone-bearing trees (the evergreen conifers) in Chugach State Park.

**Black Spruce** (*Picea mariana* ) - family Pinaceae/pine

A small spruce 15-30 feet, occasionally reaching 60 feet. It grows on cold wet flats, muskeg, north-facing slopes and lake margins to an elevation of about 2,000 feet. Black spruce commonly grow in clusters, because the lower branches take root forming a ring around the parent tree.

USDA

Black spruce is distinguished from white spruce by the shorter (<1/2 in.), blunter 4-sided needles, hairy twigs and small rounded cones which remain hanging down on the trees. From a distance the black spruce crown often appears as a dense tuft while the rest of the tree is quite narrow.

**White Spruce** *(Picea glauca)* - family Pinaceae/pine

A medium-sized spruce (40-70 ft. high). On good sites may reach 115 feet, yet above treeline it may be a prostrate shrub. When young, it is a symmetrical, cone-shaped tree becoming less so with age. White spruce occur from sea level up to 3500 feet. Most common in open forests and on south-facing slopes.

USDA

White spruce needles are 1/2 to 3/4 inches long, 4-sided, and prickly. Cones are 1 to 2 1/2 inches long and cylindrical. Scales are thin and smooth-edged. Twigs are hairless, unlike the black spruce.

**Sitka Spruce** *(Picea sitchensis)* - family Pinaceae/pine

Sitka spruce is the largest tree in Alaska. Under ideal conditions it may reach to over 225 feet in height, but around the park it averages about 80 feet. It rises to a broad open conical crown with horizontal branches. It is a maritime species which grows more rapidly and larger than the western hemlock. It extends from sea level to about 2000 feet along Turnagain Arm.

USDA

Needles are flat, almost an inch long, and pointed. Twigs are stout, stiff, and hairless. The cones are short, cylindrical, 2 to 3 inches long, and light orange-brown. Cone-scales are long, stiff, rounded but irregularly toothed.

**Western Hemlock** *(Tsuga heterophylla)* - family Pinaceae/pine

Western Hemlock reach heights of 100 to 150 feet. They grow tall and slender with the top leader in a characteristic droop. It extends along Turnagain Arm to the lower hillside in Anchorage. It is a shade-tolerant tree which grows well in areas of high soil and atmospheric moisture.

USDA

Leaves are 1/4 to 1 inch long and flat with a rounded tip. Twigs are slender and finely haired, becoming furrowed into scaly plates. Cones are stalkless and hang down at the end of each twig. They are small, less than an inch long, elliptical, with many papery thin scales.

**Mountain Hemlock** *(Tsuga Mertensiana)* - family Pinaceae/pine

Mountain Hemlock is a small to large tree growing up to 100 feet in ideal conditions, or a gnarled shrub near treeline. Its branches are open near crown and the long leader droops at the top. It ranges from sea level to almost 3500 feet. It grows at a higher altitude than other trees. Common treeline species around Glen Alps.

USDA

Needles are crowded on all sides on short twigs and curve inward. They are 1/4 to 1 inch long, flat above, rounded below. Cones are cylindrical, 1 - 2 1/2 inches long and 3/4 inches wide, purplish but turning brown with many thin papery scales.

**Common Juniper** *(Juniperus communis)* - family Cupressaceae/cypress

USDA

Often called the Prickly Juniper, it is a common subalpine shrub growing in mats or clumps to 10 feet in diameter and only 2 feet high. Most often found on well-drained rocky slopes, and sunny forest openings.

Needles are in whorled groups of 3, at right angles or slightly downward 1/4 to 1/2 inch long, stiff, and very sharp. Cones berry-like, blue and covered with a sweetish hard, mealy bloom, maturing in 2 - 3 years, and persistent.

## TREES, DECIDUOUS

**Balsam Poplar** *(Populus balsamifera)* - family Salicaceae/willow

USDA

Medium-sized deciduous tree 30 - 50 feet high with a thin open crown. Balsam poplars are a fast growing tree which prefers life along montane and subalpine river valleys, and stream flood plains. It extends higher up into the mountains than white spruce, to 3500 feet. Found in openings of mixed forests of white spruce, birch and aspen.

Leaves are larger and more elongated than aspen, dark glossy green on upper surface, paler underneath. Bark is gray becoming rough, thick and furrowed. In July balsam poplar produces cottony seeds in a 2 part pod. This differentiates it from black cottonwood which has a 3 part pod.

**Black Cottonwood** *(Populus trichocarpa)* - family Salicaceae/willow

USDA

The largest broadleaf tree in northwestern North America reaching heights of 100 feet or more with deeply grooved, rough bark. It closely resembles the balsam poplar, but black cottonwoods are usually larger and heavier-looking. Found in lowlands around the park along river bottoms and sandbars, forming pure stands with undergrowth of willows and alders. Can be seen up Eagle River valley.

Leaves are larger and broader than balsam poplar. Black cottonwood have a cotton-fluff filled pod which opens into 3 parts. This distinguishes it from balsam poplar which only has a 2-part pod.

**Quaking Aspen** *(Populus tremuloides)* - family Salicaceae/willow

Small to medium-sized deciduous tree 20 - 40 feet high with short irregular bent limbs creating a narrow dome-shaped crown. It is a fast growing tree often found on southern slopes, well-drained benches and creek bottoms. Aspens are the shortest-lived of the poplars, averaging less than 80 years.

Aspen branches are fairly short, foliage is sparse;bark is a smooth gray-green. Leaves are waxy green, nearly round 1 - 2 inches across, and pointed at the tip. They rustle quietly in the wind. In the fall the leaves turn from brilliant yellow to orange to red. Aspens propagate by sucker roots, thus groves of aspen are actually clones of genetically identical individuals. Each clone grove has a slightly different color leaves in fall .

USDA

**Paper Birch** *(Betula papyrifera)* - family Betulaceae/birch

Paper birch is a small to medium-sized deciduous tree 20 - 60 feet high with white peeling bark. Characteristic of spruce-birch forests particularly with white spruce and aspen. It occupies drier sites around Anchorage and lower slopes of Chugach State Park up to about 800 feet.

USDA

Leaves are a dull yellow-green heart-shaped with toothed edges. Willow-like catkins appear in early spring. Seeds are not cottony.

## TALL SHRUBS (over 6 feet)

**Willows** *(Salix)*, which belongs to the family Salicaceae, are the largest genus of trees in Alaska. Of the 33 species known to inhabit Alaska, at least 16 are found in Chugach State Park. There is great variation and hybridization among willows, making identification difficult at best. With considerable persistence, one can begin to distinguish between the myriad species. For the purpose of this book, willows will be keyed by habitat as an aid in identification.

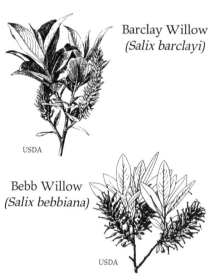

Barclay Willow
(Salix barclayi)

Bebb Willow
(Salix bebbiana)

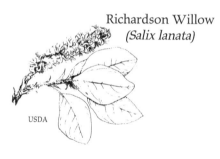

USDA

USDA

## TREELINE THICKETS
## *Tall Shrubs 3-25 feet high:

Barclay Willow (Salix barclayi)

Most common thicket-forming shrub at treeline; leaves yellow-green top, whitish below, no hairs on lower surface.

Bebb Willow (Salix bebbiana)

Leaves dull green above, light gray below and roughly net-veined; slightly hairy both sides.

## *Shrubs <10 feet in height

Richardson Willow (Salix lanata)

Leaves green-gray above, dull hairy gray below; prefers wet sites.

Richardson Willow
(Salix lanata)

USDA

## OPEN AREAS, OR DISTURBED SITES
## *Shrubs <10 feet high

Grayleaf Willow (Salix glauca)

Smooth green-gray above, dull hairy gray below; pioneer species on disturbed sites.

Grayleaf Willow
(Salix glauca)

USDA

Barren-ground Willow
(Salix brachycarpa)

Barren-ground Willow
(Salix brachycarpa)

Prostrate above treeline; leaves green on upper surface, whitish hairy beneath.

**\*Tall shrubs <20 feet tall**

**Sitka Willow** *(Salix sitchensis)*

Upper surface leaves green, beneath hairy satiny sheen; prefers sunny, open sites.

Sitka Willow
*(Salix sitchensis)*
USDA

**Scouler Willow** *(Salix scouleriana)*

Most common of all willows in park;earliest flowering, catkins develop before snow has melted; leaves green above, hairy reddish below; habitats variable.

Scouler Willow
*(Salix scouleriana)*
USDA

**WET BOREAL FOREST**
**\*small shrub <10 feet high**

**Diamondleaf Willow**
*(Salix planifolia)*

Leaves shiny green above, pale below and hairless;leaves persistent; prefers boggy sites.

**Barclay Willow** - See opposite page.

USDA    Diamondleaf Willow
*(Salix planifolia)*

**RIPARIAN HABITAT**
**\*Small Shrub <10 feet high**

**Halberd Willow** *(Salix hastata)*

Leaves dull light green oval; uncommon willow even in its prefered riparian habitat.

Halberd Willow
*(Salix hastata)*
USDA

**\*Tall shrubs or trees up to 30 feet high**

**Feltleaf Willow** *(Salix alaxensis)*

Leaves dull green above, white felt beneath; preferred moose browse.

Feltleaf Willow
*(Salix alaxensis)*
USDA

**Littletree Willow** *(Salix arbusculoides)*

USDA

Leaves shiny dark above, whitish sparsely haired beneath.

**American Green Alder** *(Alnus crispa )* - family Betulaceae/birch

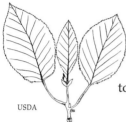

USDA

Common in thickets along gravelly slopes and flood plains. Tall shrub 3-13 feet high. The twigs and buds are important winter food for ptarmigan. Leaves yellow-green, shiny on both sides; sticky when young, toothed edges, but not lobed.

**Sitka Alder** *(Alnus sinuata)* - family Betulaceae/birch

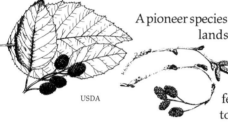

USDA

A pioneer species from sea level to alpine along streams, landslides, or glacial retreat. Becomes established with Sitka spruce. Intolerant of shade, and disappears when overtopped. Tall shrub 5-15 feet. Shiny yellow-green leaves with toothed wavy lobed edges.

**Thinleaf Alder** *(Alnus tenuifolia)* - family Betulaceae/birch

USDA

Large shrub 15-30 feet high. Thinleaf alders with larger willows commonly form tall shrub riparian thickets in the park. Its wood is used by Natives for smoking salmon. Leaves are a dull dark green and edged with short pointed teeth finely haired beneath.

**Highbush Cranberry** *(Viburnum edule)* - family Caprifoliaceae/honeysuckle

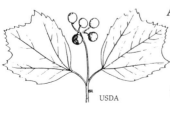

USDA

A deciduous shrub 2-12 feet high with edible red fruit when picked before mature. Leaves variable to 3-lobed, toothed, and turn red in fall. Small 5-petaled flowers, white to pink, in clusters. Scattered to common in thickets, forest openings, and along streams.

**Pacific Serviceberry** *(Amelanchier florida)* - family Rosaceae/rose

A deciduous shrub which reaches heights of over 12 ft high with toothed oval leaves to 2 inches long. Flowers with 5 narrow petals at ends of branches. Sweet, edible, purple fruit which ripens in early September. Prefers rocky slope in forest openings and cliffs. Common along Turnagain Arm.

USDA

**Rusty Menziesia** *(Menziesia ferriginea)* - family Ericaceae/heath

An odorous deciduous shrub 6-10 feet. Leaves thin, blue-green with wavy margin. Flowers bell-shaped, rust-colored. Often confused with huckleberry, but Menziesia do not have berries. Common undergrowth in spruce-hemlock forests along Turnagain Arm.

USDA

**Green Mountain Ash** *(Sorbus scopulina)* - family Rosaceae/rose

Deciduous shrub 3-13 feet with 11-15 oblong hair-less leaves with toothed edges nearly to base of leaf. Shiny bright red bitter fruit, persistent in winter. Prefers openings and clearings in forests.

**Red-berried Elder** *(Sambucus racemosa)* - family Caprifoliaceae/honeysuckle

USDA

Deciduous clump-forming shrub 5-12 feet high with 5-7 paired, oblong, toothed leaves. Clumps of red berries at ends of branches appear in August. Easily detected by strong odor when leaves or stems are crushed. Common on moist open sites. Clumps of small red berries hang from ends of branches in August. **All parts of Elder are poisonous - except flowers and berries.** (No illustration).

## SHORT SHRUBS BELOW TREELINE

**Devil's Club** *(Echinopanax horridum)* - family Araliaceae/ginseng

A deciduous shrub 4-8 feet high with thick spiny stems and few branches. Contact with spines causes inflammation. Leaves are large, 6-14 inches in diameter, irregularly toothed, deeply notched and spiny on underside. Forms dense understory in moist shaded forests.

USDA

**Prickly Rose** *(Rosa acicularis)* - family Rosaceae/rose

A prickly shrub 1-6 feet high with toothed pointed oblong leaves. Large, showy pink flowers. Fruit is an edible fleshy reddish berry called a rose hip, high in vitamin C, which is gathered in fall. Similar species, Nootka Rose *(Rosa nutkatensis)*, has only a few spines and is found along Turnagain Arm.

USDA

**Soapberry** *(Shepherdia canadensis)* - family Elaeagnaceae/oleaster

A deciduous shrub up to 3 feet tall with distinctive brown scales on twigs and undersides of shiny dark green leaves. Small yellowish flowers, and small bitter red berry which was whipped by Indians into froth. Common in dry, rocky areas along Turnagain Arm.

USDA

**Labrador Tea** *(Ledum palustris* ssp. groenlandicum) - family Ericaceae/heath

A short evergreen shrub 10-30 inches tall easily recognized by its shiny dark green upper leaves, rusty and fuzzy below and on stem, fragrant odor. Conspicuous small white flower clusters at end of stems. Common in black spruce forests and bogs. Narrow-leaf Labrador Tea *(Ledum palustre* ssp. decumbens) is smaller with very narrow leaves, and is found in alpine tundra and bogs.

USDA

**Northern Red Currant** *(Ribes triste)* - family Grossulariaceae/gooseberry

A low spreading shrub 2-3 feet tall with shreading reddish-brown bark. Leaves toothed with 3-5 lobes, turn red in fall. Drooping inconspicuous pinkish flowers, tasty red berries edible by August. Found in moist woods and meadows to treeline.

USDA

**Bog Blueberry** *(Vaccinium uliginosum)* - family Ericaceae/heath

A deciduous shrub up to 2 feet high with small oval dull green leaves (<1 in.). Flowers are small, pink, and bell-shaped. Berries are dark blue, tasty, slightly tart from July to early September. Found in bogs and heaths.

USDA

**Shrubby Cinquefoil** *(Potentilla fruticosa)* - family Rosaceae/rose

A many branched deciduous shrub 1-3 feet tall with reddish shredding bark. Leaves are thick bluish-green above, whitish hairs below. Flowers large (1-1 1/2 in.) with 5 bright yellow petals. Common on both dry and wet sites, forests, bogs, to alpine tundra.

USDA

**Beauverd's Spirea** *(Spirea beauverdiana)* - family Rosaceae/rose

Low shrub < 3 feet tall with delicate reddish-brown branches. Leaves are dark green above, pale below, oblong and finely toothed. Clusters of small white flowers. Common in muskeg, moist black spruce forests to alpine.

USDA

**Bog Rosemary** *(Andromeda polifolia)* - family Ericaceae/heath

Small, delicate spreading evergreen shrub < 1 foot high, occasionally prostrate. Leaves are narrow, to 1 inch long, green above and whitish beneath with edges rolled under. Flowers early with pink urnshaped blossoms. Common in bogs, moist depressions in forest, and wet tundra.

USDA

**Kinnikinnick** *(Arctostaphylos uva-ursi)* - family Ericaceae/heath

Prostrate deciduous shrub to 4 inches high forming large mats. Leaves are rounded, smooth, leathery, and persistent. Flowers are small, pink-white, urn-shaped. Berries not edible, too dry and mealy. Found in dry woods and open, dry rocky sites.

USDA

**Lowbush Cranberry** *(Vaccinium vitis-idaea)* - family Ericaceae/heath

Evergreen, creeping, mat-forming shrub to 6 inches high. Numerous small, shiny, hard leaves with slightly rolled edges. Flowers pink-white bell-shaped cluster at ends of branches. Abundant fruit is an edible tasty, tart red berry best picked after first frost in September. Found in dry or moist spruce and birch woods, on rocky alpine slopes throughout the park.

USDA

## SHORT SHRUBS ABOVE TREELINE

Low-growing shrubs found above treeline comprise the alpine heath community. The majority, but not all, are heaths and heathers, and most are evergreen, a mechanism which favors survival in the exposed environment above treeline.

**ALPINE WILLOWS** *-Salix sp.* - (family Salicaceae/willow)

**\*Low, creeping < 6 inches high**

**Ovalleaf Willow** *(Salix ovalifolia)*

Leaves > 3/4 inches, green above, whitish below, many catkins; found on wet sites in alpine tundra.

USDA

**Least Willow** *(Salix rotundifolia)*

Leaves <3/4 inches, green on both sides, few dead leaves; few catkins; found on lichen tundra and dry, rocky areas.

USDA

## Low, prostrate < 1 foot high

### Netleaf Willow *(Salix reticulata)*

Leaves round, strong-veined, dark green above, light gray below; commonly found on both dry and wet tundra sites.

USDA

### Arctic Willow *(Salix arctica)*

Leaves ovate, light green above and below, not strongly veined; prefers dry alpine tundra.

USDA

## Low, prostrate on tundra <3 feet

### Barren-ground Willow *(Salix brachycarpa)*
See Page 106.

## ALPINE and below (creeping to 30 inches tall)

### Alaska Bog Willow *(Salix fuscescens)*

Leaves are hanging and blade-like, light shiny blue-green on upper surface; prefers wet meadows, muskeg, and tundra bogs.

USDA

### Dwarf Birch *(Betula nana)* - family Betulaceae/birch

Low spreading deciduous shrub to 3 feet tall. Leaves round, green, hairless, with wavy toothed edges; turning copper red in fall. Twigs slightly resinous with minute warty glands. Found in moist soil of rocky alpine slopes and wet alpine tundra.

USDA

**Dwarf Blueberry** *(Vaccinium caespitosum)* - family Ericaceae/heath

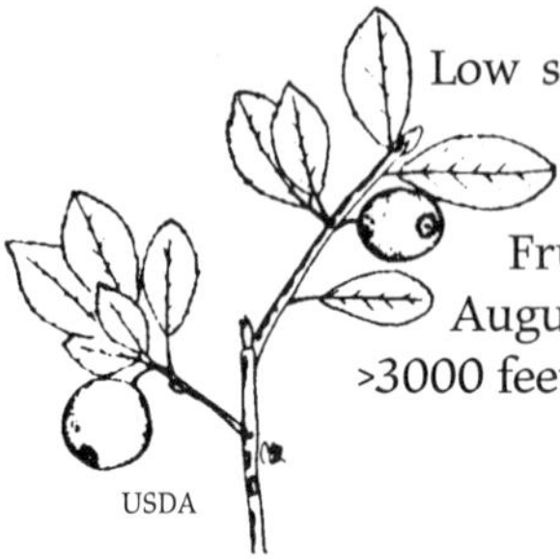

Low spreading mat-forming shrub to 16 inches high Leaves are small, elliptic, finely toothed edge Flowers are white-pink bell-shaped, grow singly Fruit is a sweet, round blueberry ripening in earl August. Found in bogs, subalpine and alpine meadows t >3000 feet.

USDA

**Bell Heather** *(Cassiope tetragona)* - family Ericaceae/heath

Low, trailing evergreen, mat-forming shrub 4-8 inches high Short, stout leaves cover stem in 4 vertical rows formin square-edged look. Flowers are white, hanging from ends branches. Very common in protected areas of alpine tundra

USDA

**Mountain Heather** *(Phyllodoce glanduliflora)* - family Ericaceae/heath

Low, ground-covering shrub, 2-6 inches tall, forming extensiv mats. Leaves are needle-like, thick and blunt with groove on lowe surface and crowded on upper 1-2 inches of rough stem. Flowers ar yellow-green with 5-15 nodding urn-shaped blossoms at tip of erec hairy stem. No berries are produced.

USDA

**Alpine Bearberry** *(Arctostaphylos alpina)* - family Ericaceae/heath

Prostrate decidudous shrub up to 4 inches high formin large mats. Leaves are long, coarse, leathery, prominentl veined with hairs along margins, and persistent. Leave turn bright red in fall. Fruit is juicy; black berry, edible bu not tasty. Found in rocky alpine areas and tundra through out the park.

USDA

**Crowberry** *(Empetrum nigrum)* - family Empetraceae/crowberry

Low, creeping evergreen shrub to 6 inches with small, narrow needle-like leaves. Flowers small, maroon colored, inconspicuous. Berries firm, round, juicy, edible but not tasty; persist through winter. Fall/winter food for ptarmigan, grouse, and bear. Abundant ground cover on alpine tundra, rocky slopes, down into subalpine forests.

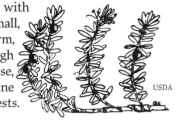

USDA

**Mountain Avens** *(Dryas octopetala)* - family Rosaceae/rose

Mat-forming prostrate evergreen shrub with many small oblong wavy, toothed leaves; shiny green above, white, densely haired below. Flowers are solitary, white with 8 petals and bright yellow stamens. When gone to seed, head forms characteristic twist. Abundant on tundra and high alpine slopes in park.

USDA

**One-flowered Cinquefoil** *(Potentilla uniflora)* - family Rosaceae/rose

Low, tufted shrub 4-8 inches tall growing from single stout stem. Dark green leaves divided into 3 leaflets with toothed edges and few hairs beneath. Flowers with 5 bright yellow petals and orange dot at base. Found on rocky exposed slopes and ridges throughout the park. *(Potentilla biflora* to 12 inches tall with 5-part leaves and grows in alpine meadows.)

SUP

**Lapland Diapensia** *(Diapensia lapponicum)* - family Diapensiaceae/diapensia

A minute ground-hugging shrub with densely crowded rosettes of tiny, hard, oval evergreen leaves forming mats to 2 feet. Cup-shaped large, showy, white flowers on erect stems. Common on dry rocky or gravelly alpine slopes and tundra.

USDA

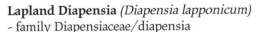

## FLOWERING PLANTS above TREELINE

Flowering plants above treeline are subjected to severe conditions during their short growing season and must adapt or perish . Alpine species tend to be shorter, more slender, less branched with fewer and smaller leaves, and fewer flowers than their lowland counterparts. Most alpine plants are perennials to save energy (rather than producing new stems, leaves, flowers and fruit all in one short growing season).

One of the earliest places to see alpine wildflowers is on Bird Ridge in late May/ early June. The easiest places to see alpine wildflowers are up Arctic Valley and Glen Alps. They bloom later in the summer than their lowland relatives, peaking in late July.

**Mountain Harebell** *(Campanula lasiocarpa)* - family Campanulaceae/bluebell

Small alpine plant 2-4 inches with small oblong toothed leaves at base of stem. Over-sized, bell-shaped flowers are usually singular, violet-blue. Found on rocky alpine slopes and ridges.

SUP

**Alpine Forget-me-not** *(Myosotis alpestris)* - family Boraginaceae/borage

The Alaska State Flower is a perennial plant 6-15 inches tall with long blue-green leaves with many stiff hairs. Long hairy stem is is topped by cluster of blue flowers with 5 petals joined at base with yellow eye ringed by white. Found in alpine and sub-alpine meadows and slopes.

SUP

**Glaucous Gentian** *(Gentiana glauca)* - family Gentianaceae/gentian

Small stout plant 2-6 inches tall with tight rosette of round yellow-green leaves at base of stem. Flowers are solitary, blue-green fused petals forming a tube at end of stem. Found on moist alpine slopes and tundra.

SUP

**Blackish Oxytrope** *(Oxytropis nigrescens)* - family Fabaceae/pea

Low matted plant branching out from single tap root. Leaves gray-green, hairy with 9-13 small pointed leaflets, dead leaf stalks crowd base. Flowers are purple, usually in pairs. Found on exposed, dry, rocky alpine areas throughout the Park.

SUP

**Dwarf Fireweed** *(Epilobium latifolium)* - family Onagraceae/evening primrose

Short sprawling plant to 20 inches high, is a pioneer species; one of the first plants to appear on disturbed sites. Leaves blade-like, alternate up stem turning bright red in fall. Flowers with 4 bright pink ovate petals all equal size. Found on alpine scree slopes and stream and river bars.

SUP

**Spring Beauty** *(Claytonia sarmentosa)* - family Portulacaceae/purslane

Small delicate flower with light green edible leaves and small 5-petaled white to pink flowers with dark veins. Found on wet, rocky alpine slopes, near streams and snowbanks.

SUP

**Moss Campion** *(Silene acaulis)* - family Caryophyllaceae/pink

Low plant forming cushion-like mounds. Leaves are narrow, short and crow the stem. Mat is covered with small (1/2 inch) pink 5-petaled aromatic flowers. Common on dry, rocky or well-drained alpine sites.

SUP

**Frigid Shooting Star** *(Dodecatheon frigidum)* - family Primulaceae/primrose

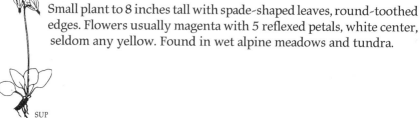

Small plant to 8 inches tall with spade-shaped leaves, round-toothed edges. Flowers usually magenta with 5 reflexed petals, white center, seldom any yellow. Found in wet alpine meadows and tundra.

SUP

**Purple Mountain Saxifrage** *(Saxifraga oppositifolia)* - family Saxifragaceae/saxifrage

Small plant with many tiny, dark green rosettes of leaves forming a mat. Flowers are magenta to purple with 5 clawed petals. Found on wet, gravelly slopes, ridges, and rock crevices in alpine sites.

SUP

**Alpine Azalea** *(Loiseleuria procumbens)* - family Ericaceae/heath

Dwarf evergreen shrub with small oval leaves forming mats. Flowers in tiny, pink, 5-petaled clusters across mat surface. Found on acidic soil, southfacing alpine slopes and ridges.

SUP

**Wooly Lousewort** *(Pedicularis Kanei)* - family Scrophulariaceae/figwort

Short and wooly plant in bud, in seed to 10 inches high. Leaves feather-like, with leaflets arranged in rowson either side of a midrib, serrated, growing from base surrounding a thick, woolly flower stalk rising from a long fibrous root. Numerous dark pink flowers surround central stem. Found on dry, rocky alpine slopes in park.

SUP

**Capitate Lousewort** *(Pedicularis capitata)*
- family Scrophulariaceae/figwort

Small plant 3-5 inches high; flower stalk appears to be separate from the rounded, feather-like leaves. A few large, hooded yellow flowers cluster around top of stem. Top of flowers becoming pink to rusty with age. Found in rocky alpine slopes and tundra.

SUP

**Coastal Fleabane** *(Erigeron peregrinus)* - family Asteraceae/aster

Tall daisy-like flower 6-14 inches high with narrow, pink to lavender ray flowers and yellow disk flowers in center. Leaves are blade-like, hairy, and alternate up stem. Found in alpine and subalpine meadows.

SUP

**Triangular-leafed Fleabane** *(Senecio triangularis)*
- family Asteraceae/Aster

Large plant 2-2 1/2 feet with many triangular, toothed leaves becoming smaller up the stem. Daisy-type flowers are ragged, yellow, in flat-topped clusters. Found in moist alpine meadows and stream banks.

SUP

**Western Buttercup** *(Ranunculus occidentalis)*
- family Ranunculaceae/buttercup

Small plant 8-12 inches tall with 5 shiny yellow petals and 3-part leaves slightly hairy. Found in alpine meadows around the Park. **ALL BUTTERCUPS ARE POISONOUS.**

SUP

## Frigid Arnica *(Arnica frigida)* - family Asteraceae/aster

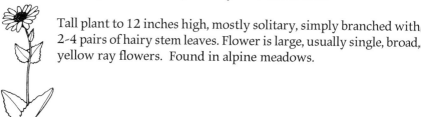

Short perennial plant 7-12 inches tall with narrow, pointed hairy leaves at base of stem. Flower stems have 1-3 sets of leaves. Flowers are usually single, large, pale yellow drooping and daisy-like with broad rays. Found on dry, rocky alpine slopes.

## Meadow Arnica *(Arnica latifolia)* - family Asteraceae/aster

Tall plant to 12 inches high, mostly solitary, simply branched with 2-4 pairs of hairy stem leaves. Flower is large, usually single, broad, yellow ray flowers. Found in alpine meadows.

## Alp Lily *(Lloydia serotina )* - family Liliaceae/lily

Small plant 4-6 inches tall with narrow grass-like leaves. Flowers have 3 petals and 3 sepals, which give appearance of 6 petals. Plant has one or two funnel-shaped flowers per stem. Found in dry alpine areas in park.

## Alpine Spirea *(Luetkea pectinata)* - family Rosaceae/rose

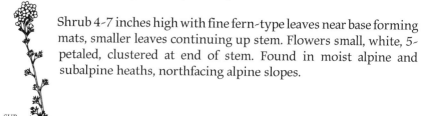

Shrub 4-7 inches high with fine fern-type leaves near base forming mats, smaller leaves continuing up stem. Flowers small, white, 5-petaled, clustered at end of stem. Found in moist alpine and subalpine heaths, northfacing alpine slopes.

**Alpine Meadow Bistort** *(Polygonum viviparum)*
~ family Polygonaceae/buckwheat

A short plant 5~8 inches tall arising from a thick, hard rhizome. Long, narrow leaves dark green smooth above, grayish below. Flowers are tiny, 5~petaled, white to pink rapidly replaced by bulblets which sprout leaves and roots before they fall from the adult plant. Found in dry meadows, heaths, and tundra.

SUP

**Prickly Saxifrage** *(Saxifraga tricuspidata)*
~ family Saxifragaceae/saxifrage

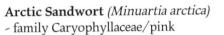

Low evergreen plant of loosely matted rosettes of small, leathery leaves with 3 pointed teeth at the end. When dry, they become very prickly. In winter and spring, leaves very red. Flower stem 4-6 inches tall with small flower clusters of 5 lavender spotted, pointed, cream-colored petals. Found on dry, rocky, open subalpine and alpine slopes.

SUP

**Arctic Sandwort** *(Minuartia arctica)*
~ family Caryophyllaceae/pink

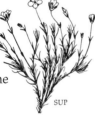

Low mat-forming plant with very small needle-like leaves. Flowers are singular 1/2 to 3/4 inches on short stems with 5 white to rosy petals. Found on dry, gravelly and rocky alpine sites.

SUP

**Windflower** *(Anemone parviflora )* ~ family Ranunculaceae/buttercup

Perennial plant to 12 inches tall with smooth dark green leaves that are 3-5 lobed, rounded, slightly dissected, modified leaf on stem below flowers. Flowers are solitary, showy, >1 inch round, 4-10 white sepals with very bluish underside. Found in moist alpine meadows, near receding snowbeds, moist woods. *(Anemone narcissiflora* is taller with hairy leaves and 1-2 inch flowers, also in alpine meadows. *Anemone multifida* has hairy, more finely dissected leaves with smaller white flowers <1 inch, rosey to lavender beneath, on dry, open hillsides and woods.)

SUP

**Capitate Valerian** *(Valeriana capitata)* - family Valerianaceae/valerian

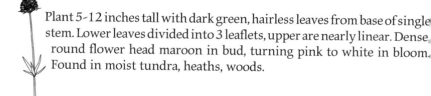

Plant 5-12 inches tall with dark green, hairless leaves from base of single stem. Lower leaves divided into 3 leaflets, upper are nearly linear. Dense, round flower head maroon in bud, turning pink to white in bloom. Found in moist tundra, heaths, woods.

**Roseroot** *(Sedum rosea)* - family Crassulaceae/stonecrop

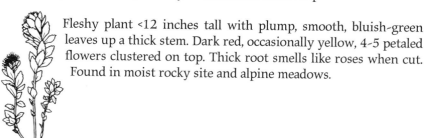

Fleshy plant <12 inches tall with plump, smooth, bluish-green leaves up a thick stem. Dark red, occasionally yellow, 4-5 petaled flowers clustered on top. Thick root smells like roses when cut. Found in moist rocky site and alpine meadows.

**False Hellebore** *(Veratrum viride)* - family Liliaceae/lily

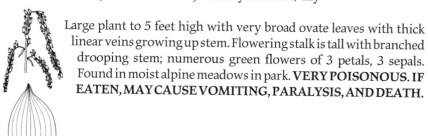

Large plant to 5 feet high with very broad ovate leaves with thick linear veins growing up stem. Flowering stalk is tall with branched drooping stem; numerous green flowers of 3 petals, 3 sepals. Found in moist alpine meadows in park. **VERY POISONOUS. IF EATEN, MAY CAUSE VOMITING, PARALYSIS, AND DEATH.**

## FLOWERING PLANTS BELOW TREELINE

The best places to see wildflowers of the boreal forest and lowland meadows are along Turnagain Trail in early June, and in late June along the trails around Eagle River Visitor Center. By mid-July most of the wildflowers below treeline are past their prime.

**Bluebells** *(Mertensia paniculata)* - family Boraginaceae/borage

Tall plant 18-30 inches high with long, pointed, dark green, hairy leaves. Flowers are funnel-shaped, pink in bud, turning blue; occasionally remain pink. Found in moist woods and alpine meadows.

SUP

**Tall Jacob's Ladder** *(Polemonium acutiflorum)* - family Polemoniaceae/phlox

Tall perennial plant 10-36 inches tall with hairy, sticky stems, 7-11 smooth pointed leaflets. Flowers with 5 pointed violet-blue leaves joined at base with white hairy centers and hairy, sticky sepals. Found in wet meadows and near streams.

SUP

**Monkshood** *(Aconitum delphinifolium)* - family Ranunculaceae/buttercup

Tall plant 24-48 inches high (smaller on alpine sites) with 5 narrow deeply-divided leaves which are divided again into 3 linear segments. Flowers are blue to navy and helmet-shaped, scattered up stem above leaves. Found in woods and meadows into alpine. POISONOUS!

SUP

**Larkspur** *(Delphinium glaucum)* - family Ranunculaceae/buttercup

Very tall plant 4-6 feet high with many deeply divided, 5-lobed leaves. Flowers are deep purple with 5 petals and a spur projecting off back. Found in moist woods and meadows. **POISONOUS!**

SUP

**Nootka Lupine** *(Lupinus nootkatensis)* - family Fabaceae/pea

Tall plant 15-36 inches high with blunt palmate leaves. Stems are stout with numerous purple flowerheads with white patches at base of petals. Found in moist woods to alpine meadows.

SUP

**Wild Geranium** *(Geranium erianthum)* - family Geraniaceae/geranium

Tall perennial plant 18-30 inches high with large, hairy, deeply toothed, palm-like leaves. Flowers at top of stem with 5 large, round, lavender petals with dark stripes. Found in woods and meadows to alpine areas. Common along trails from Prospect Heights trailhead to treeline, and around Eagle River Visitors Center.

SUP

**Alpine Milk Vetch** *(Astragalus alpinus)* - family Fabaceae/pea

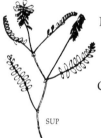

Low, creeping plant to 8 inches high with many small feather-like divided leaves. Small flowers clustered at end of stem, white with hint of lavender. Found in woods, fields to alpine; seen along Albert Trail at Eagle River Visitor Center.

SUP

**Common Fireweed** *(Epilobium angustifolium)*
- family Onagraceae/evening primrose

Tall plant 2-5 feet high growing from deep horizontal roots which escape fire damage; hence the name "fireweed." Leaves are blade-like, growing alternately on stem; leaves turn bright red in fall. Flowers are bright pink with 2 large round petals at base and 2 smaller petals above. The 4 sepals are narrow, pointed, and purple. Lower flowers bloom first. Found in open meadows and woods of the park.

SUP

**Wintergreen** *(Pyrola asarifolia)* - family Pyrolaceae/wintergreen

Evergreen plant 8-10 inches high growing out of a rosette of round, thick, shiny leaves. Flowers grow up stem in a spike of many 5-petaled, drooping pink blossoms. Found in moist woods and meadows.

**Shooting Star** *(Dodecatheon pulchellum)* - family Primulaceae/primrose

Perennial plant 10-15 inches tall with smooth blade-like leaves at base of stem. Flowers at top of leafless stalk with many 5-petaled, reflexed, bright pink petals with yellow ring at base. Found in wet meadows

**Twin Flower** *(Linnea borealis)* - family Caprifoliaceae/honeysuckle

Trailing plant to 4 inches high with small, round, light green evergreen leaves. Bell-shaped flowers, usually in pairs, at top of stem. Found in open woods and dry slopes.

**Yellow Monkeyflower** *(Mimulus guttatus)* - family Scrophulariaceae/figwort

Sprawling plant 8-16 inches tall round; dark green leaves with toothed edges grow up stem. Flowers are bright yellow with reddish spots in throat of 5-petaled irregular-shaped tube (similar to snapdragon). Found in wet areas near streams, lakes, and wet rocky slopes.

**Coastal Paintbrush** *(Castilleja unalaschensis)* - family Scrophulariaceae/figwort

Medium plant 12-18 inches high with long pointed, hairy leaves with 3-5 ribs. Flowers are minute, almost hidden in yellowish leaves, or bracts, at end of stem. Found in woods and subalpine meadows. Common up around Arctic Valley.

SUP

**Yellow Anemone** *(Anemone Richardsonii)* - family Ranunculaceae/buttercup

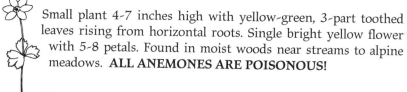

Small plant 4-7 inches high with yellow-green, 3-part toothed leaves rising from horizontal roots. Single bright yellow flower with 5-8 petals. Found in moist woods near streams to alpine meadows. **ALL ANEMONES ARE POISONOUS!**

SUP

**Elegant Goldenrod** *(Solidago lepida)* - family Asteraceae/aster

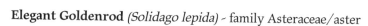

Tall plant 12-24 inches high with numerous pointed, blade-like, slightly toothed leaves. Yellow flowers in dense flower cluster at tip of stem. Found in meadows, fields, and open woods. A shorter version is the Northern Goldenrod, *Solidago multiradiata*, with shallow toothed leaves, flatter flower head, and found in drier, rockier sites in park. Common along Turnagain Arm.

SUP

**Cow Parsnip** *(Heraclaum lanatum)* - family Apiaceae/parsley

Very tall distinctive plant 4-8 feet high with large, hollow stems and very large palm-like leaves which are deeply divided into threes. Leaves attach to main stem with clasping sheath. Small white flowers with 5 petals grow in double umbrella-like flower cluster at end of stem. Common in moist woods, fields and alpine meadows. **CAUTION: Hairs on leaves and stems are very irritating. May cause itching and rash and blistering.**

SUP

**Wild Celery** *(Angelica lucida)* - family Apiaceae/parsley

Large plant 18-36 inches tall with numerous serrated leaflets.
Flowers greenish-white in umbrella-like flower cluster at end of
stem. Found along riverbanks and meadows.

SUP

**Dwarf Dogwood** *(Cornus canadensis)*
- family Cornaceae/dogwood

Low herbaceous shrub 4-8 inches tall with a single pair
of veined leaves near base and whorl of veined leaves at
top. Flowers are in a cluster in the middle of 4 large, white
bracts, or leaves, and each flower has 4 greenish sepals.
Found in woods to low alpine meadows. Common from forests
to alpine.

SUP

**Northern Yarrow** *(Achillea borealis )*
- family Asteraceae/aster

Perennial weed to 2 feet tall with fine, fern-like
pinnate aromatic leaves. Small white flat-topped
flowers clustered around the stem. Found in fields,
open woods to alpine meadows.

SUP

**Star Flower** *(Trientalis europea)*
- family Primulaceae/primrose

Low perennial with stem from rhizome and reddish runners. Leaves
blade-like, 5-6 inch whorl around stem. Flowers usually single with
7 pointed white petals. Found in woods and low alpine slopes.

SUP

**Western Columbine** *(Aquilegia formosa)* - family Ranunculaceae/buttercup

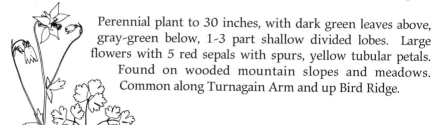

Perennial plant to 30 inches, with dark green leaves above, gray-green below, 1-3 part shallow divided lobes. Large flowers with 5 red sepals with spurs, yellow tubular petals. Found on wooded mountain slopes and meadows. Common along Turnagain Arm and up Bird Ridge.

SUP

**Broomrape** *(Boschniakia rossica)* - family Orobanchaceae/broomrape

A thick fleshy stem to 12 inches, covered with scale-like brownish leaves resembling an upright pine cone. Flowers tiny, reddish-brown on spikes between leaves. A parasite on alder roots. Found wherever alder grows, as well as in the mountains to 4000 feet. Seen scattered on tundra along trail to Wolverine Peak. Remains standing all year.

SUP

## GRASSES and GRASS-LIKE PLANTS

Grass has been described as "that long, thin plant with long, skinny leaves". This is the way grasses, sedges, and rushes have often been clumped by non-botanists, but they are less similar than they appear. All three are in separate families. Although they appear drab, they all produce minute flowers. The flowers are brownish-purple, and some of the grasses and sedges have bright yellow anthers. So when you see a "grass-like" plant ,remember this simple saying to differentiate between grasses and grass-like species:

*Sedges have edges, rushes are round, but grasses have joints.*

### GRASSES (Family Graminae)
Grasses have round hollow stems with joints rather than a continuous single tube. Grass leaves are flat. All members of the grass family produce minute drab flowers. Their color tends to brownish-purple.

## Bent Grass *(Agrostis* sp)

Up to 16 inches; tufted spikelets; erect thin leaves from base; hybridizes easily so it is difficult to distinguish species. Found in moist snow-free areas and disturbed sites.

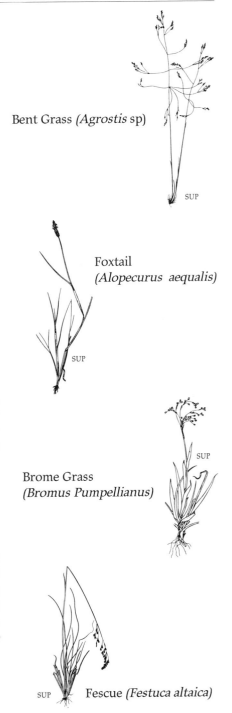

Bent Grass *(Agrostis* sp)

## Foxtail *(Alopecurus aequalis)*

Tall grass growing over 2 feet high; Lower section of plant creeping; anthers orange. Found in wet areas, or in ponds.

Foxtail
*(Alopecurus aequalis)*

## FESCUE TRIBE

### Brome Grass
*(Bromus Pumpellianus)*

Leaves are broad; heads are loose with spikelets at ends of long slender branches; found in meadows, dry grassyslopes from lowlands to alpine tundra.

Brome Grass
*(Bromus Pumpellianus)*

### Fescue *(Festuca altaica)*

This common grass grows in compact tufts from base of narrow leaves and stalk up to 3 feet high; spikelets with 2-5 flowers; heads branched. Found in variety of plant communities to 2200 feet in the mountains. *Festuca rubra* is found in drier sites.

Fescue *(Festuca altaica)*

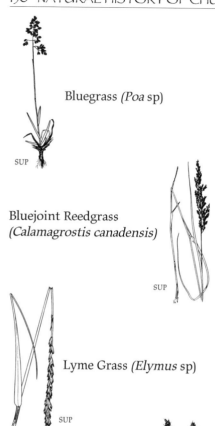

## Bluegrass *(Poa* sp)

This species is difficult to tell apart;Heads well-branched; grows in tufts. Grows in dry meadows and slopes from lowlands to alpine meadows.

Bluegrass *(Poa* sp)

SUP

## Bluejoint Reedgrass *(Calamagrostis canadensis)*

Tall grass with large and feathery head; common along wet marshy alpine meadows and along lowland lakes.

Bluejoint Reedgrass *(Calamagrostis canadensis)*

SUP

## Lyme Grass *(Elymus* sp)

Leaves are broad and droopy; heads are compact; grows in tufts from creeping roots; found along shore line especially sandy beaches.

Lyme Grass *(Elymus* sp)

SUP

## Alpine Holy Grass *(Hierochloe alpina)*

Short grass to about 4 inches; tufted leaves at base of stem, reddish at base; Heads are well-divided; common in dry alpine meadows, heaths, and rocky sites from lowlands to 6000 feet.

Alpine Holy Grass *(Hierochloe alpina)*

SUP

## SEDGES (Family Cyperaceae)
Sedges have hollow stems; both leaves and stems are triangular in a cross-section. Sedges have drab flowers but bright yellow anthers.

## Carex *(Carex* sp.)

There are some 120 species of Carex found in Alaska. They are extremely difficult to identify because of their similarities. They can be distinguished by the beaked seed-carrying part of the sedge called a perigynium. Male and female flower are found on the same plant. Male flowers are usually found above with lots of stamens hanging out; female flowers are usually lower and fatter. Carex is the predominate sedge of wet, boggy areas. Carex is common throughout Chugach State Park.

Carex *(Carex* sp.)

SUP

## Cottongrass *(Eriophorum angustifolium)*

Cottongrass is one of the easiest plants to identify. They grow in abundance in wet bogs and shorelines. They have characteristic white tufts at the top of a stem. Grows to 1 foot tall.

Cottongrass
*(Eriophorum angustifolium)*

SUP

## RUSHES (Family Juncaceae)
Rushes have hollow, round stems like grass, but have continuous stems and no joints. Leaves are round rather than flat.

### Rush *(Juncus articus)*

This rush is small and easy to miss, growing to less than a foot tall singley or in small groups. Found along shores and tidal marshes.

### Woodrush *(Luzula* sp)

Small drooping heads on branched stalks; leaves wider and flatter than other rushes. Prefers drier areas than Juncus; grows in meadows and among trees.

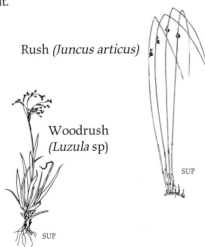

Rush *(Juncus articus)*

Woodrush
*(Luzula* sp)

SUP

SUP

## FERNS and FERN-ALLIES

Ferns and their allies, horsetails and club-mosses, are the most primitive of the vascular plants. Ferns and fern-allies are not related but grouped together by botanists because they share common characteristics. Like mosses, mushrooms, and lichens, they produce spores, not seeds. They lack flowers, so they do not bloom. They do not increase in diameter by secondary growth as do conifers and flowering plants.

## FERNS

Ferns love moist, damp sites either in deep wood and meadows, or in depressions which hold water. Ferns first poke out of the ground after snow-melt in a coiled roll called a **fiddlehead** which unrolls as the fern grows. Some species of ferns have 2 distinct, very different kinds of leaves: fertile leaves which carry the spores, and the sterile leaves, which do not.

**Wood Fern** *(Dryopteris dilatata)* - family Aspidaceae/shield fern

Tall fern to 2 feet with 3-pinnate, broadly triangular blades rising from rhizome. Stipes, or stems, are covered with coarse brown scales. Spores found on underside by mid-summer. Found in moist woodsand meadows.

SUP

**Fragrant Shield Fern** *(Dryopteris fragrans)* - family Aspidaceae/shield fern

Small fern to 8 inches high with many stiff, dark green leafblades. Spores on underside of leaves. Leaves persist for more than a year and are coarse in texture. Found on open, dry rocky outcroppings.

SUP

**Fragile Fern** *(Cryopteris fragilis)* - family Athyriaceae/lady fern

Small delicate fern to 7 inches high in small clumps from spreading underground rhizomes. Spores on undersides of leaves. Found on rocky sites in woods, clearings, and alpine sites.

SUP

**Ostrich Fern** *(Matteuccia struthiopteris)* - family Athyriaceae/lady fern

Large fern with fronds to 3 feet high growing in a single tight clump. Lacks scales on leaf stalk. Spores on separate fertile frond. Found in very wet woods at low elevations.

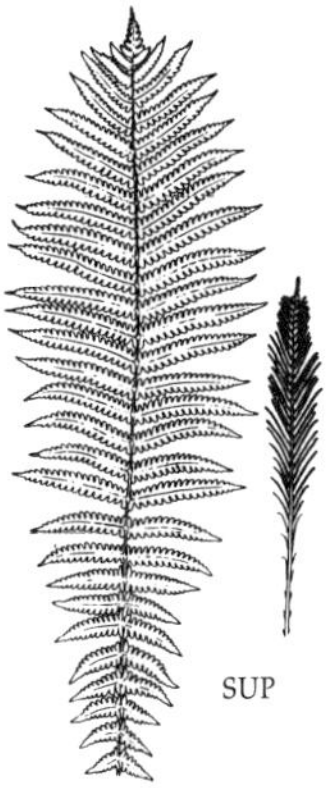

SUP

**Parsley Fern** *(Cryptogramma crispa)* - family Cryptogrammaceae/mountain parsley

Small loosely clumped fern to 6 inches from thick rootstalk with remnants of old dead leaf stalks. Spores on fertile fronds which rise above the other fronds. Found on rocky slopes and ledges.

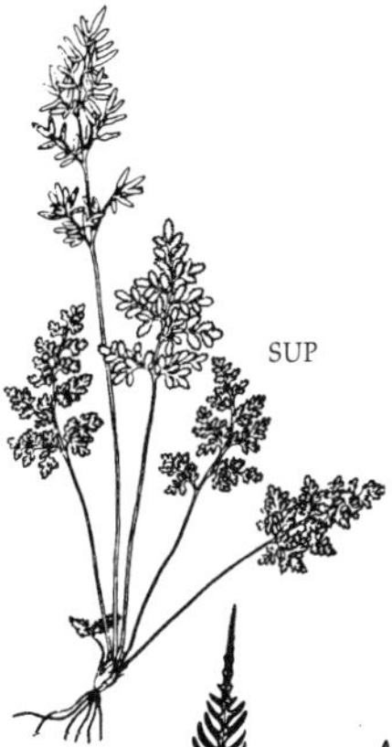

SUP

**Deer Fern** *(Blechnum spicant)* - family Polypodiaceae

Large fern to 1-5 feet tall with fronds clustering from woody rootstalk. Sterile fronds abundant, fertile fronds few and tallest. Found in wet woods and bogs.

SUP

**Oak Fern** *(Gymnocarpium dryopteris)*

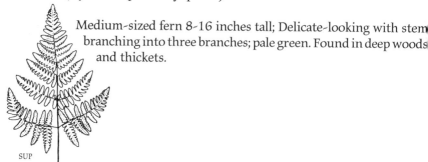

Medium-sized fern 8-16 inches tall; Delicate-looking with stem branching into three branches; pale green. Found in deep woods and thickets.

## FERN-ALLIES

**Stiff Club Moss** *(Lycopodium annotinum)* - family Lycopodiaceae/club moss

Low, creeping evergreen plant 4-7 inches high with stiff, pointed, yellow-green leaves. Branches erect from horizontal runners. Spores are in a cone at tip of branch on spore-producing plants. Found in woods and low alpine slopes.

**Creeping Jenny** *(Lycopodium complanatum)*

With flat, erect, branched cedar-like leaves to 5 inches high found in dry woods and clearings below treeline.

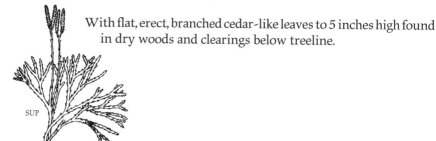

**Siberian Spike-moss** *(Selaginella sibirica)* - family Selaginellaceae/spike-moss

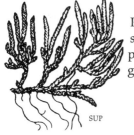

Plants forming flat, loose mats to 1 inch high with simple branching. Leaves yellow-green, stiff, flat, pointed and ascending stem. Found on rocky cliffs and gravelly, exposed alpine sites.

**Horsetail** *(Equisetum arvense)* - family Equisetaceae/horsetail

One of the most common plants in the world. Single stalked, unbranched, spore-bearing spring phase has hollow stem with vertical ridges. This dies back after production in early spring, and is replaced by sterile, simply-branched vegetative stems which die back in fall. Found in a variety of habitats,elevations and soil conditions throughout the park.

## MOSSES

SUP

Mosses are often walked on and overlooked. Yet they form vast mats on forest floors to alpine tundra. Mosses, along with liverworts, are nonvascular plants known as bryophytes. Bryophytes do not have structural features which allow them to retain water, so they must live in moist places in order to have sufficient water for growth. During periods of drought, bryophytes cannot maintain water in their bodies, so they become dormant. What appears dead and dry is actually a resting bryophyte, waiting for the drought to end.

Mosses are made up of a stem, often with many branches arising from it. Leaves are almost always a single cell layer thick and attached closely to the stem. The **seta** is the stalk that supports a **capsule**, a spore-filled sac. The **peristome**, is a specialized layer of cells at the capsule mouth with teeth and plates which open and close releasing spores. All these minute parts help differentiate the various species of mosses and liverworts, but most are so small a microscope is needed to identify them. Therefore, only the most obvious and easily identifiable are listed below.

### Feather Mosses of the Forest Floor

The most obvious and perhaps the most common bryophytes are the feather mosses of the subalpine and lowland coniferous forests. They do not do well in deciduous woodlands where falling leaves cover them. These feather mosses form a dense, soft, green, overlapping mat.

### *Hylocomnium splendens* (Stairstep Moss)

This is the most common feather moss. This moss, unlike any other, grows in tiers of curving branches representing annual growth increments. It has a light, feathery appearance. Together with *Pleurozium scheberi* it forms a continuous ground cover in boreal and subalpine coniferous forests.

MAC

## *Pleurozium scheberi* (Big Red Stem)

A common feather moss with a conspicuous red stem. Branches growing out at right angles from stem. Leaves shiny yellow-green and tightly pressed together. Found with *Hylocomnium splendens* forming a continuous green mat in boreal and subalpine coniferous forests.

MAC

## Ptilium crista-castrensis (Knight's Plum)

Golden-green leaves curl outward from branches like ostrich feather. Least common of feather mosses, found in low areas of boreal forest.

## *Polytrichum commune*

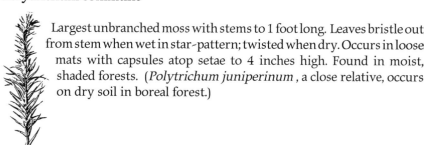

Largest unbranched moss with stems to 1 foot long. Leaves bristle out from stem when wet in star-pattern; twisted when dry. Occurs in loose mats with capsules atop setae to 4 inches high. Found in moist, shaded forests. (*Polytrichum juniperinum*, a close relative, occurs on dry soil in boreal forest.)

MAC

## MOSSES of the MUSKEG

Muskeg is a heavily vegetated wet bog of hummocks and hollows providing only the slightest changes in moisture content. Muskeg does not provide a solid surface to walk across. One may go only a few steps before sinking knee deep into black, smelly muck from years of accumulated rotting vegetation. The most readily accessible muskeg bogs are in Eagle River valley near the Eagle River Visitor Center.

Three mosses dominate the muskeg bogs of Chugach State Park. The first is a true peat moss which belongs to the genus **Sphagnum**. Colors range from red to green; branches are attached to a stem radiating to a blunt head. Peat mosses have the ability to acidify their surroundings and retain more than 20 times their dry weight in water. Second is **Drepanocladus,** a wetland genus preferring wet hollows, with curved, overlapping leaves. Third is

*Tomenhypnum,* an erect, golden-colored, fuzzy-stemmed hummock-forming moss; stem is reddish-brown.

## MOSSES of the MOUNTAIN STREAMS

*Pohlia*

Edges of perennial streams and waterways provide a steady source of moisture for water-sensitive bryophytes. Many genera, such as **Bryum, Pohlia,** and **Cratoneuron,** are found along streams with fairly constant water levels. If water levels vary, **Hygrohypnum** are found in the splash zone between high and low water. Colonies of **Scouleria aquatica** occur in the splash zone on constantly wet rocks in fast flowing mountain streams. These slimey black mats make streams crossings a tricky affair at best.

MAC

## MOSSES of the ALPINE and ROCKY CLIFFS

Cliffs at any elevation often duplicate conditions found in the alpine environment. The conditions they share are extremely variable temperatures, little or no soil, and extremes between wet and dry. Mosses in this environment depend on rain and snowmelt for water. Several common species of moss are found on cliffs and rocks above treeline.

**Grimmia** is a species of moss found growing on dry rock surfaces at all elevations. Grimmia cushions appear to be covered with fine erect hair; short capsules sit atop short setae. **Orthotrichum speciosum** is irregularly branched with long slender leaves. Capsules are long and cylindrical. Although it is primarily a moss of coastal rain forests, in Chugach State Park it occurs on dry sites on alpine tundra. **Hypnum revolutum** is the easiest to recognize. Leaf margins are revolute; that is, they are rolled under, and have no midrib. The plant, a shiney, golden-green color, is found growing in mats on dry granitic or calcareous rock. **Polytrichum piliferum** is characterized having a short bristle at the end of of each leaf. Like others in this genus, **P. piliferum** grows in a distinct star-pattern when viewed from above, and have capsules on reddish-brown setae. **Pogonatum alpinum** has conspicuously narrow, toothed-leaf margins, and is unbranched. Found at higher elevations on mineral soils; easily confused at lower elevations with others of this genus.

## LIVERWORTS

Liverworts, or hepatics, are even more inconspicuous than mosses. Most have a flat undifferentiated plant body called a **thallus** with a distinct upper and lower surface, or they are leafy with 3 ranks of leaves. Spore dispersal ranges from elaborate umbrella-headed stalks as on **Marchantia** to no mechanism at all.

## Marchantia polymorpha

One of the largest and most common of the liverworts. Bright green thalli ("leaves") with obvious pores; female portion of plant are lobed caps on raised stalks. Grows in marshy areas; very abundant after a fire (even old camp fires).

MAC

## Ptilidium ciliare

Leaf margins have numerous fine hairs; green finger-like growth form. Forms dense fuzzy mat loosely attached to ground. Occurs in depressions and wet rocky areas. Extremely slippery when wet.

## LICHENS

Lichens* have established a wonderful symbiotic relationship between fungi and certain species of algae to produce growth forms rivaling anything in the plant world for diversity and adaptation. Lichens grow only in intimate association between fungi and algae. The fungal component determines the shape of the lichen as it surrounds the alga with strands of microscopic fungal threads called HYPHAE, thus providing structural support and form.

Like mosses and liverworts, lichens must absorb moisture to survive. Lichens can absorb an amazing amount of water, but cannot retain it. A chief survival mechanism is that lichens can dry out very rapidly to become crunchy, brittle, and dormant. Or they can just as readily absorb moisture and nutrients from the surrounding air or from rainfall to begin growing again. As water content increases, so does the rate of photosynthesis. What was once a dry, drab lichen will radiates with color when wet.

Lichens are classified primarily by structure and chemical composition, which can make identification difficult, if not impossible. But most lichens can be identified to genus based on their form, and some distinctive lichens to species. Lichens develop into 3 growth forms - fruticose, foliose, and crustose. **Fruticose** lichens are radially symmetric. They spread out from a central point, and are tufted, stalked or pendent. **Foliose** lichens are leaflike and radiate from a central point as well. **Crustose** lichens have a thallus, or leaf-like structure, in intimate contact with the ground or rock. Any one of these types of lichens can be found in a variety of habitats.

*Lichens are pronounced LIKE-ens, not LITCH-ens.

# Ground-dwelling Lichens

Ground-dwelling lichens are common on the forest floor. A good place to look is along the Eagle River trail out toward Echo Bend on both dry and moist sites.

*Cladonia* species are the most diverse and common fruticose lichens of the forest floor. They develop as erect **podetia,** a hollow structure to 4 inches tall, taking 3 forms:

**1) worm-like rods** of *Cladonia cornuta,* which forms dense mats on open coniferous forests. Tan to brown; tall, slender stalks, or podetia, to 4 1/2 inches.

**2) irregular branching rods** of *Cladonia stellaris,* grow in the distinctive form of "cauliflower heads". Yellow-green branchlets form a star-shaped whorl around a central hole at the branch tip. Grows from open coniferous forests to damp depressions in alpine tundra.

**3) cupped structures which resemble golf tees,** or wine glasses, are numerous in this genus. Most common is *Cladonia chlorophaea,* "British soldiers", a goblet shaped *Cladonia* with large red knobs growing off the edge of cup. *Cladonia coccifera* and *C. bellidiflora* also have the red spore-bearing knobs.

*Cladina rangiferina,* the "reindeer lichens", are fruticose and form thick cushioned mats on the coniferous forest floor. This is a large, fast growing lichen, which is a primary food source for caribou of the arctic and subarctic.

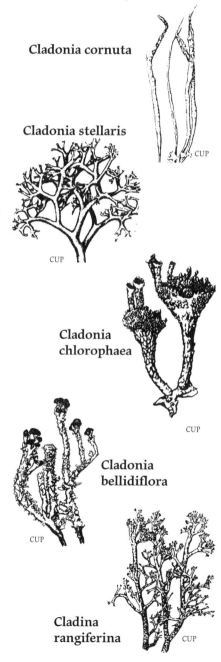

Cladonia cornuta

CUP

Cladonia stellaris

CUP

Cladonia chlorophaea

CUP

Cladonia bellidiflora

CUP

Cladina rangiferina

CUP

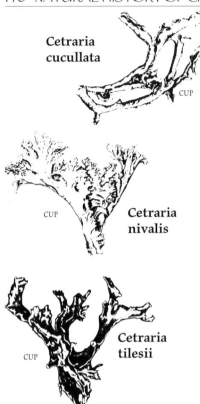

**Cetraria cucullata**

CUP

CUP

**Cetraria nivalis**

CUP

**Cetraria tilesii**

*Cetraria* species are fruticose and range from boreal forest to alpine tundra. The most common of this group, **Cetraria cucullata,** is pale yellow with deeply turned-in lobes and frilly margins; along with **C. nivalis,** a flat, wrinkled, pale yellow lichen, both are prominent lichens on drier alpine slopes. A brilliant yellow lichen is **C. tilesii** which grows in tight clumps on the dry forest floor or gravelly alpine tundra.

*Stereocaulon* species as a group are difficult to distinguish without a stereoscope and chemical analysis. These silver to rose-gray clumps of rough branchlets grow on the ground in open places above and below treeline. Especially common on old gravel river bars and bare tundra.

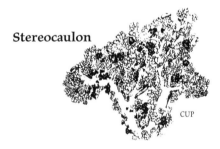

**Stereocaulon**

CUP

*Thamnolia subuliformis* is a tundra lichen. The clumps of white, hollow worm-like rods are easy to identify on dry rocky tundra. Also on the alpine tundra are stubby, hollow yellow-brown rods are **Dactylina arctica,** or "old man's fingers".

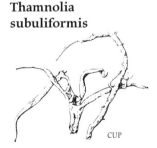

**Thamnolia subuliformis**

CUP

**Dactylina arctica**

CUP

*Alectoria ochroleuca* is a fine yellow-green lichen common on the open tundra. Its thread-like branches form dense interwoven clumps. The sun turns the upper surface dark green while lower branches remain yellow. It is found in association with *Cornicularia divergens,* a dark brown thin, branched lichen.

CUP

Alectoria ochroleuca

*Peltigera* are common lichens of the forest floor growing over and among the feather mosses. *Peltigera aphthosa* is a brilliant green (when wet), broad-lobed lichen over 2 inches across. Dark warty dots **(cephalodia)** speckle the upper surface; the underside has indistinct veins covered by fine matted hairs **(tomentum).** It may be confused with 2 similar genera below.

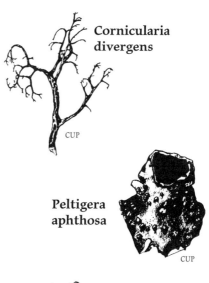

Cornicularia divergens

CUP

Peltigera aphthosa

CUP

*Lobaria linata,* a bright green (when wet), large-lobed lichen with a conspicuous pattern of hollows and ridges on surface. Its lower surface is finely haired, and a mottled white with brown. They grow with mosses in moist forests.

Lobaria linata

CUP

*Nephroma arcticum* is a smooth, light green, large-lobed lichen. Its lobe-margins tend to curl under. The lower surface is cream-colored grading from brown to black near center. They prefer moss/heath alpine tundra and open subalpine coniferous forests.

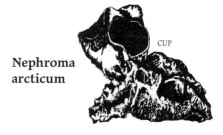

Nephroma arcticum

CUP

*Icmadophila ericetorum,* aptly called "fairy puke" lichen, is easy to recognize. It looks powdery white with pin-head sized salmon-pink dots **(apothecia)** scattered on surface. Common on moss, humus, and trail banks in moist forests of the park.

## TREE-DWELLING LICHENS

Tree-dwelling, or arboreal, lichens are common in the forests of Chugach State Park. They may appear as hair-like masses swaying in the trees, as tufts on branches, or as clumps on bark.

***Bryoria capillaris*** is a common thread-like lichen, hanging to 6 inches or more. Its gray-green color is distinctive since other *Bryoria* species are true brown. *Bryoria* are some of the more obvious arboreal lichens found hanging on spruce and hemlock trees in humid, mature forests.

CUP

***Usnea,*** or "old man's beard", is a hanging lichen attached to trees with a holdfast. These straw-colored lichens have a central cord from with branches attached at right angles. Common hanging from branches of spruce, occasionally birch.

CUP

***Cetraria pinastri*** has greenish-yellow lobes with bright yellow frilly edges It grows on old wood, branches and twigs of deciduous trees as well as on the base of conifers. Only bright yellow lichen to grow on trees and shrubs. Differs from ***C. tilesii*** which has smooth margins, is deep lemon yellow, and grows on the ground.

CUP

***Hypogymnia physodes*** has pale gray-green, hollow lobes with black margins; underside is black and lacks rhizines (root-like appendages). An abundant lichen, it forms rosettes which grow on twigs and bark of conifers as well as birch poplar, and willows. Often grows with, and is confused with, ***Parmelia sulcata,*** but *P. sulcata* has solid lobes rhizines, and a network of ridges on its surface. Both are common on conifers and deciduous trees.

CUP

*Lobaria hallii* is a large, dull green arboreal lichen with a broad ridged surface. It is common in large overlapping bunches on black cottonwood in the moist lowland forests of the park, rare on conifers. (See Lobaria linata on page 141.)

## ROCK-DWELLING LICHENS

Most of the rock-dwelling lichens are a crustose form requiring a microscope and chemical analysis to identify. Most are black or gray giving the rocky alpine ridges a monotonous drab color. A few groups have obvious physical characteristics, or color which make them easier to identify.

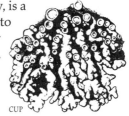

*Xanthoria elegans,* the easiest rock lichen to identify, is a bright orange with narrow foliose lobes radiating out to form a rosette to 2 inches across, but often form larger overlapping colonies. Common on exposed rocks, particularly limestone and rocks frequented by birds and their associated nitrogen release.

CUP

*Rhizocarpon geographicum,* "map lichen", is a common crustose lichen easily identified by its unique lime-green dots (spore pouches) on the black lichen. It is found in round patches on acidic rocks of alpine tundra. Called "map lichen" because of its slow, but predictable growth rate. (No Illustration)

*Xanthoparmelia centrifuga* has a concentric growth pattern which aids in identification. The flat, greenish-yellow, foliose thallus grows in concentric circles, recolonizing the inner portions as the thallus decays. Commonly found on acidic rocks in rock slides and outcroppings, talus slopes.

CUP

*Umbilicaria,* or rock tripe, are attached to the substrate by a single central point under the thallus. These brown to black lichens become extremely slippery when wet. Surface is smooth to wrinkled. Found on boulders, rock outcroppings, and slides of the alpine and subalpine.

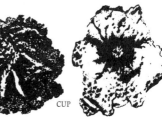

CUP

## MUSHROOMS

Mushrooms are a primitive group of plants called fungi. They lack chlorophyll so do not appear green. They cannot manufacture their own food, but obtain it elsewhere. Mushrooms are **saprophytic,** they live off dead and decaying matter.

Mushrooms lead a simple life. They begin as **mycelia,** a thread-like network of **hyphae** which spreads into a food source. The mycelium develops into a more complex organism, the **carpopore** - the mushroom itself. The carpopore is the fruiting body, the reproductive equipment of the plant, which produces spores which grow new mycelia.

The identification of mushrooms is tricky. Since they are a simple structure they have few distinguishing characteristics. Mushrooms change appearance quickly with age. Young mushrooms, when they first emerge, appear a rounded, colorful caps. Slowly they age to a flattened, pale incarnation of it former self, and finally appear as a shriveled up blackened mass.

It is important to recognize key features for correct identification:

1. Texture, color, shape and size of cap.
2. Texture of stalk, and the presence or absence of rings
3. Gill type, color, and arrangement.
4. Color of spores as seen in a SPORE PRINT.
 (A spore print should be made of every mushroom collected, if possible.)

### IF YOU CAN'T IDENTIFY IT, DON'T EAT IT.

### The Mushroom Season

Mushrooms are found "in season" anywhere food, moisture and temperature meet the requirements for mycelial growth. Most of the mushrooms in Chugach State Park are the wood and soil-loving varieties. Look for them in the moist lowland forests, bogs, and meadows for the greatest number of mushrooms. The higher up you go in the park, the fewer species you'll find Weather can affect the timing of the mushroom season. Where you found an abundance of mushrooms last season, this season you may find nothing. A late cool spring, or a hot, dry spell can delay growth. There are 3 seasons in the park

1. Mid-June to early-July (spring growth)
2. July to August (summer growth)
3. September (fall growth)

# MOST COMMON MUSHROOM FAMILIES

## Gilled Fungi (family Agaricaceae)

Gilled fungi are the largest and most common family of all the park's mushrooms. The name refers to the gills, or lamellae, on the underside of the cap which radiate out from the stem like spokes of a wheel. The gills bear millions of spores which drop from the mature mushroom. They range in color and size up to 8 inches high and 8 inches in diameter, but usually are much smaller.

SIM

There are two groups of gilled mushrooms. First are those genera with colorless, or white to yellow, spores. Second are those genera with colored pores. Know the spore color of mushrooms you are trying to identify.

**Spores colorless, white to yellow**

| | |
|---|---|
| Amanita | Lepiota |
| Armillariella | Mycena |
| Clitocybe & Hygophorus | Pleurotus |
| Collybia & Marasmius | Russula |
| Lactarius | Tricholoma |

**Spores with color**

| | |
|---|---|
| Clitopilus | Pholiota (Rizotes) |
| Pluteus | Agaricus |
| Cortinarius | Stropharia |
| Inocybe | Coprinus |
| Paxillus | Gomphidius |

## Fleshy Pore Fungi (family Boletaceae)

The boletes are a fleshy pore fungi without gills, but resemble gilled fungi in shape and grow up to 10 inches high and 8 inches across. Spores are borne in tubes or pores underneath the cap. Pores vary in color from white to red. **RED PORE MOUTHS SHOULD BE AVOIDED!** Stems and caps of some Boletes change color when bruised or cut. A few with this characteristic are considered POISONOUS. Yet some of the best edible mushrooms occur in this group. Found on ground in forests and meadows. Common genera *Boletus*, *Leccinum, Suillus*.

SIM

## Bracket Fungi (family Polyporaceae)

Bracket fungi, or woody pore, have pores under their caps, but otherwise do not resemble any other mushroom. Fruiting body is hard, woody, and tough and appear as a shelf or bracket-like growth on live or dead wood. Size is variable, but may reach 18 inches across. Common genera are *Polyporus, Caloporus,* and *Laetoporus.*

SIM

## Toothed Fungi (family Hydnaceae)

This large family bears its spores on the surface of spine-like teeth on the underside of the fruiting body. Body shapes vary from a simple flat layer on wood to bracket-like forms on wood, and occasionally on the ground. Common genera are *Hydnum and Dentinum.*

SIM

## Sponge Fungi (family Helvellaceae)

The fruiting body is sponge-like in appearance and varies in shape from a smooth to pitted, or convoluted, lobed surface, hollow inside. Range from 2 to 5 inches high. Found on wet, marshy, forested sites. Common genera are *Helvella, Morchella* and *Verpa.*

SIM

## Coral Fungi (family Clavariaceae)

SIM

Fruiting bodies are erect, simple or branched in shape to 6 inches high with no pores, gills or teeth. Entire surface of fruiting body bears spores. Family is easy to identify because they resemble coral. Identification to species is difficult. **Be careful!** One species, *Ramaria formosa,* is considered poisonous. Common genera are *Ramaria, Clavicorona, Clavariadelphus.*

## Puffball Fungi (family Lycoperdaceae)

Fruiting bodies of puffballs are globular in shape and vary in size from 1 to 10 inches in diameter. Mostly white when young, turning darker as they mature. Young puffballs are homogeneously white, solid inside, no cap, gills or stem. As it ages from white to yellow to brown, the interior dries to a fine powder - the spores. Outer skin smooth, or with warts, spines. Found singly, or in groups in meadows and mixed woods on ground or on wood. Common genera are *Calvatia* and *Lycoperdon*.

SIM

# CHAPTER THIRTEEN

# MAMMALS OF CHUGACH STATE PARK

Chugach State Park is a wonderful, wild place to look for mammals. Most of the mammals found in Alaska also reside in the park, and most can be seen year round by visitors with persistence and a keen eye. Spring is a time of renewal, and by May most animals have given birth. Bears begin to emerge from their dens with new cubs in search of fresh greens. Dall sheep ewes with newborn lambs feed on the sun-warmed slopes. Snowshoe hare dash about in the fervor of courtship, unconcerned by a human presence nearby. Cow moose become dangerously protective of their newborn calves, standing off a grizzly or a pet dog in defense of their young.

With the long days of summer, a late evening hike in the Park may be rewarded by the sight of a northern flying squirrel or little brown bat. In the cooler evening hours, many of the Park's animals become more active. Wolves, wolverine, and bear move out onto the open alpine tundra in search of voles and lemmings who emerge under the cover of twilight.

Fall brings a final burst of activity to the short, northern summer. Ripe berries provide many animals with an ideal source of food for laying down a thick layer of fat. Grizzlies and marten are frequent visitors to the copious berry patches in the Park. Other animals begin to cache seeds, grass, and berries for the bleak months beneath the mantle of snow. The elusive Northern Flying squirrel piles seed cones in the crevices around the bases of spruce trees. Lemmings spend the latter part of summer hoarding grass in their rocky subterranean homes.

Winter is the easiest time of the year for observing wildlife in Chugach State Park. The animals' passing, once hidden in the lush green of summer, is exposed for all to see on a blanket of new snow. A whole new dimension for viewing wildlife opens up to the diligent observer. Each animal's movements are imprinted in the soft snow with tracks, trails, droppings, or food remains. A walk or ski through the forests reveals trampled snowshoe hare thorough-fares and squirrel runways between spruce trees. Dark brown moose stand out

Facing page: Dall Sheep rams in rut (Michael DeYoung)

against the snow as they feed on dormant willow and alder. Antlered bulls may be visible as late as February. For the adventurous winter visitor skiing deep into the Park, the sight of a wolf or wolverine hunting ptarmigan or snowshoe hare is the rich reward.

Curiosity and patience will produce unexpected results for those who travel off the beaten path. The animals of Chugach State Park can be observed any time of the year if one takes the time to look. Knowledge of the animals' habits and habitat preferences will assist the visitor in knowing what to expect and where. Scanning the alpine tundra with binoculars may reveal Dall sheep, moose, or a grizzly going about their daily activities. It takes time. A chance encounter with any of the Park's wildlife is exciting, but animals cannot be rushed. Once in the wild, we share their world and move on their time. We must respect their right to exist and to be left alone.

## How Mammals Cope with the Long, Dark Winter

For a good part of each year, Chugach State Park is enveloped in a blanket of snow. Since mammals expend a great deal of energy to maintain body temperature, surviving the winter is tough. With food at a minimum, energy expenditure must also be kept at a minimum. Short-term physiological and behavioral changes allow individuals to cope with the stresses of winter. The Little Brown Bat is the only mammal not adapted to winter in Chugach State Park, so it migrates south each fall.

For those that remain there are a wide range of *physiological responses* to the cold and snow. Some mammals hibernate, letting their body temperature drop to conserve energy. Marmots and arctic ground squirrels may hibernate for over half the year, reducing their body temperature and heart rate dramatically. Grizzlies go into a shallow state of hibernation called topor, to save energy, and may be roused during warm spells in winter. Mammals must also add to their fat reserves with the onset of winter.

Animals which remain active throughout the winter have evolved morphological characteristics to aid in their survival. Snowshoe hare, lynx, wolverine and wolves have large well-furred feet which enable them to disperse their body weight on the snow's surface.

A few resident mammals change color to adapt to their surroundings. This is in response to changes in **photoperiod,** the length of darkness each day. Changes in photoperiod trigger changes in hormone levels which trigger color change. Short-tailed weasels and snowshoe hare change from the brown of summer to their white winter camouflage. Color change in weasels occurs through **molting** with the brown hair replaced by the white. In snowshoe hare only the tip turns white, while the base remains grey. They do not undergo a molt in fall, but shed in spring with the lengthening daylight.

*Behavioral adaptations* to the stresses of winter vary greatly. Small mammals such as meadow jumping mice take advantage of a higher surface-to-volume-ratio by hibernating together in a ball. Voles and beaver actively spend the winter beneath the snow and ice, feasting on food gathered during summer and fall. The majority of moose move out of the mountains to escape the deep wind-crusted snow in search of browse in the lowlands around the park.

## THE MAMMALS

Mammals are not abundant in Alaska, but they are some of the largest and most visible of its wildlife. Members of the class Mammalia all bear live young which may be born blind, hairless, and helpless (altricial), or they may be born fully furred, eyes open, and moving about (precocial). All mammals have hair, and nurse their young - even dolphins and whales. Chugach State Park has approximately 47 naturally occurring species of mammals, as well as an uncommon migrant, *Homo sapiens*.

## The BAT (Order Chiroptera)

**Little Brown Bat** *(Myotis lucifugus)* - Family Vespertilionidae

The only true flying mammal, and the only bat known to inhabit Chugach State Park. It is the most common bat in North America, and the only bat whose range extends beyond Canada and southeast Alaska. It is an "evening bat" who relies on echolocation to locate and catch its prey. It catches prey in its mouth, in the wing skin, or in the interfemoral skin between its legs & tail. It uses the same foraging pattern from night to night preferring to feed over water. In the fall this colonial bat will migrate south to hibernate in caves or trees, and will return in the spring to the same site where it was born. In Alaska, they reproduce at a slow rate, but live to a very old age (>20 years).

JWS

## The **SHREWS** (Order Insectivora)

Six species of shrews (Family Soricidae) inhabit Alaska, and five are found in Chugach State Park. These tiny insect-eaters are voracious and often consume more than own their weight in food each day.

**Water Shrew** *(Sorex palustris)*, pictured above, is one of the most interesting shrews. It is found in small numbers in fast-flowing streams in coniferous forests. It has stiff hairs along its hind feet to aid in swimmming. It feeds or insect larvae and freshwater invertebrates. It remains active even in winter by swimming from airpocket to airpocket under the ice.

**Dusky shrew** *(Sorex monticolus)* and **Tundra shrew** *(Sorex tundrensis)* are found in the higher montane and alpine regions of the Park. They are active year round, day and night, in search of ground-dwelling insects.

**Common,** or **Masked shrew** *(Sorex cinereus),* is the most widely distributed in North America. Like all shrews, the common shrew is active year round, day and night. They are found in forested areas of the park as well as in bogs and muskeg. They have several litters a year, and the young are on their own in two weeks.

Pygmy shrew *(Microsorex hoyi)* is the rarest shrew in North America. This tiny animal, weighing no more than a dime, is one of the smallest living mammals. It is found in the drier forests of the Park.

## The **HARES and PIKAS** (Order Lagomorpha)

**Snowshoe hares***(Lepus americanus)* - Family Leporidae

The only member of this family found in Chugach State Park. Hares are not rabbits, but are in the same family. They range in size from 13-18" long. Young are preco-cial - born fully furred, eyes open and are able to run within minutes whereas rabbits are born helpless and hairless. With abundant vegetation they may produce up to four litters a season. They usually produce 2-4 young per litter.

Hares molt twice a year. In summer their fur is rusty brown with white nostrils, tail, chin, and belly. For winter they grow a camouflage white coat but it is not solid white. The outer shaft is white, the middle is tawny, and the inner section is black. Hares are found in dense forests and brush as far as treeline where they feed on grasses, willows, alder and aspen.

**Collared Pika** *(Ochotona collaris)* - Family Ochotonidae

Small brown body 7-8" long with gray sides and pale gray collar on neck and shoulders, no visible tail, short rounded ears. Unlike hares, pikas are highly social and vocal. They are colonial and communicate with shrill bleats and barks. Pikas bear 2-6 altricial - blind and hairless - young in May-June. Pikas do not hibernate.

Pikas are found in the remote alpine valleys and talus slopes of Chugach State Park. They feed on grasses and sedges, as well as fireweed, dryas and lichens. Pikas spread the plant material in the sun to dry and then store them deep in dens for later use in winter.

**The RODENTS** (Order Rodentia)

These gnawing animals form the largest mammalian order in the world. More than half of all mammals are rodents. They are characterized by having only two pairs of incisors - one set above and one set below. Most are nocturnal (active at night) and are active year round. They are extremely prolific, usually found in high numbers, and are a major food source for many predators.

Squirrels (Family Sciuridae) are a diverse group containing marmots, ground squirrels, and tree squirrels. All are diurnal (active by day) except the flying squirrels. Ground squirrels, like chipmunks, have internal cheek pouches. Almost all squirrels store food for winter.

## Hoary Marmot *(Marmota caligata)*

This large squirrel, 18-21" long, is confined to the high alpine valleys of Chugach State Park as it requires large bouldered slopes and abundant vegetation. It is active in daylight, so listen for its high-pitched shrill whistle when passing a rocky talus slope. Look for a marmot sentry sitting upright on guard for impending danger.

HCP

The short Alaskan summer is a period of intense activity for this alpine dweller. They must consume enough food to fatten up for the 8-9 months of hibernation. In Alaska they enter hibernation by mid-September. From May to early June, 4 - 6 altricial young are born in the snow-bound nest.

## Arctic Ground Squirrel *(Spermophilus parryii)*

The largest of North American ground squirrels, 8-14" long, and the only ground squirrel in Alaska. A common inhabitant of the alpine tundra and shrub treeline areas of the Park. Even with the long days of summer, a visitor can hear the shrill peep night or day. Hibernation lasts about 7 months, from September to April. The males are the first to emerge through the receding snow. Grizzlies will gouge out their burrows in the alpine tundra in search of a tasty morsel.

JMM

## Red Squirrel *(Tamiasciurus hudsonicus0*

This is one of the most conspicuous small mammals in Chugach State Park, 11-14" long including its tail. It is a noisy inhabitant of the coniferous forests. Listen for its staccato chatter. It may be a warning of your presence, or of another animal. It is diurnally (during day) active year round, both in the trees and on the ground — as their tracks in the snow demonstrate. Remnants of spruce cones in depressions in the ground or on a stump reveal their presence. They feed on a wide variety of food from seeds, berries, bird eggs, and even fungi. Two litters are born each season - the first in March/April, the second in August.

HCP

# Northern Flying Squirrel *(Glaucomys sabrinus)*

The only strictly nocturnal squirrel. Common, although rarely seen, except in the twilight of our Alaskan summers. It has large eyes with a light brown body above and a white belly. Folds of loose skin alongside of the body between the fore and hind leg catches air as it glides from tree to tree. Found in mature stands of mixed deciduous for-ests, using old woodpecker holes for nests. Feeds on seeds, nuts, insects, bird eggs, and meat, if available.  In fall they leave telltale caches of cones at the base of white spruce.

HCP

# Meadow Jumping Mouse *(Zapus hudsonius)*

A beautiful yellowish mouse with a 3″ body, large hind feet and long tail, 4-5″; jumps 3- 4 feet when startled. It prefers moist fields, muskeg and woods with thick vegetation. Insects constitute half its diet, seeds and green plants the other half. Meadow Jumping Mice hibernate from October to late April. Since they store no food, they double their weight (6 grams of fat) in the few weeks prior to hibernation.  Males emerge first in late spring. Two litters are often produced, the first in June, and the second by mid-August.

JWS

# Red-back Vole *(Clethrionomys rutilus)*

This bright reddish hamster-sized vole, 4-5″ long, is common throughout the Park in brushy, moist areas, birch forests, and moist alpine meadows. They are seed-eaters, storing large caches for later use during winter. Red-back voles do not make elaborate burrow systems like those of their relatives in the genus *Microtus*.

JWS

**Meadow Vole** *(Microtus pennsylvanicus)*

A grizzled gray-brown hamster-sized rodent 4-7" with a medium long tail. Lives in a system of burrows year round, and active day and night. Common in moist areas at low elevations throughout the Park. Their ability to digest cellulose through fermentation by microbacteria in their stomach allows them to feed on grass.

**Tundra Vole** *(Microtus oeconomus)*

This dull brown vole, 5-9" long, is very specific in its habitat requirements. It prefers disturbed areas, burn areas, and scoured gravel bars in rivers. It feeds on new vegetation, and stores some for winter. A rarely seen resident.

**Singing Vole** *(Microtus gregalis)*

Small pale gray vole, 4-7" long, has a very short tail and thick fur. Is found above treeline on dry ground near water. This species may be found foraging up in the lower branches of low brush. Its common name refers to the high-pitched trill given as a warning.

**Long-tailed Vole** *(Microtus longicaudus)* and **Yellow-cheeked Vole** *(Microtus xanthognathus)* may occur in the Park, but sightings have not been confirmed.

**Northern Bog Lemming** *(Synaptomys borealis)*

This brownish-gray rodent, 5-7" long, is the only lemming known to inhabit the park. The ears are hidden in dense fur like all lemmings. Feeds on grasses, sedges, and leafy plants. Inhabits lowland boggy areas and birch forests up to treeline. It uses runways and a burrow system similar to voles. It is active year round, day or night.

JMM

**Muskrat** *(Ondatra zibethicus)*

A large brown aquatic rodent with a 16-25" body; scaly tail 7-12" is laterally flattened and used as a rudder; hind feet are webbed. Muskrats can close their mouths behind their incisors which allows them to chew underwater. They inhabit bogs, marshes, ponds, lakes and slow-moving streams below treeline.

JWS

R.P.Grossenheider

They are active year round, but primarily at night, feeding on cattails, sedges, rushes, frogs, fish and snails. Breeding season is in September, and 4-7 young are born May-June. They are a major prey species for mink, owls, and Northern Harriers within Chugach State Park.

## Porcupine *(Erethizon dorsatum)*

Porcupine are the second largest rodent in North America with a large stocky body, 18-22", and a club-like 7-9" tail. Their yellowish fur is interspersed with quills, or modified hairs on the rump and tail. Individuals may have up to 30,000 quills at any time. Porcupines do not throw quills, but when in danger they will erect them for protection. Barbs on the ends of the quills cause them to become firmly embedded in the victim. Porcupine are adept climbers, with claws and unique small fleshy knobs on the soles of their feet.

Porcupines are solitary, slow-moving animals. Occasionally seen or heard scurrying off in the spruce-hardwood forests. They mate in October-November, and after a long gestation period of 7 months a single young is born. The baby's quills are soft at birth, but harden within half an hour; it will leave its mother in September, before breeding season begins anew. Porcupines are vegetarians, feeding on hemlock, spruce, birch and willow in winter. Ground feeding commences in spring after the snows recede. Porcupine relish new buds, catkins, and succulent leaves of aspen and birch, as well as grasses, sedges, dandelions, and aquatic plants.

## Beaver *(Castor canadensis)*

The largest rodent in North America can weigh up to 60 pounds. They are a well-muscled animal measuring 35-46 inches with a large, flat, black, scaly tail 11-18 inches. Front legs are shorter than their rear legs. They are well-adapted to an aquatic life, with webbed feet and oily guard hairs which measure 10 times the diameter of the undercoat hairs; closeable nos-trils and ears; an inner eyelid, and lips which close behind the incisors to facilitate chewing under water. Incisors are orange to 5 mm wide. In the lakes and waterways of Chugach State Park beavers may be heard before they are seen as they slap their broad tail against the water surface in alarm.

(continued)

Beaver colonies contain 5-12 adults, first and second-year young, and kits. Two year olds disperse to form new colonies. Beavers breed in late January-February, and are believed to mate for life. By June 1-8 kits are born (precocial) and will be swimming in the inner lodge within a week. The mother carry the kits on her back, in her front paws, and on her tail. Beavers are vegetarians feeding on bark, twigs and leaves of poplar, aspen, birch, willow, and alder. They store branches with foliage under water near their lodge for the icebound months of winter. They remain active day and night all winter beneath the ice.

Beaver are beneficial to other wildlife. As they cut and clear trees, it opens areas for new vegetation growth. They create ponds for waterfowl and other water-loving creatures which feed on aquatic vegetation and insects. Construction of dams occurs from April to June, and again from late August to freeze-up. Lodge construction and repair using poplar, aspen, willow, birch, and alder occurs only in fall. This work is completed before food caching begins.

## The FLESH-EATERS (Order Carnivora)

The carnivores are the major predators in Chugach State Park. Carnivores have large canine teeth and live mainly on freshly killed meat, although some supplement a mostly vegetarian diet with an occasional meat meal.

## Least Weasel *(Mustela nivalis)*

Smallest carnivore in North America, body 5-6"; brown above with a white belly and feet. Its tail is short, 1-2", brown (no black tip). It mates year round with up to 3 litters a year. In any month 3-6 young are born in a burrow; weaned in 4-7 weeks.

Ferocious predator of small rodents. Hunts in a "random search" pattern, investigating burrows, nests, or other potential hiding places in bogs, muskeg, tundra or open forest. Active year round, but in summer it is diurnal, and in winter it is nocturnal.

## Short-tailed Weasel *(Mustela erminea)*

This small weasel, or ermine, has a body 6-9" long with a tail 2-4". In summer its coat is dark brown with white belly and feet. Ermine are known for their luxurious white winter coat. In summer and winter the tip of the tail is black.

Ermine mate in July and 4-9 altricial young are born the following spring undergoing up to 200 days of delayed implantation of the egg. The young are

cared for by both parents. Weasels are carnivo-
rous, preying on voles, lemmings, shrews, baby
hare, and birds. It inhabits open areas of bogs,
marshes, muskeg, wet tundra, and open
forests. They avoid dense coniferous forests.

JWS

## Marten *(Martes americana)*

A medium-sized weasel with a brown body, 14-17", an orange-buff throat
patch and a long bushy tail 7-9". There is a slight seasonal variation in coat color
with the summer coat the lightest. New fur growth
begins at the tip of the tail in early September and
is completed by mid-October. Its claws are semi-
retractile, but not sheathed.

Marten are solitary except in mid-
summer during mating season. In
March or April, 3 young
(altricial) are born in a den and
disperse by autumn. Marten
are active throughout the year
especially in the morning, late

JWS

afternoon and on overcast days. They are arboreal (tree-dwellers), but will hunt
on the ground. Most common in mature old-growth forests in the Park.
Red-back Vole is the primary food, but marten will eat other rodents, birds and
eggs and are extremely fond of berries. Occasionally, a marten may be found
sharing a berry patch with human berry pickers.

## Mink *(Mustela vison)*

Long body, 12-17", with long tail,
5-9"; rich thick brown fur with
distinguishing white spots on its throat.
Molts twice a year. Adapted for life in the
water with semi-webbed toes and semi-

JWS

retractile claws, and oily guard hairs. Mink are generally nocturnal and
solitary except in family groups.

They breed from late February to early April. They bear 1-8 altricial young in
May. The young are weaned by September and sexually active by 10 months.
They inhabit areas along rivers, creeks, lakes, bogs, and saltwater mudflats.
Mink are carnivores who search out small mammals, fish, frogs, birds, eggs, and
insects. Mink in turn are preyed upon by wolves, lynx, and owls.

**River Otter** *(Lutra canadensis)*

Larger than mink, body 26-30", tail 12-17". Otters are adapted to life in water with webbed toes and thick brown fur. Away from human disturbance, otters are active by day - especially in the morning and evening.

Otters breed early in the spring after the birth of that year's litter of 1-4 pups, and are weaned at 4 months, dispersing by 8 months. They are strong swimmers who are agile on land, where they play along river banks, ponds and lakes. They feed on small mammals, fish, insects, birds, and occasionally plants. They attack waterfowl by seizing them from under the water surface.

**Wolverine** *(Gulo gulo)*

Largest and most powerful member of the weasel family. Body, 29-32", resembles a small bear with dark brown fur, a pale yellow band from the shoulders to the base of its short 7-9"tail, with light patches on its brow. Fur is course with long guard hairs - ideal for shedding snow; feet densely furred with semi-retractile claws. Does not hibernate, but remains active in the park day or night. It has a 3-4 hour activity cycle, but this varies with weather and food availability. A small population of less than a dozen are found in moist areas of alpine tundra down major drainages in the park to river bottoms of Chugach State Park.

Wolverine are opportunistic hunters ferocious enough to drive a grizzly or wolves from a kill. Capable of bringing down a moose, especially when snow hinders escape. Feeds on anything from moose to rodents, birds to plants and carrion. When drinking water, a wolverine automatically paddles the water's edge with its forefeet, causing the water to puddle.

## The **DOGS** (Family Canidae)

### Red Fox *(Vulpes vulpes)*

Foxes have a small reddish body and stand approximately 16″ at the shoulder. Color can vary from black to silver; belly, throat and chin as the tip of their long bushy tail are white; back of the ears, lower legs, and feet are black. Unlike other canids, foxes have elliptical pupils. Primarily nocturnal and very secretive, preferring open forests, upland hardwoods and marshes. Foxes avoid dense vegetation.

Foxes breed from January to March; 1-10 kits are born April-May. Young are weaned and dispersed by 4 months. Dens are established after mating, and abandoned when kits leave. A scattered population of red fox prefer the more remote northern half of the Park, although on rare occasions fox have been seen as far south as Ship Creek.

### Coyote *(Canis latrans)*

Coyotes vary in color from grizzled gray to reddish, standing 23-26″ at shoulder. Hair is long and coarse; the tail is bushy with a black tip, and hangs down when running. (Wolves run with their tails out horizontal.) Coyotes are the fastest runners among canids going up to 40 mph for short distances. Coyotes, less social than wolves, are usually seen alone, in pairs, or a mother with pups. No pair bonding as with wolves. Breeding season occurs from February to April. In May, 1-19 pups are born (altricial), cared for by their mother and last year's siblings. Pups emerge from the den after about three weeks at which time they begin eating solid food. Coyotes are omnivores, eating small mammals, birds, eggs, insects, berries, and just about anything they can get their mouths on.

**Wolf** *(Canis lupus)*

Wolves in Chugach State Park? Yes, a healthy population. Wolves in the park are usually gray, but vary in color from white to black. Distinguished from coyotes by their large size ( 26-38" at shoulder), and tail held horizontal when running (Coyotes' tails drop down when they run.). Wolves usually mate for life; sexually mature at 2 years; do not breed until their third year, between March and April in Alaska. An average of six pups are born in a den. At two months the pups venture out of the den, and in October they join the pack on hunting forays. Two to three packs share the vast Chugach wilderness, and occasionally a pack strays into the outskirts of Anchorage.

JMM

A pack usually consists of the "Alpha" mated pair, pups, the previous year's siblings, and occasionally other unmated adults. This social organization allows the wolf to hunt larger prey, such as moose and Dall sheep, which comprise 80% of their diet. Rodents, birds, fish, and insects make up the rest. In winter months, wolves must expand their range in search of food. Wolves locate prey by direct scent and tracking, or by chance encounter. Availability of the "right" prey and the presence of man affect the distribution of wolves in the park.

**The CAT** (Family Felidae)

**Lynx** *(Felis lynx)*

This medium-sized tawny cat, 29-42" long, with a short tail (2-5" long tipped with black); long black ear tufts, and a ruff around its face is the only member of the cat family in the Park. They have long legs and large well-furred paws for walking on snow. A small population of about a dozen lynx inhabit the park. Lynx are solitary and elusive, inhabiting deep forests of the park. In May-June, 2-6 young are born, and remain with their mother through the first winter until the next breeding season begins.

JWS

Snowshoe hair are the primary prey species, and the lynx population parallels the cyclic swings of the hare. They also feed on squirrels, grouse, ptarmigan, voles, shrews and carrion. Lynx are active year-round, although they are primarily nocturnal.

C.G.Pritchard

## The **BEARS** (Family Ursidae)

### Black Bear *(Ursus americanus)*

Black bear are the smallest (3 feet at shoulder) of the two bears inhabiting the Park. Their color varies from cinnamon to black with a white blaze on the chest; muzzle is tan and profile is straight; short claws which allow them to climb trees. Black bear enter dens between October and December; footpads are shed and regrow during denning. Black bears emerge in March-May; females with cubs leave their dens last. Breeding occurs during the summer months, peaking in June-July. In January-February, 2-4 cubs (altricial) are born and stay with their mother into the second year before dispersing as yearlings.

About 70-80 black bear inhabit the park with the highest concentration in Eagle River valley. Black bear are shy and secretive, preferring dense understory vegetation, and treeline thickets. Active primarily in evenings, they can be seen any time of the day or night. Almost strict vegetarians, they forage for grasses and grass-like forbs, or peeling bark to get at the rich cambium layer in spring and summer. In late summer and early fall, they feed on shrubs and berries to build up a thick layer of fat for winter. If available, they eat carrion, insects or fish.

### Brown Bear / Grizzly *(Ursus arctos)*

Grows to twice the size of a black bear, standing 4-5 feet at the shoulder, 6-7 feet long. They have features which distinguish them from their smaller, darker, more reserved cousin. Grizzlies are larger and have longer legs with a thick golden brown coat. Each of their five toes has 4 inch long claws which are a visible feature of their tracks. Long claws makes it difficult to climb trees, although they try. Their facial profile is concave, or dishface, with large ears. They have excellent hearing, but terrible eyesight. Curiosity has often been mistaken as a charge. They can attain speeds of up to 35 mph.

(continued)

Sows have their first litter around 5 years old, and may continue breeding until 25 years old. They have a three-year rearing cycle. One to four cubs are born in February, following an 8-month gestation period. Cubs den with the sow the second winter and are weaned as 2-year olds. Denning is well-developed in Alaskan grizzlies; they begin to excavate between September and November, entering dens by November. Dens are usually found in the upper reaches of the subalpine zone (1000 - 5000 feet) on 30 - 45  slopes. Bears emerge from their dens between April and May, although mid-winter warm spells may bring some out for a look around.

About 40 grizzlies are found within the park. They will cross high mountain ridges, glaciers, and rivers in search of food. Grizzlies are omnivores, eating anything they can get their mouths on. Grizzlies need large areas away from excessive human use. Their home ranges extend 42 to 1500 square miles, depending on food availability.

**The CLOVEN-HOOFED HERD** - (Order Artiodactyla includes the sheep/goat family (Bovidae) and the deer family (Cervidae). The difference is that bovids grown true horns which continue growing each year, and the deer family grow antlers which they shed each year.

### Mountain Goat *(Oreamnos americanus)*

This bovid is not true goat, but related to the European Chamois. Their conical horns are hollow and are present on both sexes; hooves are cloven and widely splayed; horns, hooves, eyelids, and nose are black. Mountain goats are stocky 4-5 feet long, 3 feet high with a slight hump on their shoulders. They have a long yellowish-white coat; males have a "beard" which is an extension of their throat hair. In late fall during rut, battles between rival males are rare. One or two kids are born between mid-May and mid-June, and within a few hours the kids can negotiate all but the steepest slopes. Kids are weaned in late August-September.

Between 500-600 goats are found in the park above treeline adjacent to the safety of rock outcroppings, but may enter old growth hemlock-spruce forests to feed. Goats avoid areas of high human use, secluding themselves in the remote high valleys deep within the park. They are most active in morning and evening, but may be seen feeding in the twilight of the Alaskan summer nights. They are vegetarians which eat grasses and sedges, as well as lupine, mountain bluebells, dwarf huckleberry, willows, mosses, lichens, and ferns.

## Dall Sheep *(Ovis dall)*

A northern relative of the Bighorn sheep, Dall sheep are all white, body 4-5 feet long, 3-4 feet at shoulder. Both sexes have yellow-brown horns, but ewes just have spikes; hooves yellowish-brown. Huge curled horns of rams are used in loud collisions with rival males during breeding season, conflicts which usually amount to nothing more than a shoving match. Lambs walk in about 3-4 hours, and begin feeding on vegetation at about 10 days. In spring and summer bands are composed of ewes, lambs, and yearlings. Rams do not join the bands until fall, when they begin to form harems for breeding.

JWS
C.G.Pritchard

Around 2000 sheep are found in the Park, usually on rocky ridges and south-facing alpine slopes, occasionally venturing below treeline to reach adjacent feeding areas such as Windy Corner on the Seward Highway. Dall sheep feed on grasses, willow, fireweed, horsetails, crowberry, cranberry, mosses, and lichens. They are drawn to natural salt licks such the Twin Peaks area at Eklutna. Sheep have separate winter and summer ranges within the Park, but movement is primarily altitudinal. They are active during the day as the band moves across mountain slopes feeding and resting.

## Moose *(Alces alces)*

Moose are the largest member of the deer family in the world, and the only family representative in Chugach State Park. They stand 6 to 7 1/2 feet at the shoulder and weigh up to 1400 pounds. Males have massive palmate antlers, 4-5 feet across, which begin growing from a pedicle

JMM

(a bony outgrowth on the skull) in late spring and are covered by a velvet skin which protects the extensive vascular system feeding the growing antler.

Growth stops in late August/early September when bulls begin to rub the velvet off on trees and shrubs as a prelude to rut.  Bull moose are most dangerous during rut. Following breeding season in September-October, the bone is reduced between the antler and the pedicle until the antler is shed between November and April. Older bulls shed first.

In May and June, a cow gives birth to 1-3 calves, charging unsuspecting hikers to protect her calves. **CAUTION: COWS WITH CALVES ARE DANGER-OUS!** Moose do not form harems, but may be seen in loose groups of 2 to 30 individuals, especially in winter when food is scarce.

Several hundred moose reside in the park where they feed on willow, birch, alder, mosses, lichens, and aquatic vegetation. Moose are active day or night. Loss of leaves and snow cause a decrease in food availability within the Park. A seasonal migration begins in October-November as moose come down out of the mountains into the Anchorage bowl. Some moose remain at treeline within the Park.  In spring they follow the the greeningvegetation up the drainages back into the park.

## MARINE MAMMALS

### WHALES and DOLPHINS (Cetaceans)

They are warm-blooded, air breathing mammals, bearing living young who suckle. Their body shape is fish-like with a tail fluke which is horizontal. Their nostrils are located on top of their head, the blow-holes. They surface periodically, blowing air from lungs as, or just before they break the surface of the water.

### Beluga Whale *(Delphinapterus leucas)*

Beluga, or white, whales inhabit the marine waters along Turnagain Arm from Anchorage to Twenty Mile River near Portage. Belugas are small white whales up to 14 feet long weighing 1400-2400 pounds. They reach maximum size at about 15-20 years. Young are a gray-brown and don't begin to whiten until 6 or 7 years old. Belugas

JWS

have small peg-like teeth on upper and lower jaws which they use to catch fish. They have a blunt snout and no dorsal fin.

Their primary food is eulachon (hooligan), as well as salmon, squid, and marine worms. They begin arriving up Turnagain Arm in May and June following the eulachon, an oily smelt. As many as 200 to 400 Beluga return in search of food during the summer months. They move up the Arm with each high tide and are obvious against the silty gray waters. By November they will have moved out as ice begins to form in Upper Cook Inlet.

**Killer Whales** *(Orcinus orca)*

Family groups of killer whales are known to travel up Turnagain Arm in pursuit of prey, and may become stranded on the mudflats with the ebb tide. Killer whales have distinctive tall dorsal fin to 45 inches high, and striking black and white color pattern. They attain lengths of over 30 feet and weights of 8 tons or more. Killer whales are a top marine predator, feeding on a variety of marine mammals, and sea birds, as well as eulachon and salmon.

HCP

**Minke Whale** *(Balaenoptera acutorostrata)*

This small baleen whale has been sighted up Turnagain Arm as far up as Twenty Mile River near Portage, possibly caught in the incoming tide. A dark whale 30 feet long weighing 10 tons with tipped (falcate) dorsal fin and distinctive prominent narrow head ridge. They feed on krill and small shoaling fish such as herring, cod, and pollack.

**Harbor Porpoise** *(Phocoena phocoena)*

Harbor porpoise, on rare occasions, have drifted up Turnagain Arm with the incoming tide as far as Twenty Mile River. Their distinctive features are no beak, no obvious color pattern, and a triangular dorsal fin. They are small and chunky to over 7 feet long.

HCP

## OTHER MARINE MAMMALS

### Pacific Harbor Seal *(Phoca vitulina)*

This is a small phocid, or earless, seal grows up to 5 feet long and weighs up to 255 pounds. Its color varies from buff with a darker dorsal surface and dark spots to all dark Both color variations have light areas around the eyes and snout Flippers are turned back, geared for an aquatic existence.

Harbor seals venture on land to give birth to a single pup which is born during May-June in the Gulf of Alaska. Pups have a woolly white coat called "lanugo" which is shed within a month when they change to the adult brown. These seals are found in the eastern North Pacific. They feed on flounder, herring, squid, and lamprey. Occasionally, the seals may follow salmon and hooligan up Cook Inlet, feeding with the incoming tide.

### Northern Sea Lion *(Eumetopias jubatus)*

The northern, or Steller's sea lion is the largest eared seal. Males are 8-10 feet long, weighing more than one ton; they develop a heavy, muscular neck with a mane of long coarse hair; females one third the size of males. They use all 4 flippers to move on land, but are most at home in the ocean. Sea lions primarily feed on squid, but will eat herring, halibut, rockfish and occasionally salmon. On rare occasions they enter Turnagain Arm in search of food.

## The PRIMATE (Family Hominidae)

### Human *(Homo sapiens)*

The park's only primate is highly variable in appearance. Adult males range from 5-6 feet tall or more; females smaller, less than 6 feet. Diagnostic habit of walking on hind legs; thinly haired over most of its body, except on head, groin and under front arms. Coat color highly variable. Sexes difficult to distinguish because this species conceals diagnostic features year round. No distinctive call, highly varied.

Females are sexually responsive all year, but rarely produce young - averaging 2-3 during the lifetime. Young are born helpless, but not blind or deaf as in rodents. Sexual maturity at 13-14 years, but successful mating usually does not occur for several more years. Humans do not survive for long in the wild, but have been known to live more than 100 years in captivity. (Thank you, Ben Gadd)

In summer, this species occurs regularly around the park, but uses little of suitable habitat. Active diurnally and year round. Found in small numbers of 2 or more on well-established trails from boreal forests to alpine tundra. Occasionally small groups will remain in alpine valleys or on mountain ridges for several days. Omnivorous, feeding on anything from nuts and dried fruit to foods of no nutritive value at all; occasionally seen feeding in berry patches along with bears and marten.

# CHAPTER FOURTEEN

# BIRDS OF
# CHUGACH STATE PARK

Chugach State Park is at the crossroads of two main bird migration routes, the Coastal and Pacific routes which converge out in the Gulf of Alaska. Birds either follow Cook Inlet north, or cross over the Chugach Mountains flying down Turnagain Arm or down the Knik River drainage. The two best habitats in the park for birdwatching are the waterways and alpine tundra. In June and July the park is alive with birdsong. By August most birds are heading south for warmer weather, but a few species brave the Alaskan winters.

## Avian Adaptations to the Long, Cold Winter

To control heat loss, birds, like mammals, must adjust the thickness of their insulation. An increased thickness of feathers can reduce heat loss. Birds, such as redpolls, may increase their total feather weight by 50% during the winter months. Fluffing up feathers while roosting may reduce heat loss by another 30 to 50%. In winter, birds shiver to produce heat when not generating heat in flight. Northern species, such as ptarmigan, will use the insulating properties of snow by tunneling into the snowpack or by nestling into moose tracks.

Although birds lack the long-lasting brown fat, they can add to fat reserves on a short-term basis. Year-round avian residents show seasonal and daily changes in temporary white-fat reserves. Accumulated fat is generally only sufficient to get them through one long, cold night (16-24 hours) before they must forage again.

Of the approximately 100 species of birds known to occur in Chugach State Park, only those most likely to be seen by the casual observer and/or birds of unusual interest are described below. For easier identification birds are grouped by primary habitat. Most birds are adapted to specific habitat types by their food preference and tend to remain in a specific area during the winter or summer season. See Appendix A for complete bird list.

Facing page: Great Horned Owl (John Warden)

## BIRDS OF THE LAKES, PONDS, and RIVERS

**Northern Pintail** *(Anas acuta)* - Family Anatidae

**ID:** Large slender duck, 20-29 inches long. Male has brown head, long neck with white breast continuing in a fine strip up side of neck, gray body and long pointed tail feathers. Female plain brown, no eye stripe, gray bill and shorter but pointed tail. Slender appearance of both sexes in flight.

**Habitat: Common**/year-round resident.  Prefers lowland marshes, ponds, and slow streams.  Dabbles in shallow water primarily for seeds of sedges and grasses, pondweed; also eats snails, aquatic insects, and leeches. Nests in late spring in a hollow depression in the ground, often away from water.

**Common Merganser** *(Mergus merganser)* - Family Anatidae

Largest Merganser, 22-28 inches long. Male has black head and back, white chest and wings, gray tail. It has long, slender red-orange bill and no crest. Female has gray body and red-brown head with a slight crest.

**Habitat:** Year-round resident. Prefers clear water lakes, ponds, and streams of the lowland forests. Swims with head down or dives in search of small fish, frogs, leeches, or anything it can get. May nest in tree cavities, cliff ledges, or on ground.

**Barrow's Goldeneye** *(Bucephala islandica)* - Family Anatidae

**ID:** Smallish duck to 18 inches long. Male has striking black and white plumage with a white crescent on cheek and black bill. Male has more black on back than Common Goldeneye.  Female has mottled gray body with dark brown head and yellow bill in winter and spring. Eyes of both sexes bright yellow.

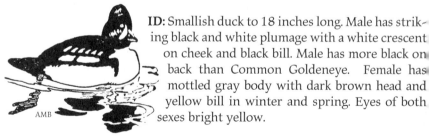

**Habitat:** Year-round resident.  Prefers wooded lakes and ponds. Dives for dragonfly and damselfly larvae; eats pondweed and an occasional small fish and salmon eggs. Nests in tree cavities, or holes in ground.

**Common Goldeneye** *(Bucephala clangula)* - Family Anatidae

**ID:** Similar to Barrow's to 18 inches long, but facial spot on male is smaller and head more green-black, body whiter. Female difficult to distinguish with gray body and brown head except the Common has yellow-tipped bill. Both sexes have bright yellow eyes.

AMB

**Habitat:** Similar to Barrow's Goldeneye, ranges overlap. Also feeds on aquatic insects, pondweed, and snails. Nests in a dead tree cavity 6-60 feet above ground.

**American Dipper** *(Cinclus mexicanus)* - Family Cinclidae

**ID:** Round solid gray bird to $7^1/_2$ inches long with a short tail and large yellow legs; eyelid is white. Adapted to life in the water with oil glands to waterproof feathers, flaps to seal nostrils, and a nictating membrane (transparent eyelid) to protect eye. Call is a loud, sharp "zeet", or cheep and warble at rest. Sings throughout the year.

**Habitat:** Year-round resident. Common from lowlands to treeline in fast-moving streams that remain open all year. Feeds by walking or diving

AMB

into the current where it walks along bottom in search of aquatic larvae, snails, and tiny fish, then jumps up on to a rock and bobs up and down. Female builds a domed nest of mosses on cliff ledge, behind waterfall, or on rock in midstream early spring.

**Harlequin Duck** *(Histrionicus histrionicus)* - Family Anatidae

**ID:** Large duck, 14-17 incheslong. Male in breeding plumage is a boldly patterned slate-blue and rust with white stripes and ear spots; female pale brown with 2-3 white spots on head. Agile fliers; pair often seen flying just above water surface with shallow wing beats.

AMB

**Habitat:** Found along the fast-moving mountain streams and rivers in the park after its arrival in March. Highly adapted to aquatic life; like Dippers they swim and walk underwater in search of caddisfly larvae and other aquatic insects. Nest along shore of a stream.

## BIRDS OF THE MUSKEG and MARSHES

**Bohemian Waxwing** *(Bombycilla garrulus)* - Family Bombycillidae

**ID:** Crested soft gray bird, 8 inches long with black eye mask, distinctive yellow-tipped tail and red waxy dots on each wing. Call is a high quiet hissing twitter "*sirr*", often while in flight. Year-round resident.

**Habitat:** Nest in late spring in isolated conifers in open muskeg where they feed on insects. By fall they are flocking down out of the Park into the Anchorage bowl where they will winter feeding on berries, especially mountain ash and wild raspberries.

**Common Snipe** *(Gallinago gallinago)* - Family Scolopacidae

**ID:** Sandpiper-like bird, 11 inches long with an extremely long bill, brown with vertical striping and short dark tail, no white on wings or lower back. More often heard before seen by the winnowing sound of territorial acrobatics. In this spring mating ritual, male snipes fly up and plunge down at high speeds with tail feathers spread to catch the wind. The feathers vibrate, creating the hollow woo-woo-woo sound in the evening air.

**Habitat:** Found in open wet mixed coniferous-deciduous woods to open subalpine forests, muskeg and marshes. Arrives in the park and vicinity usually by the last week of April. Walks around probing the mud for worms and insect larvae. Nests on dry ground, well-camouflaged in the grass or moss.

**Lesser Yellowlegs** *(Tringa flavipes)* - Family Scolopacidae

**D:** Smaller of the 2 Yellowlegs in Chugach State Park, to 11 inches long with long, bright yellow legs (only sandpipers with this leg color), dark wings, white rump, finely barred tail. Distinguishing feature is thin straight black bill shorter than Greater Yellowlegs *T. melanoleuca*); Greater has a long 2-toned slightly upturned bill with black at tip. Lesser breeding plumage shows white belly with streaked breast; Greater is 15 inches long, has streaked and spotted belly. Call is a high soft *tew-tew,*;both species bob head and tail when alarmed.

AMB

**Habitat:** Prefers muskeg and freshwater marshes; often seen below Eagle River Visitor Center. Arrives in park by the end of April. Feeds by pecking in shallow waters or snatching passing minnows. Often calls from atop a spruce during nesting season. Nests in late spring in hollow on mossy ground. Both species share similar habitat.


# BIRDS OF THE FORESTS and OPEN WOODLANDS

**Common Redpoll** *(Carduelis flammea)* - Family Fringillidae

**D:** Stout little streaked bird to 5 inches with black chin, bright red cap, and stubby bill. Both sexes have pink rumps; some males have red breast. Distinguished from uncommon Hoary Redpoll *(C. hornemanni)*, which has a white rump. Travels in large mixed flocks of Common and a few Hoary Redpolls.

**Habitat:** Year-round resident; can survive colder temperatures than any other songbird. Prefers seeds from cones of birch, alder, and willows, as well as weed seed. Redpolls have an enlarged esophagus which others in this family don't have. It allows them to take in and hold more food, which can be digested over a long cold night. Nests in lower branches of spruce, alder or willow, 3-6 feet off ground.

AMB

**White-winged Crossbill** *(Loxia leucoptera)* - Family Fringillidae

**ID:** Male has pink-red body, 6 inches long, dark wings with two conspicuous white wing bars. Female is dull olive-gray with wing bars. Both sexes have crossed bills which allow them to extract seeds from spruce cones. Male's song is a quiet *sweet-sweet-sweet*

**Habitat:** Year-round resident. Found in coniferous forests just below treeline where it feeds on spruce seeds, other seeds, as well as an occasional insect. Nests in conifers 5 to 80 feet above ground.

AMB

**Pine Grosbeak** *(Pinicola enucleator).-* Family Fringillidae

**ID:** Male is a stout, a robin-sized 9 inches; red on head, breast and back with mottled gray sides, 2 conspicuous white wing bars and slightly forked tail. Female is gray with a yellow tinge to head and rump, white wing bars.

**Habitat:** Year round resident. Found in open coniferous forests, usually less than 15 feet above ground. Feed on seeds of deciduous trees and shrubs, spring buds, and insects coming to the ground to feed. Nests in spruce or tall shrub from 6-30 feet above ground. Moves out of the park down into Anchorage during the winter months.

AMB

**Pine Siskin** *(Carduelis pinus).-* Family Fringillidae

**ID:** Small bird to 5 inches long. Both sexes are a heavily streaked gray-brown, buff underside, and yellow in wings and base of notched tail. Utters tsee-tsee-*tsee* in flight also a long buzzing *shreeee*. Usually in large flocks undulating through the trees.

**Habitat:** Year round resident. Prefers coniferous or mixed forests where flocks of siskins search for a variety of seeds, and insects. Nests in well-concealed branches of spruce or cottonwood high above the ground.

AMB

## Dark-eyed Junco *(Junco hyemalis)* - Subfamily Emberizinae

**ID:** Small unmarked slate-colored bird to 5 1/2 inches long with white breast and white outside tail feathers. Call is a one pitch trill. Also say "tick-*tick*" to each other as they flit among the branches.

**Habitat:** Year round resident. Abundant in small flocks from lowland coniferous forests to treeline. Feeds on ground for insects and seeds. Nests on ground in cavity hidden among roots, deadfall or grass.

AMB

## White-crowned Sparrow *(Zonotrichia leucophrys)* - Subfamily Emberizinae

**ID:** Small bird 6 inches long with prominent black and white striping on head, streaked above, plain gray face, chin, and breast, throat and belly white. Brown back, rump and long tail. Two white wing bars. Easily recognized and often heard song of 6 notes which begins with 2 notes followed by a wheezy 'chee-zee-zee" and a trill.

AMB

**Habitat:** Year round resident. Abundant in small flocks, often with Golden-crowned sparrows( See page 184), and most often along forest edges and open thickets to alpine. Feed on ground, scratching noisily for insects and seeds. Nests May-June on ground to 3 feet up in grassy or brushy areas with nest concealed in moss or undergrowth.

## Ruby-crowned Kinglet *(Regulus calendula)*
- Family Muscicapidae

**ID:** Tiny gray bird 4 inches long with conspicuous white eye ring, no eye striping and red crown on males (not always visible). Two white wing bars; flicks wings nervously when perched. Loud, distinctive song in 3 parts: first is a high tee-*tee-tee*, followed by a loud finchlike warble of *chur-chur-chur* , finishing with a harsh chattering *teedadee*.

(continued)

AMB

## Ruby-crowned Kinglet (continued)

**Habitat:** Prefers open spruce forests and mixed deciduous forests and shrub thickets to treeline following its arrival in mid-April. Moves through trees singly or in pairs searching for insects. Nests in late spring in spruce from 2-60 feet from ground, building a deep nest of grasses and lichens lined with feathers.

**Golden-crowned Kinglet** *(Regulus satrapa)* - Family Muscicapidae

**ID:** Small olive-gray bird, 3 1/2 inches long with white eyebrow stripe in both sexes. Male has yellow-red stripe down middle of head with black borders, female has yellow crown only. Year round resident. Song is a constant high *"tzee-tzee-tzee"* from the tops of trees. More often heard than seen.

AMB

**Habitat:** Common in coniferous forests where they feed on insects, their eggs and larvae. Builds round nest in spruce 30-60 feet above the ground.

**Black-capped Chickadee** *(Parus atricapillus)* - Family Paridae

**ID:** Small round bird, 5 inches long. Both sexes have a large head with black cap, black throat, white cheek patches, gray back and gray-buff. Call is *chick-a-dee-dee;* also a *phoebe* whistle.

**Habitat:** Year round resident. Common in mixed deciduous-coniferous forests to treeline. Birds search branches for small insects, insect larvae, ants, and aphids, occasionally seeds and berries. Nest built by the pair in dead tree cavity 1-10 feet above ground.

AMB

**Boreal Chickadee** *(Parus hudsonicus)* - Family Paridae

**D:** Similar to Black-capped, but it has a dark brown cap, brown back, reddish sides and white chest - generally duller appearance. Call is similar to the others, but more drawn out and wheezy.

**Habitat:** Year-round resident. Found in high coniferous-deciduous forests. Feeding habits similar to Black-capped. Nest built only by female in tree cavity 1-10 feet above ground; nests later that Black-capped .

**Steller's Jay** *(Cyanocitta stelleri)* - Family Corvidae

**D:** Dark blue bird, 13 inches long with conspicuous smoky black crest and upper back. Call is a harsh raucous *shack-shack-shack.* Imitates shrill screams of hawks.

**Habitat:** Year-round resident found in forested areas throughout the park. Feeds on seeds, berries and insects. Builds stick nest in early spring, 10 feet or more above the ground, usually in a spruce. Comes down out of the high country in winter.

AMB

**Gray Jay** *(Perisoreus canadensis)* - Family Corvidae

**D:** Smoky gray jay, 11 inches long, light gray face and dark back of head, short bill and long tail. Soft call is *whee-ooo,* or scolding *cla-cla-cla-cla.*

**Habitat:** Common year-round in open subalpine spruce forests where they glide from tree to tree feeding on seeds, insects, carrion, even other birds' unattended chicks. Store food for winter in tree cavities. Nest in early spring in spruce trees.

AMB

**Northern Shrike** *(Lanius excubitor)* - Family Laniidae

**ID:** Robin-sized gray songbird, 10 inches long with a black mask and black wings and tail, and large hooked bill. Song is variable, but usually quiet. Often seen sitting on the top of a tree in open country.

**Habitat:** Uncommon. Found singly or in pairs in open subalpine forests, shrub thickets to alpine tundra, usually sitting atop a spruce. Feeds on small rodents and many small birds. Often saves excess by impaling prey on thorn, broken tree, or suspends it in crotch of a tree. Nests in small deciduous tree, or conife spruce in mid spring.

AMB

**Northern Goshawk** *(Accipiter gentilis)* - Family Accipitridae

**ID:** Distinctive dark blue-gray back, white underside streaked with gray and distinctive white stripe over orange eye. Immature with mottled streaking below. Call is a high *eck eck-eck.*

**Habitat:** Found year-round in forests and forest edges to treeline, pursuing primarily grouse and ptarmigan, snowshoe hare and any other small game that moves. It kills hard and fast with talons open. Nests next to tree trunk 20-60 feet up in spring deep in boreal forest. Extremely protective of nest and will attack human intruders.

**Merlin** *(Falco columbarius)* - Family Falconidae

**ID:** Small falcon, 12 inches long with a 2-foot wingspan, dark gray back streaked breast and barred tail with white tip, no conspicuous facial markings. Female larger than male. Call is high screaming trill.

**Habitat:** Uncommon. Found in forest clearings and edges near marshes and muskeg such as those around Eagle River Visitor Center and Upper Hillside area. Hunts at treetop level for small birds, squirrels, voles, insects and an occasional bat. Nests in old tree cavities or hole in cutbank.

AMB

## Great Horned Owl *(Bubo virginianus)* - Family Strigidae

ID: Large brown owl, 18-25 inches, with dark cross-barring on breast, prominent ear tufts. Call is a deep *hoo-hoo-oo-oo-hoo*. Most vocal in winter months of January-February during courtship. Active at night and in twilight of the long Alaskan summers.

Habitat: Uncommon. Found in boreal and subalpine forests to treeline. Glides through trees to swoop down on snowshoe hares, voles, squirrels, perching birds, and an occasional ski hat. Nests in January-February in tree cavity or abandoned hawk nest. CAUTION: Known to attack humans in defense of nest.

AMB

## Boreal Owl *(Aegolius funereus)* - Family Strigidae

ID: Dark brown and white owl, 10 inches long with short tail, striped breast and no ear tufts. Framed facial disks, yellow bill and spotted forehead. Distinctive call is rapid high-pitched *hoo-hoo-hoo-hoo-hoo*.

Habitat: Found in boreal forests where it hunts at night for voles, shrews, small birds and insects. Nests in mid-spring in tree cavities. Active at night, hides in dense shrubs or trees by day.

AMB

## Northern Saw-whet Owl *(Aegolius acadicus)* - Family Strigidae

ID: Small version of Boreal Owl except with dark bill and streaking on forehead rather than spots, no ear tufts. Call varies from a high-pitched raspy wheeze to separate hoots.

Habitat: Prefers boreal forest and thickets where it hunts for insects, occasionally small birds and rodents. Nests in early spring in abandoned woodpecker holes and natural tree cavities 14-60 feet above ground. Active only at night, a sound sleeper during day and easily approached at roost.

AMB

**Spruce Grouse** *(Dendragapus canadensis)* - Family Phasianidae

**ID:** Chicken-sized bird, 16 inches long. Male is mottled gray above, black throat and breast. Red visible above each eye. Female is a barred rusty-brown with a rusty-orange band a tip of blackish tail. Call is a deep hoot at low pitch, barely audible to human ear. Often called "fool's hen" for its apparent tameness when approached by man.

**Habitat:** Common in open spruce and spruce-birch woodlands, forest edges, and muskeg. Feeds primarily on spruce needles and buds, as well as berries, seeds, plants, and insects. Nests in mid-spring in a well-hidden depression on the ground usually under a spruce branch or bushes.

**Downy Woodpecker** *(Picoides pubescens)* - Family Picidae

**ID:** Smallest woodpecker, 6-7 inches long, almost identical to Hairy woodpecker (next entry) with black and white markings, but smaller bill and less wary. Downy (and Hairy) have white backs; all others have black backs. Males have bright red patch on back of head. Drums on trees as territorial and courtship display.

**Habitat:** Found in coniferous and deciduous forests, and shrub thickets. Feeds on beetle larvae by hacking into their galleries under the bark. Also eats other insects and occasionally berries. Excavates hole in dead tree in early spring.

**Hairy Woodpecker** *(Picoides villosus)* - Family Picidae

**ID:** Larger version of black and white Downy up to 9 inches long, large bill and white back, longer heavier bill. Males have bright red patch on back of head. Call is loud sharp *pweek-pweek.*

**Habitat:** Found climbing on tree trunks or hanging upside down from tree branches in spruce and deciduous forests. Diet similar to Downy. Also nests in tree cavity.

## Three-toed Woodpecker *(Picoides tridactylus)* - Family Picidae

**ID:** A dull black and white woodpecker to 8 1/2 inches long, with barred back and sides. Males have yellow cap; females lack yellow crown. Only woodpecker with 3 toes. Call is *perk-perk*. Less active than other woodpeckers.

**Habitat:** Prefers mixed coniferous-deciduous forests to subalpine. Feeds on beetles and their larvae found under bark. Usually nests in cavity of a dead conifer.

AMB

## Olive-side Flycatcher *(Contopus borealis)* - Family Tyrannidae

**ID:** Large, dark olive-gray bird, 7 inches long with white line down breast; large bill. Song is distinctive 3-syllable *whip-three-beers*. Often conspicuously perched atop high, dead branches.

**Habitat:** Begin arriving in May where they reside in spruce forests where it feeds on flying insects. Nests deep in spruce tree near trunk.

AMB

## Alder Flycatcher *(Empidonax alnorum)* - Family Tyrannidae

**ID:** Greenish above, pale yellowish breast, white throat, dark wings and tail. Faint eye ring. Song is wee-*bee-o* with accent on second syllable. May be confused with Hammond's or Yellow-bellied flycatchers.

**Habitat:** Prefers moist dense alder and willow thickets after its migration north to raise its young. It nests in crotch of a shrub. Feeds on flying insects.

AMB

**Varied Thrush** *(Ixoreus naevius)* - Family Muscicapidae

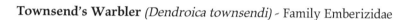

**ID:** Robin-size bird, 9-10 inches long; top of head and breast band is gray-black orange eye stripe, chin and breast, and wing bars Male sings long melancholy whistle.

**Habitat:** After its arrival in May the Varied Thrush remains deep moist woods where it forages on ground for a variety of insects, as well as berries Nests on horizontal branch, usually a spruce 5-15 feet above ground in late spring.

AMB

**Townsend's Warbler** *(Dendroica townsendi)* - Family Emberizidae

**ID:** Only warbler in Chugach State Park with olive above, yellow below and streaked sides. Male has black throat, cheek patch and cap. Female has yellow throat. Male song is *weazy-weazy-weazy-weazy-tweea.*

**Habitat:** Prefers spruce forests, but also found in mixed deciduous-coniferous woods spending most of time at tops of trees after its arrival in May. Hunts for insects on tree branches. Nests 10 feet or more in spruce trees in late spring.

AMB

## BIRDS OF THE TREELINE THICKETS and ALPINE KRUMMHOLZ

**Golden-crowned Sparrow** *(Zonotrichia atricapilla)* - Family Emberizidae

**ID:** Similar to White-crowned sparrow, but larger (6 $1/_2$ inches long), has a black cap with a bright yellow center. Song is 3 slow notes descending the scale in a minor key (like Three Blind Mice). Migrates south in fall, although some remain all winter; returns in large numbers by first week of May.

**Habitat:** Common in alpine and subalpine shrub thickets from early May to September. Feeds mostly on ground, picking up seeds and insects. Nests in early summer on ground among willows and grasses.

AMB

## Willow Ptarmigan *(Lagopus lagopus)* - Family Phasianidae

**ID:** The Alaska state bird and largest of the 3 resident ptarmigan, to 16" long. Summer plumage is mottled red-brown body with white wings; winter plumage is all white except for black outer tail feathers. Males have a red "eyebrow" in spring and summer. Molting begins at head and moves down neck to the body by summer. Call has been interpreted to sound like go back-go back, or *look out-look out.* Unique in the grouse/ptarmigan family, both male and female care for the young.

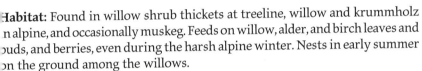

**Habitat:** Found in willow shrub thickets at treeline, willow and krummholz in alpine, and occasionally muskeg. Feeds on willow, alder, and birch leaves and buds, and berries, even during the harsh alpine winter. Nests in early summer on the ground among the willows.

Its cousin, the **Rock Ptarmigan** *(L. mutus),* prefers the higher, more exposed rocky slopes of the park and is distinguished in winter by black bar through eye. The **White-Tailed Ptarmigan** *(L. leucurus)* is the smallest of the 3 alpine birds. It has no black on tail, more gray-brown and more white showing in summer; both sexes have red "eyebrow" during breeding season.

## Wilson's Warbler *(Wilsonia pusilla)* - Family Emberizidae

**ID:** Small bird, 4-5 inches long; olive above, bright yellow below, no obvious markings. Male has black cap in breeding plumage. Male's song is even chip-chi*p-chip-chip.*

**Habitat:** Prefers shrub thickets, commonly seen at treeline by late April or early May. Usually stays within 10 feet of ground, searching for insects. Nests on ground in mosses or sedges.

## BIRDS OF THE ALPINE TUNDRA and RIDGES

**Northern Harrier** *(Circus cyaneus)* - Family Accipitridae

**ID:** Thin gray-brown bird to 23 inches long, with streaked light underside. White rump patch and owl-like facial disk in both sexes are diagnostic. Long narrow lightly-barred tail and long black-tipped wings.

**Habitat:** Year-round resident found in alpine tundra, and over freshwater and tidal marshes. It hunts close to the ground in search of mice, voles and small birds. Only hawk to nest and roost on the ground.

AMB

**Horned Lark** *(Eremophila alpestris)* - Family Alaudidae

**ID:** Brownish bird, 7-8 inches long; male has black face mask which curves down from eye, yellowish face and throat, black feather tufts ("horns") on head, black collar; underside white, tail black; female duller version of male. Walks, does not hop. Flight undulating. Male sings a tinkling *pit-wit, wee-pit, pit-wee, wee-pit* while in flight.

**Habitat:** Arrives in alpine tundra, by late April where it walks or runs across ground in search of seeds; may also eat ants, wasps, and spiders. Nests on bare ground in slight hollow lined with grasses.

AMB

**Rosy Finch** *(Leucosticte arctoa)* - Family Fringillidae

**ID:** Medium-sized brown bird, 6 inches long; rose-colored wings, breast and rump; occasionally with black cap and gray crown.

**Habitat:** Migrates up to alpine tundra and mountain ridges from the Anchorage Bowl and surrounding lowlands by late April. Feeds on insects in moist meadows and around melting snowbanks. Nests in rocky crevices in cliffs. Moves down out of Chugach Mountains for the winter in flocks.

AMB

**Water Pipit** *(Anthus spinoletta)* - Family Motacillidae

**ID:** Sparrow-sized bird, 6-7 inches long; gray-brown above, pale streaking below. Conspicuous white outer tail feathers; tail long. Walks, does not hop; may bob or wag tail while on the move. Male sings in flight a soft tsi-*tsip*.

**Habitat:** Arrives in alpine tundra by late April where it is found near mountain lakes and streams. Walks around plucking insects and seeds from ground and off plants; also feeds on mudflats. Sheltered nest among rocks, bank, or hummocks in early summer.

AMB

**Northern Wheatear** *(Oenanthe oenanthe)* - Family Muscicapidae

**ID:** Small bird, 5-6 inches long; buff-gray with black mark through eye; pale below. Distinctive white rump patch and tail white with inverted black T; wings also black. Call is a scolding *chuck-chuck*. When perched on a rock it spreads its tailfeathers and bobs tail up and down.

**Habitat:** Casual visitor found in alpine tundra, rocky slopes and ridges by June. Feeds on mainly on insects, but may eat seeds, berries.

AMB

**Surfbird** *(Aphriza virgata)* - Family Scolopacidae

**ID:** Short, chunky sandpiper, 10 inches long; in breeding plumage breast and back heavily streaked; pale gray. Short black bill with yellow at base of lower mandible. Legs and feet yellow. Broad white stripe on wing and rump to tail; black tip of tail. Unlike its relatives, the turnstones, surfbirds are usually quiet.

**Habitat:** Uncommon resident of alpine tundra and mountain ridges during summer, where it runs around ground picking up flies, beetles, bees, ants, as well as seeds. Nests in small depression on rocky ridge.

AMB

## COSMOPOLITAN SPECIES

**Black-billed Magpie** *(Pica pica)* - Family Corvidae

**ID:** Large black and white bird to 20 inches, with black bill and long black tail. Call is a series of *Ack-Ack-Ack.* They fly low above the ground in a flap and glide pattern. Year-round resident.

**Habitat:** Common singly or in small flocks in open woodlands, forest edges and treeline thickets and spruce krummholz. Feeds on ground as it searches for insects, carrion, as well as small rodents. Nests in mid-spring in tall shrubs, or krummholz above treeline, building a coarse stick nest with a stick canopy.

AMB

**Common Raven** *(Corvus corax)* - Family Corvidae

**ID:** Large black bird, 22-27 inches long with large bill and a wedge-shaped tail; shaggy throat feathers especially when perched. Calls highly varied from gro*nk-gronk*; a hoarse *craak*; a melodious *kloo-klok*; to a knocking sound. Flaps and soars in flight.

**Habitat:** Common from tidal flats to alpine ridges, singly or in small groups, often performing acrobatic feats on the wind. A scavenger feeding on carrion, also insects, berries, occasionally hunting voles and lemmings. Nests in mid-spring in conifer trees or rocky ledges on large nest of sticks 2-3 feet wide and 4 feet high. Pairs mate for life.

AMB

# BIRD NOTES

# CHAPTER FIFTEEN

# THE AMPHIBIAN

Alaska has no reptiles; no snakes slither across the tundra. However, a few amphibians manage to survive the harsh arctic environment. Although some salamanders, newts, toads and frogs have found their way into Alaska, only the **wood frog** occurs in Chugach State Park. Most amphibians are limited to the more southern latitudes because their body temperature is dependent on external sources of heat. It is the lack of heat in summer, not the cold of winter, that limits their northern expansion.

Wood Frog *(Rana sylvatica)* - Family Ranidae/true-frog

**ID:** It is the most abundant and most northerly frog in North America. It reaches 3 inches in length. Color varies from dark brown to gray-green with distinctive dark eye stripe, occasionally with pale stripe down back, or some spots on back. Underside creamy white. Call is a repetitive duck-like quack. Active in temperatures just above freezing.

**Habitat:** Common in moist lowland woods, muskeg to tundra. They enter the water to breed as soon as the ice is off the water, usually in early May at lower elevations. Wood frogs must complete their development cycle in one summer. Adults overwinter out of the water in shallow depressions beneath dead vegetation, below an insulating snowcover.

# CHAPTER SIXTEEN

# FISH OF
# CHUGACH STATE PARK

Only 9 species of fish are found in and around Chugach State Park. Fish are not abundant in the park because the numerous glacially-fed streams create silty gray water in the lakes and waterways. Bird Creek and Eagle River are the primary salmon spawning streams in the park. Penguin, Indian, Rabbit, Campbell, Ship, Peters, Thunderbird, and Hunter creeks also have fish. Rabbit and Eklutna lakes also support a small fish population. Numerous sea run species are found in Cook Inlet off Chugach State Park.

**SALMON, TROUT and SMELT** (Order Salmoniformes)

**Family Salmonidae**

Trout and salmon are members of the same family. Salmon live an **anadromous** life cycle which means they hatch in fresh water and return to the sea as adults. After a number of years at sea they return to fresh water to spawn and die.

Trout remain in fresh water throughout their lives, spawning many times before they die. Some members of the salmon family may occur in either salt or fresh water. Steelhead and rainbow are the same species; steelhead are anadromous and rainbow are not. Anadromous forms tend to grow much larger than their freshwater equivalent.

Facing page: Gone fishin' (Brenda Ralston )

## SALTWATER TO FRESHWATER

### Pink or Humped-back Salmon *(Oncorhynchus gorbuscha)*

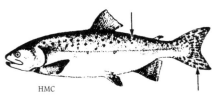

HMC

ID: Metallic blue-green above; silver below. Distinctive large oval black spots on tail and upper body. Spawning males have humped back, reddish-yellow upper side, and beaked upper jaw. To 30 inches long. Sometimes called "humpies."

### Silver or Coho Salmon *(Oncorhynchus kisutch)*

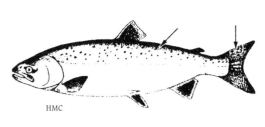

HMC

ID: Metallic blue above; silver below. Black spots on back and upper part of tail. Gums white at base of teeth. Spawning males are gray-green upper, bright red on side and blackish below. Females bronze-pink on sides. To 38 inches long.

### Red or Sockeye Salmon *(Oncorhynchus nerka)*

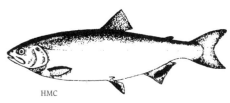

HMC

ID: Metallic blue-green above, silver below. No dark spots on back or tail; tail not edged in black like Chum. Fins not tipped with white. To 33 inches long.

### Chum or Dog Salmon *(Oncorhynchus keta)*

HMC

ID: Metallic blue above; silver below. Flecks above, but no spots. Spawning they become dark olive above, reddish blotches on sides, lower fins tipped with white. Males' front teeth enlarge more than other salmon. To 40 inches long.

## King or Chinook Salmon *(Oncorhynchus tshawytscha)*

**ID:** Largest salmon, to 58 inches long. Dark blue-green upper; silver below with irregular black spots on upper back and entire tail. Gums black at base of teeth. Very dark when mature with blotchy dull red on sides. The official name is "chinook salmon," but it is more commonly called "king salmon" in Alaska.

## Smelt

## Family Osmeridae

## Eulachon, or Hooligan *(Thaleichthys pacificus)*

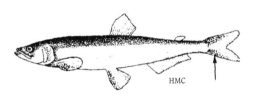

**ID:** The only smelt with striations on gill covers, to 9 inches in length. Upper jaw extends to rear of eye. Blue-brown above with fine black flecks on back; silver below. Tail often flecked with black. Spawn from April-May in Turnagain Arm; dies after spawning. Also called "Candlefish" because Indians inserted a wick into this oily fish for a lamp.

## FRESHWATER STREAMS AND LAKES

## Dolly Varden *(Salvelinus malma)*

**ID:** Troutlike char, 18-36 inches long, found in freshwater. Dark blue above; silver on side to white below. Fins may be yellowish. Cream-colored spots on most of body with yellow to red spots on back and sides. Arctic Char *(Salvelinus alpinus)* is the anadromous relative of the Dolly Varden, but does not occur in the Park.

**Rainbow Trout** *(Salmo gairdneri)*

HMC

**ID:** In freshwater, greenish above; creamy-silver below. Small black dots on back and most of fins. Often have a reddish side stripe. Usually about 24″ long.

**Grayling** *(Thymallus arcticus)*

HCP

**ID:** Grayling do not normally range south of the Matanuska River. A long bluish-black fish to 30 inches and 6 pounds with silvery sides and dark stripe along sides. Large dark dorsal fin.

## WHERE TO FIND THE FISH

| | |
|---|---|
| **Bird Creek** | **Pink Salmon** |
| | **King Salmon** |
| | **Silver Salmon** |
| | **Chum Salmon** |
| | **Dolly Varden** |
| **Penguin Creek** | Same as Bird Creek |
| **Indian Creek** | **Pink Salmon** |
| | **Dolly Varden** |
| **Rabbit Creek** | **Dolly Varden** |
| **Rabbit Lake** | **Dolly Varden** |
| | **Grayling**[1] |
| **Ship Creek** | **Dolly Varden** |

**[1] Stocked by Alaska Department of Fish and Game**

| | |
|---|---|
| Eagle River | King Salmon |
| | Pink Salmon |
| | Silver Salmon |
| | Chum Salmon |
| | Red Salmon[2] |
| | Rainbow Trout |
| | Dolly Varden |
| Peters Creek | Dolly Varden |
| Thunderbird Creek | Dolly Varden |
| Eklutna River | Dolly Varden |
| Eklutna Lake | Dolly Varden |
| | Rainbow (stocked) |
| Hunter Creek | Dolly Varden |
| Cook Inlet | Eulachon, or Hooligan, |
| | All salmon species |
| | (during migration) |

[1] Stocked by Alaska Department of Fish and Game
[2] Seen below Eagle River Visitor Center

# CHAPTER SEVENTEEN

# INSECTS OF CHUGACH STATE PARK

Insects are a misunderstood and overlooked lot. We squash, slap, beat, and flail at them any chance we get. Yet without insects, flowers would not get pollinated, moose pellets would not get broken down, and some birds, rodents, and fish would starve.

There are approximately 88,600 species of insects in North America, far too many to include in a general guide book. So this chapter will describe a few of the more common orders of insects and their representative species found in Chugach State Park. Distinguishing characteristics and descriptions of the more obvious but overlooked bugs are included to help de-mystify the insect world.

**WHAT IS AN INSECT?**

Adult insects have two distinguishing characteristics.

1. Three major body segments - head, thorax, & abdomen.
2. Three pairs of legs, all attached to the thorax. Most adults have one or two pair of wings, also attached at the thorax, although some are wingless.

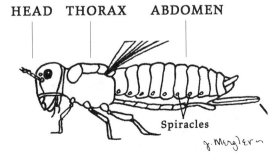

HEAD    THORAX    ABDOMEN

Spiracles

Facing page: Water Strider (Cynthia Cassell)

The HEAD contains the sensory structures - a single pair of antenna and a pai of compound eyes. Small simple eyes and mouthparts are also found on th head.

The THORAX contains the movable parts - usually two pair of wings, thre pair of legs, and spiracles, through which the insect breathes.

The ABDOMEN is the last segment. It is the location of insect reproductiv organs. On female insects a distinct ovipositor is found - the structure she use to deposit her eggs. The abdomen also contains additional spiracles, as well a a tympanum, the hearing mechanism.

Other small creatures often incorrectly called insects are daddy longlegs spiders, and mites. They have only two body segments and eight legs, thus are not insects.]


## INSECT DEVELOPMENT

Insects go through dramatic and varied changes in their short lives. These changes are known as **metamorphosis** and aid in identification. Two of the most common kinds are simple metamorphosis and complete metamorphosis

### 1. Simple Metamorphosis

The insect emerges from the egg as a nymph. Nymphs shed their skin gradually, looking more and more like the adult with each shedding until they have fully-developed and can reproduce.

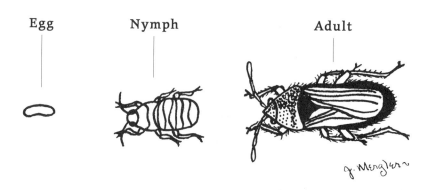

Egg          Nymph          Adult

## 2. Complete Metamorphosis

An insect hatches from an egg to the larval stage. The larvae, resembling small worms, occasionally shed their skin as they grow. Then their skin hardens into a tough casing called a pupa (in some, it is a cocoon). During the pupal stage, the insect undergoes dramatic changes and emerges as an adult, ready to reproduce. The best example of complete metamorphosis is butterflies.

| Egg | Larvae | Pupa | Adult |

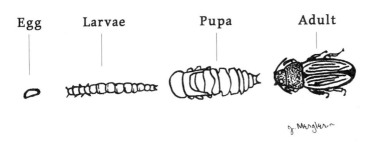

## INSECTS OF THE LAND, WATER & AIR

The BEETLES (Order Coleoptera): "sheath wings" - beetles.

A stout body with a pair of hardened front wings covering a pair of membranous hind wings underneath; outer wings meet in a straight line down back. Chewing mouth parts. Lives in all habitats: plant eaters, scavengers or predaceous, as well as aquatic, subterranean or terrestrial. Metamorphosis is complete.

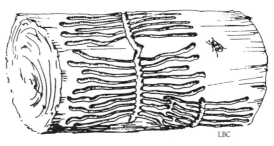

LBC

Common species and habitat:

**Spruce bark beetle** *(Dendroctonus rufipennis)* is found on spruce trees.

**Burying Beetle** *(Nicrophorus* sp.) is found on dung and decaying organic matter.

**Leaf Beetle** *(Chrysomela* sp.) is found on most deciduous trees.

**The SPRINGTAILS** (Order Collembola): "tassel wings" - springtails, snow fleas.

These minute insects lack wings, but have a **furcula**, a structure on their underside which acts as a spring to propel them. Chewing mouth parts. Primitive metamorphosis - no change from birth to maturity. Occurs in leaf litter, soil, and bark, feeding on decaying vegetation in moist areas as well as on freshwater ponds and streams.

**Common species and habitat:**

**Springtail** *(Isotomurus* sp.) are extremely abundant with millions of individuals per acre. They occur in moist woods in the soil and leaf litter. Color may be mottled, or a brownish-white.

RHI

**The FLIES** (order Diptera): "two wings" -mosquitoes, gnats, flies & midges.

Larvae have chewing mouth parts. Adults have only one pair of wings and sponging or piercing-sucking mouthparts. Found on plants or decomposing organic matter. Undergoes complete metamorphosis.

**Common Flies and their Habitat:**

**Mosquitoes** Of the 27 species found in Alaska, only 16 are found in Chugach State Park. The Family Cuculidae are the most common and widely distributed. *Aedes* is the most common genus in this family.

Mosquitoes have aquatic larvae which stay just beneath the surface, actively feeding on algae, pollen, and dead organic matter. Mosquito pupae differ from most other insects in that the pupa can swim away if threatened. Adults have long narrow wings, a proboscis, and a pair of palps or feelers.

Male mosquitoes have feathery antennae, long palps, and do not bite. Females have thin antennae, short palps, and do bite. Adults use their slender proboscus to feed on plant juices, but females require a blood meal to obtain protein for egg production. She

HRW

nomes in on the carbon dioxide from a breathing mammal. Most bug repellants, such as DEET, act to block her $CO_2$ receptors. Mosquitoes are most abundant in the Park from mid-June through mid-July.

**Black Flies or White Socks** The Family Simuliidae have a humpback, stocky body with short antenna and wings broad at base. Larvae occur in streams, often attached to underwater objects. Adult females are vicious biters and appear in late spring-early summer.

HRW

**Blow Flies** The Family Calliphoridae are a large group of large-bodied metallic bluish-green flies. Larvae are scavengers feeding on carrion and dung. These are the most common maggots on dead animals.

**Syrphid Flies** The Family Syrphidae are very common. They vary in appearance, color and size. Often brightly colored with yellow and black. Many resemble Hymenopterans, the bees and wasps, but syrphids do not bite or sting. All are excellent fliers and are capable of hovering - thus their common name of Hover Fly.

**The TRUE-BUGS** (Order Hemiptera): "half wings" - true-bugs, backswimmers, water striders.

Two pairs of wings - one hard, the other membranous - form triangle on back when folded at rest. Look like beetles except for cross "X" patterned wings. Piercing-sucking mouth parts. Found on plants, in debris, or in water. Simple metamorphosis.

## Common species:

**Stink bug** Family Pentatomidae - Oval, shield-shaped insect with a triangular plate on back. Colors range from plain brown to bright metallic colors. Bugs produce a disagreeable odor. Feed primarily on plants.

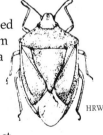
HRW

**Waterstriders** - Family Gerridae - An aquatic insect usually found running on surface of slow streams and ponds. Bodies are slender; front legs are short, other legs long. Feed on other insects which fall on the water surface.

**The APHIDS and LEAFHOPPERS** (Order Homoptera): "same wings" - aphids, leafhoppers, whiteflies, scale insects.

Most have small, delicate bodies which may or may not have two pairs of membranous wings held in tent-like position over body when at rest. Piercing-sucking mouth parts. Found feeding on plants. Metamorphosis is simple

**Common species:**

**Aphids** Family Aphidae is a large group of small, soft-bodied insects which suck sap from leaves and stems of plants. Aphids produce a "honeydew" which is fed on by carpenter ants. Aphids occur in large numbers, they often cause damage to plants.

LBC

**The BEES, WASPS, & HORNETS** (Order Hymenoptera): "membrane winged" - bees, wasps, ants, sawflies, & hornets.

All have two pairs of thin, clear, membranous wings; female abdomen ends in well-developed egg-laying organ and/or stinger. Chewing or chewing-lapping mouthparts. Found on ground, on plants, or on woody material. Most specialized order of insects. Metamorphosis is complete.

**Common species and their Habitat:**

**Family Apidae** - Bumble bees, carpenter bees, honey bees

**Bumble Bees** (*Bombus* sp.) - along with honey bees - are social. They are the most important bee in the pollination of plants. Bumble bees are a large black and yellow insect up to 3/4 inch long. They are found in most habitats in the park. Even over high alpine ridges. They nest in the ground. Bee colonies form each year with only the fertilized queens overwintering. In spring the queen selects a nest site and begins nest construction.

HRW

## Family Vespidae - Vespid wasps

Yellowjackets (*Vespula* spp.) are the wasps most often encountered along the Eagle River trail. Don't antagonize them by waving your arms. They can sting you repeatedly. Most vespid wasps hang their gray papery nests high up in deciduous trees, but yellowjackets nest in the ground.

HRW

## Family Formicidae - ants

Carpenter Ants *(Camponotus herculeanus)* are some of the largest ants in North America. They are social insects with a three caste system in their colonies - queens, males, and workers. Carpenter ants excavate extensive nesting galleries in wood. The occasionally feed on the "honeydew" produced by aphids.

LBC

**The BUTTERFLIES and MOTHS** (Order Lepidoptera): "scale wings" - butterflies, moths.

Two pairs of wings covered with scales which rub off easily. Butterflies are diurnal; moths are nocturnal. Larvae have chewing mouth parts and feed on plants. Adults have siphoning mouthparts and are harmless to plants. Found on plants. Metamorphosis is complete.

## Common Butterflies:

Family Nymphalidae - Mourning Cloak *(Nymphalis antiopa)* is most common in the forested regions of the park (shown in illustration).
Family Lycaenidae - Blues
Family Papilionidae
   - Tiger Swallowtail *(Papilio glaucus);*
*Parnassius phoebus* is a large showy tailless swallowtail of the late summer tundra.
Family Pieridae - Sulphurs - *(Colias)* are the most common suphur of the tundra.
Family Satyridae - The Arctics, of the genus *Oeneis*, are common in the alpine tundra of Chugach State Park.

LBC

Common moths:

Family Tortricidae - Spruce Budworm *(Choristoneura* sp.) are destructive to spruce trees because the adult beetles lay larvae under the bark. Larvae then create feeding tunnels throught the phloem, the food- conducting tissue just below the bark. These tunnels can girdle and kill a spruce.

Family Noctuidae - Noctuid moths most common moth of the park.

**The DRAGONFLIES** (Order Odonata): "tooth" - dragonflies, damselflies.

Two pairs of long, narrow membranous wings of roughly equal size; adults have two large eyes on large head and extremely long narrow abdomen. Chewing mouth parts for feeding on other insects. Found near water. Metamorphosis is simple.

Family Aeschnidae -

**Darners** genus are the largest group of dragonflies, reaching lengths of 3 inches long. Thorax and abdomen dark- colored to a metallic blue-green. At rest, they hold their wings horizontal. Large compound eyes. Strong fliers found around ponds, slow streams, and bogs.

RHI

**The GRASSHOPPERS** (Order Orthoptera): "straight wings" - grasshoppers, crickets, cockroaches.

Have long back legs for hopping; thin, leathery forewings that cover larger hind wings, which fold like a fan at rest. Chewing mouth parts. Found on plants or on ground. Metamorphosis is simple.

Family Acrididae - grasshoppers
Spur-throatedgrasshoppers *(Melanoplus* sp) are
very common in the park.

HRW

# The CADDISFLIES ( Order Trichoptera): "hair wings" - caddisflies.

Small to medium insects with 4 hairy wings usually held over back when at rest. Chewing mouthparts; feed on plant juices. Larvae are aquatic and an important fish food. Caddisfly larvae build and live in cases constructed of grains of sand, pebbles, twigs, bits of leaves and silk. Each case is characteristic of the species. After the larvae pupate, they swim to the surface and emerge as adults. Once the wings dry, the adult flies away but always remains near water.

HRW

Part Four

# Visiting the Park

# CHAPTER EIGHTEEN

# ENJOYING THE PARK

**WALK ON THE WILD SIDE**

Traversing Chugach State Park can be done on well-worn hiking or animal trails or by setting off cross-country in search of peace and solitude. The hiking season is short. The snow has barely left the high country in early June before the leaves suddenly change color in August. Always be prepared for bad weather any month of the year; even if it's nice and sunny in town, weather changes rapidly in the mountains. Always bring raingear, hat, gloves, water, and food - even on a short hike.

**TURNAGAIN ARM TRAILS**

### Historic Iditarod/Crow Pass Trail

Access:      Exit at Mile 90 of the Seward Highway 2.5 miles toward the town of Girdwood; take Crow Creek Road 5 miles to trailhead.

Distance:     26 miles one way from trailhead; 8 miles round trip to Crow Pass (3883 feet)

Elevation gain:  2000 feet

Difficulty:    Moderate to difficult

Special Interest: Follows the original Seward-Iditarod Trail over Crow Pass, past the ruins of old Monarch Mine.

Flora & Fauna: Moose, black and brown bear usually seen, Dall sheep, ground squirrels; wonderful woodland and alpine wildflower displays.

Comments:   Ford Eagle River at marked crossing (Mile 13). Get clean water before crossing river and heading down the valley — only silty water is available between Eagle River and Icicle Creek — a 6-mile section of trail. Not recommended for winter route due to high avalanche danger. The trail passes through coniferous forests to alpine tundra, and descends into mixed coniferous forest in Eagle River valley.

Facing page: Hikers rest below summit of Mount Rumble (Steve Johnson)

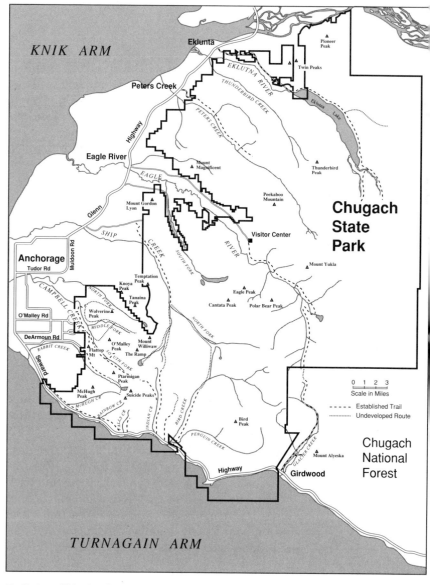

Trails & Facilities in Chugach State Park (Ron Engstrom)

## Bird Ridge

| | |
|---|---|
| Access: | Mile 101 of Seward Highway. |
| Distance: | 4.5 miles round trip from trailhead. |
| Elevation Gain: | 3500 feet, high point is 3505 feet. |
| Difficulty: | Moderate to difficult. |
| Special Interest: | Fantastic views; abundant wildflowers. |
| Wildlife: | Moose, Dall sheep, birds. |
| Comments: | Earliest hiking and earliest floral display in the spring; trail passes from mixed deciduous forest to alpine tundra at the top of Bird Ridge. |

## Bird Creek

| | |
|---|---|
| Access: | Mile 100 of Seward Highway (past Bird House Bar) one mile to trailhead. |
| Distance: | Approximately 5 miles one way to trails end. |
| Elevation Gain: | over 800 feet |
| Difficulty: | Moderate |
| Special Interest: | Old prospectors trail. |
| Flora & Fauna: | Heavily forested valley; moose, birds. |
| Comments: | Bird Creek was prospected in the early 1900s. |

## Indian Creek

| | |
|---|---|
| Access: | Mile 102 of Seward highway (before Turnagain House Restaurant); drive .5 miles back to trailhead. |
| Distance: | 12 miles round trip to the pass; traverse to Arctic Valley via Ship Creek, 21 miles one way. |
| Elevation Gain: | 2100 feet, high point is 2350 feet |
| Difficulty: | Moderate |
| Special Interest: | Trail follows alternate route for the Iditarod Trail used by gold seekers |
| Flora & Fauna: | Moose, Dall sheep, birds, wolves rarely may be seen or heard on a traverse of Ship Creek; travel through forest through treeline to alpine tundra at pass. |
| Comments: | Ruins of "Fats" roadhouse are barely visible on the west side of Ship Creek about a mile above its confluence with the North Fork of Ship Creek, although it's vanishing into the brush. Trail passes from mixed deciduous forest to alpine tundra. |

## Turnagain Trail (formerly Old Johnson Trail)

| | |
|---|---|
| Access: | Potter Trailhead, Mile 116 Seward Highway; McHugh Creek Wayside, Mile 112; Rainbow, Mile 108; Windy Corner, Mile 106; Falls Creek, Mile 105. |
| Distance: | 9.4 miles one way from Potter Trailhead to Windy Corner |

Trail Milepost:  0  -  Potter Trailhead
              3.3  -  McHugh Trailhead
              7.5  -  Rainbow Trailhead
              9.4  -  Windy Corner Trailhead

| | |
|---|---|
| Elevation gain: | Minimal, several hundred feet |
| Difficulty: | Easy to Moderate |
| Special Interest: | Follows early railroad survey trail; earliest spring hiking with views of Turnagain Arm; |
| Flora & fauna: | Moose, Dall sheep, beluga whales, spruce grouse, earliest wildflowers of boreal forest, most northerly extent of Sitka spruce & Western Hemlock. |
| Comments: | Rarely has much snow, so it's not a great ski trail. Trail passes through thick mixed coniferous-deciduous forests. |

## McHugh Peak

| | |
|---|---|
| Access: | McHugh Creek Wayside, Mile 112 of Seward Highway. |
| Distance: | Approximately 7.5 miles one-way to Rabbit Lake. |
| Difficulty: | Moderate to Difficult. |
| Special Interest: | Many glacially-rounded rocks. |
| Flora & fauna: | Dall sheep, moose, an occasional bear; early wildflowers in late May/early June. Travel through forest through treeline to alpine tundra. |
| Comments: | First section follows steep switchbacks then gradual climb to Rabbit Lake. |

## HILLSIDE TRAILS

### Rabbit Lake

| | |
|---|---|
| Access: | Glen Alps parking area. Take trail to pass at base of Flat Top Mountain, traverse hillside around the base, and follow trail approximately 5.5 miles to Rabbit Lake. |
| Distance: | 11 miles round trip |
| Elevation Gain: | 500 feet |

| Difficulty: | Easy to moderate. |
| --- | --- |
| Special Interest: | See glacially sculpted valleys, lakes, and peaks |
| Flora & Fauna: | Alpine tundra plants; ground squirrels, marmots. |
| Comments: | This is the preferred alternative to the DeArmoun Road route. Travels from treeline to alpine tundra. |

## Powerline Pass

| Access: | Glen Alps - Take O'Malley Road, turn left on Upper Huffman, and take a right on Toilsome Hill Road - Proceed slowly - tight turn ahead. |
| --- | --- |
| Distance: | 11 miles round trip |
| Elevation Gain: | 1,300 feet |
| Difficulty: | Easy to moderate. |
| Special Interest: | The trail takes you into the heart of the Chugach foothills. |
| Flora & Fauna: | Treeline thickets & Krummholz attracts varied wildlife from birds to moose and rarely, grizzlies. |
| Comments: | Good hiking, biking, and jogging on old road bed. Avoid pass in winter - high avalanche danger. Otherwise, there's great skiing, mushing, and snowmachining on the trail to the pass. Begins at treeline and moves to alpine tundra. |

## Williwaw Lakes

| Access: | Prospect Heights (or Glen Alps) trailheads - Follow Abbot Road or O'Malley Road to Upper O'malley, and take a left on Prospect Drive |
| --- | --- |
| Distance: | 13 miles round trip from either trailhead |
| Elevation gain: | 742 feet |
| Difficulty: | Easy to moderate |
| Special Interest: | Spectacular valley with several alpine lakes with Mt. Williwaw and O'Malley as back drops. |
| Flora & Fauna: | Moose, Dall sheep, ptarmigan, Arctic ground squirrels |
| Comments: | Parts of trail remain wet throughout the summer; trail begins in mixed deciduous forest, but crosses treeline to alpine tundra. |

**Long Lake**

| | |
|---|---|
| Access: | Prospect Heights trailhead - From either Abbott Road or O'Malley Road, take Upper O'Malley Road, and left on Prospect Drive to trailhead entrance. |
| Distance: | 16 miles round trip |
| Elevation gain: | 1600 feet |
| Difficulty: | Moderate |
| Flora & Fauna: | Moose, brown bear, willow ptarmigan |
| Comments: | Trail is primarily above treeline on tundra. It goes up and over Near Point to North Fork Campbell Creek; sidehilling around the right side of Near Point is optional. Easiest, driest hiking is across the creek on north side, but use care when crossing creek. |

## KNIK ARM TRAILS

**Ship Creek**

| | |
|---|---|
| Access: | Arctic Valley Road Exit at Mile 7 of Glenn Highway to the trailhead located at a pullout one-half mile below the military ski area; trail parallels hillside for almost a mile before dropping down into the valley. |
| Distance: | 14 miles one way to Indian Pass |
| Elevation gain: | 1050 feet, highest point is 2350 feet at the pass |
| Difficulty: | Moderate |
| Special Interest: | Follows alternate Iditarod Trail winter route; ruins of "Fats" roadhouse still visible 1 mile above confluence with the North Fork of Ship Creek. |
| Flora & Fauna: | Moose, black and brown bear, wolves, beaver; riparian habitat to alpine tundra. |
| Comments: | Primarily cross-country and bushwacking trail until treeline, then clear hiking to passes. Best done as a ski traverse of 1-2 days, depending on conditions. |

Springtime in Ship Creek valley (Todd Frankiewicz)

## Arctic Valley

| | |
|---|---|
| Access: | Arctic Valley Road Exit, Mile 7 of Glenn Highway, to end of Arctic Valley Road at Alpenglow Ski Area parking area. |
| Distance: | Variable from 3-5 miles roundtrip. |
| Elevation gain: | 1500 feet |
| Difficulty: | Easy to moderate. |
| Flora & Fauna: | Colorful alpine meadows filled with wildlfowers to dry alpine tundra; moose and wolf tracks and droppings along trail on south ridge off Rendezvous Peak. |
| Comments: | Trail is all above treeline in alpine tundra; a variety of areas to chose from. |

## Eagle River

| | |
|---|---|
| Access: | Southbound take Eagle River Exit at Mile 14 of Glenn Highway; turn right on Eagle River Road and go 12 miles to the Visitor Center at the end of the road; northbound take Hiland Road Exit at Mile 10 of Glenn Highway, bear right, and go 2.5 miles to intersection with Eagle River Road. Turn right and go 10.6 miles to Eagle River Visitor Center. |
| Distance: | Albert Nature Trail - 3.2 miles round trip<br>Rodak Nature Trail - .6 miles round trip<br>Rapids Camp - 3.4 miles round trip<br>Echo Bend - 6 miles round trip |
| Elevation gain: | Minimal. |
| Difficulty: | Easy |
| Flora & Fauna: | Albert Loops takes you through boreal forest to Eagle River; Rodak Nature Trail takes you through boreal forest to viewing platform. |
| Comments: | Albert Trail is handicapped accessible to Eagle River from Visitor Center. Trails travel through mixed deciduous-coniferous woodlands. Great views. |

## Eagle River - South Fork Eagle River to Eagle and Symphony lakes

| | |
|---|---|
| Access: | Hiland Road Exit, turn right, go to Mile 7.3, take right on South Creek Drive, turn right on West River Drive to trailhead. |
| Distance: | 11 miles round trip |
| Elevation gain: | 650 feet |
| Difficulty: | easy to moderate |
| Flora & Fauna: | Alpine tundra and shrub thickets; watch for moose, brown or black bear, Dall sheep and mountain goat. |
| Comments: | Trail begins in treeline thickets and travels into alpine tundra. |

## Peters Creek

| | |
|---|---|
| Access: | Peters Creek Exit at Mile 22 of Glenn Highway - Take a right on Ski Road, a right on Whaley, a left on Chugach Park Road, a left on Kullberg, a left on Sullins, and a right on Malcolm Drive to trailhead. Park on the road. Locked gate 1/2 mile in from trailhead on a bad road. |
| Distance: | 5 miles one way to end of old road; 9 miles one way to upper valley. |

| | |
|---|---|
| Elevation gain: | 800 feet |
| Difficulty: | Easy to moderate. |
| Flora & Fauna: | Moose, brown and black bear, spruce grouse; abundant wildflowers in open meadows; berries in season. |
| Comments: | Trail meanders through private inholdings - Respect private property. Several shallow creek crossings. Trail traverses mixed woodlands to alpine tundra at its terminus below Mount Rumble. |

## Eklutna Lakeside Trail

| | |
|---|---|
| Access: | Take the Thunderbird Falls Exit at Mile 25 of Glenn Highwy, follow road half a mile and turn right to Eklutna Lake. The park is another 10 miles up the valley. |
| Distance: | 28 miles round trip to terminus of Eklutna Glacier |
| Elevation gain: | Minimal |
| Difficulty: | Easy, follows old road bed. |
| Special Interest: | Excellent views of spectacular peaks. |
| Flora & Fauna: | Dall sheep and mountain goats on upper slopes; moose, black and brown bear occasionally seen in forests; waterfowl commonly stop to rest on lake, golden eagles and hawks may be seen soaring overhead; berries in season. |
| Comments: | Provides access to more difficult hiking:<br>Twin Peaks trail, 7 miles round trip;<br>Bold Ridge Trail, 7 miles round trip from Mile 5 of Lakeside Trail;<br><br>East Fork Trail, 11 miles round trip from Mile 10.5 of Lakeside Trail. |

## Thunderbird Falls

| | |
|---|---|
| Access: | Take Thunderbird Falls exit at Mile 25 of Glenn Highway; go .3 miles to Thunderbird Falls parking area — on your right before the bridge. To return to Glenn Highway - turn right from parking area towards Eklutna & go a half mile to Eklutna overpass. |
| Distance: | 2 miles round trip |
| Elevation gain: | 300 feet |
| Difficulty: | Easy to moderate; trail traverses hillside; |
| Flora & Fauna: | Trail travels through mixed deciduous-spruce forest. |
| Comments: | A popular ice climbing area in winter and early spring; outhouses at parking area. |

Climbers on the summit of Whiteout Peak (John Bauman)

**Pioneer Ridge Trail**

| | |
|---|---|
| Access: | Take right off Old Glenn Highway/Palmer Alternate onto Knik River Road - Parking is on your right at Mile 3.6. |
| Distance: | 6 miles one way to Chugach State Park boundary (9 miles one way to Pioneer Peak summit) |
| Elevation gain: | 5120 feet to trail's end at main ridge crest. |
| Difficulty: | Moderate to difficult (Summit should be attempted by experienced rock climbers only!). |
| Flora & Fauna: | Moose, Dall sheep, black bear, ptarmigan. |
| Comments: | Trail ends at park boundary. It does not continue into park. Climbing Pioneer Peak should be attempted ONLY by people experienced in rock climbing techiniques. Trail follows through mixed deciduous woodlands to alpine tundra. |

## MOUNTAINEERING

This book is not a definitive guide to mountaineering in Chugach State Park. I offer only basic information to let park visitors know what types of activities are available.

The benign-looking mountains within sight of Anchorage can be dangerous. Without proper knowledge, skills and equipment, someone could get hurt, or killed. Several organizations offer classes. Take advantage of their expertise on rock and ice climbing, before venturing in over your head. Contact the following organizations for more information:

Mountaineering Club of Alaska
American Alpine Club - Alaska Chapter
Alaska Pacific University Outdoor Program
Alaska Wilderness Studies Program, University of Alaska, Anchorage

### PEAKS OF CHUGACH STATE PARK

| | |
|---|---|
| Bird Peak (5505') | Flattop Mountain (3,550') |
| Penguin Peak (4305') | Ptarmigan Peak (4,950') |
| McHugh Peak (4,301') | The Wedge (4,660') |
| North Suicide Peak (5,065') | The Ramp (5,240') |
| South Suicide Peak (5,005') | O'Malley Peak (5,105') |
| | |
| Mt. Willawaw (5445') | Cantata Peak (6410') |
| Near Point (3,050') | Calliope Peak (6810') |
| Wolverine Peak (4455') | Organ Mtn (6980') |
| Knoya Peak (4,650') | Eagle Peak (6955') |
| Tikishla Peak (5,150') | Polar Bear Peak (6614') |
| Tanaina (5300') | Hurdy Gurdy Peak (5130') |
| | |
| Peek-aboo Mtn (6795') | Bellicose Peak (7640') |
| Raina Peak (6795') | Benign Peak (7200') |
| Korohusk Peak (7000') | Peril Peak (7040') |
| Mt Kiliak (7460') | Mt Rumble (7530') |
| Mt Yukla (7535') | Thunderbird Peak (6575') |
| Beelzebub (7280') | The Mitre (6000') |
| | |
| Baleful Peak (7500') | |
| Bold Peak (7522') | Pioneer Peak (6398') |
| Twin Peaks | Mt Palmer (6940') |
| (East Twin-5050' | Bashful Peak (8005') |
| West Twin-5401') | (tallest in park) |

Ice climbing up Eagle River valley (John Bauman)

# ICE CLIMBING

There are a number of areas around the park which are accessible to ice climbing. Before venturing out, be prepared for the unexpected.

**Seward Highway** along road cuts between Indian and Potter Creek Weigh Station (Grades III through IV, varies from 50-200').

**O'Malley Peak Waterfalls** - north side of peak (Grades II through III, 100-400').

**Eagle River Valley** beyond Visitor Center to Thunder Gorge (Grade III) and Heritage Falls (Grade II), Echo Bend and Twin Falls (Grade IV, 300').

**Eklutna Canyon** at Thunderbird Falls - Cheap Wine Series (Grades II through IV, 65-180").

**Eklutna Lake Area** - The Mitre (Grade V, 1400" )

# ROCK CLIMBING

The rock climbing season is short in Alaska. The south-facing rock along the Seward Highway south of Anchorage is a popular place for local climbers to go after they've put away their ice climbing tools. Boy Scout Rock at Milepost 112.1, Longs Crack at Milepost 110.7, and Boulder Stadium Milepost 102.5, in Chugach State Park, offer one of the warmest and earliest rock climbing locations in Southcentral Alaska. These areas may be crowded on sunny, summer days. Again - be prepared for anything even though you are along a highway.

# SKI TOURING

Opportunities for cross-country skiers abound in Chugach State Park. Ski trails are not set for track skiing, but the park offers miles of backcountry touring. The numerous valleys form a natural pathway into the park. CAUTION: Be aware of weather and snow conditions. Avalanches can occur when you least expect them. Some trails must be shared with snowmachines, so watch out.

# BERRY PICKING

By August, the leaves begin to change color. Thoughts turn to the abundant berries ripe for the picking. But where to go?

Open sunny woods of McHugh and Bird creeks offer rose hips, raspberries and lowbush cranberries. The deep moist woods along Turnagain Trail, Campbell Creek, and Eklutna Lake area offer currants, highbush cranberries, trailing raspberry, and bog blueberry. Alpine blueberry and lowbush cranberries grow in abundance on open slopes and alpine tundra throughout the Park. The farther off the trail you venture, the greater your reward.

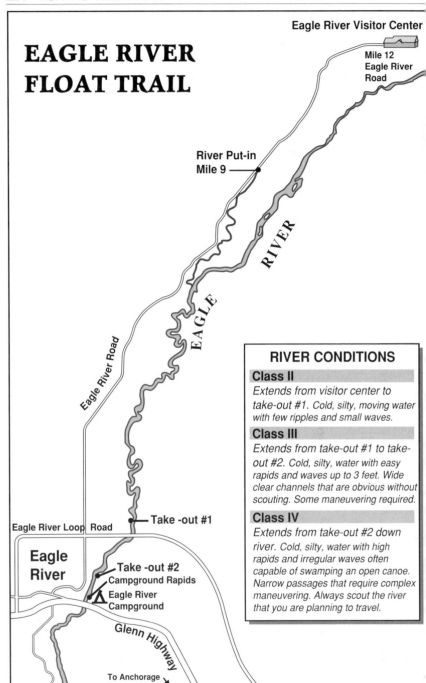

Eagle River Float Trail (Ron Engstrom)

# BOATING

## Eklutna Lake

This 7-mile long glacially carved lake is the largest in the Chugach State Park. It powers an electrical plant, and provides Anchorage with much of its water. It is an excellent place to canoe, kayak, or windsurf in summer (or ski, snowmachine or dogmush in winter ). The water level drops dramatically — by as much as 40 feet — from spring to fall. Weather changes rapidly in the mountains with winds suddenly kicking up waves.

Campgounds are located at both ends of the lake (See Chapter 20) and a Ranger Station is located near the parking area at the end of Eklutna Lake Road.

## Eagle River

**Put in:** North Fork Eagle River Access - Mile 9 Eagle River Road (Six miles from the intersection of Eagle River Loop and Eagle River Road.)

**Take outs:**

1. Eagle River Loop Road (Access road down to the river is on the west side of bridge.)
2. Eagle River Campground above Campground Rapids
3. South of Glenn Hwy bridge on Fort Richardson - call ahead for permission.

Rafting Eagle River (Dave Albert)

## Difficulty:

The Class rating has been upgraded by a factor of one because of the extremely cold, silty water.

**Class II** - Cold, silty, moving water with a few riffles and small waves above Take Out #1 (Novices).

**Class III** - Cold, silty water with easy rapids and waves to three feet. Wide clear channels are obvious without scouting. Some maneuvering required between Take Out #1 and #2 (1/5 mile above Campground) Don't get caught going through Campground Rapids!!!! (Moderate paddlers.)

**Class IV** - Cold, silty water with high rapids and irregular waves ofter capable of swamping an open canoe. Narrow passages that often require complex maneuvering. Always scout the river below Take Out #2 (Experts Only !!)

## HORSEBACK RIDING

The use of horses, mules, and burros is allowed in Chugach State Park, excep for:

- Designated campgrounds, swimming beaches, and picnic areas;
- Eagle river valley from Crow Pass to Eagle River Visitor Center, except by permit from the Director of Parks & Outdoor Recreation;
- Meadow Creek drainage in Eagle River;
- Turnagain Trail from Potter to Indian;
- Section 29,T12N, R2W, S.M., west of the powerline easement, except on trail between the powerline easement and Glen Alps parking lot will be designated for summer use of horses;
- Flattop Mountain Trails;
- All trails in the Hillside Trail System which may be closed seasonally to horse use to control break-up problems and to avoid use conflicts with sk trails.

Groups of 10 or more animals must obtain authorization from the director o Parks & Outdoor Recreation before entering Chugach State Park. Tying horse mules, or burros within 100 feet of fresh water is prohibited. Loose herdin, of animals is prohibited.

## MOUNTAIN BIKING

- Bird Creek-Penguin Creek valley: 11 miles roundtrip
- Powerline Pass-Indian valley traverse: 12 miles one way from Glen Alp to Indian.

- Powerline Pass: 11 miles round trip
- Near Point Trail: 6 miles round trip on old homestead road at Prospect Heights; follow gasline right-of-way to Glen Alps.
- Peters Creek: 10 miles round trip to road's end.
- Eklutna Lakeside Trail: 26 miles round trip to glacier.

## MOTOR VEHICLE USE

Winter snowmachine and ATV use is restricted to designated areas only at Eklutna Lake, Peters Creek, Eagle River, South Fork Campbell Creek and Bird Creek when snow cover is adequate. Before heading out, contact the Park for information on conditions, and to learn which days vehicle use is permitted.

Summer ATV use is restricted to Eklutna Lakeside trail and Bird Creek logging roads only, Sunday through Wednesday.

Aircraft may be used on Eklutna Lake surface, or Bold Airstrip at the southeast end of Eklutna Lake.

## FISHING and HUNTING

Chugach State Park is a part of Game Management Unit 14 (C) which does allow fishing and hunting in specifically designated areas. Contact the Alaska Department of Fish and Game for current regulations, 344-0541, or Fish and Wildlife Protection, 269-5751, or Chugach State Park, 345-5014 or 694-2108. **If you see or hear of a fish or wildlife violation, please report it by calling (800) 478-3377.**

- No target practice is allowed within Chugach State Park.
- Weapons may be carried, but not discharged unless hunting.
- No discharge of firearms within one-half mile of the Seward Highway, or on any road or trailhead, or at any facility.

## PANNING for GOLD

Recreational gold panning is permitted in Chugach State Park in all streams except anadromous salmon streams. Salmon streams are open to gold panning May 16 through July 14.

- No mechanized equipment.
- No chemicals.
- Only gold pan and shovel can be used.
- Work below high water line below vegetation.
- NO CLAIMS!

## AND STILL MORE REGULATIONS

### Campfires:

- No open campfires except in contained metal fire pits, or on gravel river bars below the high water mark in these drainages: Eklutna River, Peters Creek, North Fork Eagle River (except Meadow Creek) and Bird Creek.
- Only dead and down wood may be burned.
- Stoves are recommended for convenience and safety.

### Disturbance of Natural Objects

- Edible plants and berries may be collected within the park
- Dead and down wood may be collected for personal use in park
- Illegal to dig up or pick flowers, to collect insects or rocks
- No digging of trenches around tents
- DO NOT DISTURB THE WILDLIFE.

### Organized Activities

- Any organized activity - i.e. wedding, race, etc. - requires a permit.
- An activity with 20 or more people requires a permit.
- Call Chugach State Park Headquarters for further information, 345-5014.

Sheep viewing at Windy Corner along the Seward Highway (Michael Goodwin)

Mountain biking the Eklutna Lakeside Trail (Todd Frankiewicz)

# CHAPTER NINETEEN

# BACKCOUNTRY PRECAUTIONS

The beauty of Chugach State Park draws us in. It's alluringly close to the largest city in Alaska. We look down from the Park on the city below and feel naively secure. Our senses in this way become dulled by the protective wrap of civilization. "What could possibly go wrong?" we ask.

1971 - 2 climbers killed in avalanche while descending Eklutna Glacier.
1973 - Man killed in avalanche when descending Flattop Mountain.
1974 - Man killed by avalanche while descending Tanaina Peak.
1986 - Hiker died of hypothermia returning from a day hike along Powerline Pass trail.
1990 - Snowmachiner killed in avalanche below Powerline Pass.
1991 - 9-year old boy fell while descending Flattop Mountain and died as a result of his injuries.
1992 - 2 men killed in avalanche behind Flattop

Scare tactics? Perhaps they are. But accidents continue to happen. Just because you're on the outskirts of Alaska's largest city, don't let yourself be lulled into a false sense of security. Remember: Chugach is a wilderness park. Be aware of conditions. Help is often a long time in coming, so be prepared for anything.

## BEARS & PEOPLE

Bears are interesting and exciting to see, but they are powerful, wild animals. Both black and brown bears inhabit the Park and are potentially dangerous. Bears are out there just being bears, and there is a good chance some day you will see one. The best way to avoid a close encounter is to take a few precautions in the wilds. But remember — bear encounters are rare.

(continued)

Facing page: AVALANCHE!! (Doug Fesler)

HIKING: Always be aware of your surroundings and be prepared. Avoid seasonal areas where bears are likely to hang out, such as dense brush, berry patches, and salmon streams. If you see a bear in the distance above treeline, move away from its direction of travel. They're not hunting you; you're just in their space.

In areas of limited visibility, make noise. Announce your presence by singing or talking loudly. Give a bear the opportunity to leave the area unnoticed. Larger human groups tend to make more noise and rarely see a bear. It is debatable whether bells and other noise-makers are effective; some argue they attract curious bruins. Strong winds or a roaring river may mask your noise, so remain aware of your environment.

CAMPING: When above treeline, cook and store food in airtight containers, well away from your campsite. Hang food in a tree, when available. Don't smell good - no food odors, no perfumed lotions. If camping above treeline, hide food in an inconspicuous, difficult-to-reach spot away from tent. Stay Clean !!

MENSTRUATION: Use internal tampons. Pack used tampons out in a ziplock bag. Don't use external pads. Don't bury supplies. Stay clean !!

Watch for bear signs: fresh tracks; droppings of berries, vegetation, or hair; animal carcasses covered with dirt; torn up logs or stumps; ground squirrel holes gouged out in the alpine tundra; claw marks on trees, any one of these indicate a bear has been in the area. Are the signs fresh? Be aware.

Warning signs in Chugach State Park: (Jenny Zimmerman)

## Bears - What's the Difference?

**GRIZZLY BEAR**
Dish-shaped face — Shoulder hump

**BLACK BEAR**
Straight profile — No hump

Long front claws
Toes close together

Short claws
Toes spread

Illustration: Joanna Mergler Mayer

## How To React To A Bear Encounter

Most of the time a bear will flee when encountering humans, but a chance close encounter may occur. There is no standard method of behavior when encountering a bear, but a calm head and common sense will be the most help. Although it's not easy - try and stay calm. Look around for cubs or a recent kill. A bear is more aggressive under these circumstances.

Remember: bears have poor eyesight. They may not know you are a human and often are just curious. Don't run unless you know you can reach safety before the bear can catch you. Bears instinctively chase anything that runs. It is best to slowly move away from the bear, reducing the threat the bear feels. For this reason, do not make eye contact. Let it think you are a powerful predator "pretending" to have little interest in it. Talk calmly to the bear as you back up, letting it know you are human. If a bear begins to snort and slap the ground, it still feels threatened and is about to charge.

Black bears are less likely to charge than grizzlies, but if a black bear tries to intimidate you - **don't play dead.** If the black bear continues to pursue you, it wants dinner. Fighting back against the smaller, but more aggressive, black bear is your best chance of survival.

If charged by a grizzly, stand your ground (if at all possible), drop an object between you and the bear to distract it. In the last resort - if you are facing a charging grizzly, you have two options. If you have a gun, shoot to kill. A wounded bear is extremely dangerous. If you are unarmed, drop down and play dead. They tend to bite the head, neck, and shoulders, so protect your neck with your hands or pack. Do not play dead prior to an attack, because it may arouse the bear's curiosity to investigate you more closely. Dropping a pack or food is another "last resort" option.

Despite the fear and foreboding of meeting a bear in the wild, the chances of getting hurt by a bear are less than the chances of injury climbing Flattop Mountain. According to state park officials, there have been few bear-human encounters since the park was established, and none have been fatal.

## MOOSE & PEOPLE

Although they appear harmless, moose may charge humans. However, these situations are predictable and avoidable. In September, bull moose begin rut, a prelude to the mating season. They enter into shoving matches with other bulls, occasionally stabbing out with their hooves. Humans have been pursued in cases of mistaken identity. It is best to avoid bulls in rut.

Cows with calves are extremely protective and dangerous, especially when calves are less than a month old. Cows will agressively charge with ears flattened back and hackles straight up. It is best to beat a hasty retreat. Moose want you out of their immediate space and are satisfied when you leave the area.

Illustration: Angry cow moose with calf. (Joanna Mergler Mayer)

## HOW SAFE IS THE WATER?

### Giardia

Often called "beaver fever", *Giardia lamblia* is a protozoan parasite that is ingested with water and attaches itself to the small intestine, and occasionally the gall bladder. It enters lakes and streams as cysts from the feces of a carrier.

If you drink water infested with *Giardia*, symptoms begin in about 15 days. You may experience diarrhea, abdominal cramps, gas, weakness, and lack of appetite. Occasionally sharp pain is felt in the lower abdomen. This is annoying, but seldom incapacitating. Treatment is an anti-protozoan drug. Better to prevent ingestion by either boiling water for 5 minutes, or pumping it through a ceramic water filter. Cysts are resistant to iodine, chlorine, and halizone tablets, although the parasite is not.

Water presents another problem for the back country traveller. Many rivers and streams are a milky gray from glacial runoff. Although safe to drink, the water may be somewhat unpalatable, and water filters often become clogged.

### Crossing Rivers and Streams

Chugach is a wilderness park with few established trail systems and even fewer bridges. A rushing mountain stream can present a formidable obstacle. Streams and rivers vary from crystal clear to milky gray, from knee-deep pools to waist-deep icy torrents. A current of icy cold water tumbling over slick boulders can be a real danger with a pack on.

Safely crossing Eagle River (Frankie Barker)

236 VISITING THE PARK

If the decision is made to cross, look for a wide straight stretch. These are often the shallower sections, where water is more placid. A narrow corner may look easy to cross but the water is usually being forced through at a higher flow rate. When examining the water, consider the options in case you are swept off your feet. Can you get ashore easily downstream? What is the current like below you? Choose the time of your crossing with care. Has it been raining? Should you wait for water to recede? Has the day been hot and sunny with late afternoon runoff? Early morning crossings are usually best.

If you anticipate a river crossing, you may want to carry neoprene socks or booties. They are light and save having cold feet and wet boots. Always wear footgear, however, if you are carrying a pack, and undo the waistbelt. Stand sideways to the current with feet wide apart. Take short steps, feeling the bottom as you go, and keep feet apart. An ice ax or walking stick will help you brace yourself. If you are in a group, you get extra support crossing in pairs by linking arms, facing across the stream, and slowly working your way across. Stay as dry as possible, changing into dry clothes if you get wet. If you lose your footing and go down, shed your pack immediately. Start swimming on your back and keep your feet facing downstream to fend off boulders. GET DRY AND WARM QUICKLY TO PREVENT HYPOTHERMIA.

## MUDFLATS

**Mudflats** along Turnagain Arm and Knik Arm are deadly. The silty glacial sediment is not as solid as it appears. It is a thick ooze, the consistency of peanut butter, and just as sticky. Anyone who ventures out on the flats risks becoming stuck fast. A rapid incoming tide may arrive before a victim can be freed.

## AVALANCHES

Snow avalanches are a major killer of park visitors. The number of accidents has been increasing as winter use by skiers, climbers, hikers, and snowmachiners escalates. The majority of the avalanches that catch, injure, and sometime kill, park visitors are human-triggered. With proper training, you can learn to recognize and avoid avalanche hazards.

### What Causes an Avalanche?

Avalanches are not random events. They occur as a result of the interaction between three critical ingredients: terrain, snowpack, and weather. An avalanche hazard exists if a fourth ingredient - people or property - is present.

First, the *terrain* must be steep enough to produce avalanches. Slope angles of between 25 and 60+ degrees are dangerous, but 35-45 is the critical angle.

Snow tends to slide on the steeper slopes, and hold on the shallower slopes. A slope may only be 50 feet high, but if it is steep enough, it may be an avalanche path. Within the Park, many such terrain traps exist, even near trailheads. Second, layers of snow within the *snowpack* may be poorly bonded to each other. Third, the *weather* often contributes to instability because new snow, rain, or wind-loading (deposition of wind-transported snow) increases the stress on the snowpack. The stability of the snowpack continues to change throughout the winter. Most of the time the snowpack is stable because its bond-strength far exceeds the stress being exerted on it. When stress and strength are in a near equilibrium balance (an unstable condition), it often takes little additional stress to tip the balance and trigger an avalanche. Again, the weight of a traveler on or near a steep slope is the most common trigger in avalanche accidents.

## How to Avoid Getting Caught

LEARN TO RECOGNIZE AVALANCHE TERRAIN. This is a critical first step because it enables you to decide whether or not you want to expose yourself to a possible hazard. An invaluable and inexpensive tool, to carry and know how to use, is an inclinometer, used to measure slope angles. Stay off cornices (overhanging deposits of windblown snow), especially along ridgetops, as cornice failure is a common type of avalanche.

BE ALERT FOR CLUES TO INSTABILITY. These include recent avalanches on similar slope, recent new snow or wind-loading, "whump" noises indicating the collapse of a buried weak layer, hollow-sounding snow, and shooting cracks radiating out around you in the snow. It is possible to trigger an avalanche even when none of these clues are evident, but these are important signals that should not be ignored.

LEARN TO EVALUATE AVALANCHE HAZARD. The Alaska Mountain Safety Center, Inc. at 345-3566 offers intensive workshops in avalanche hazard evaluation and rescue through its Alaska Avalanche School.

DON'T MAKE ASSUMPTIONS. Assumptions can kill. Do not assume that experienced skiers or climbers are also experienced at evaluating avalanche hazard, or that rangers will be able to tell you what the snow conditions are in the backcountry. Do not assume because it's a clear, sunny day that snow conditions are safe. Do not assume that a trail which is safe in summer is also safe in winter, or a route is safe because you've travelled it before. Do not assume that you will be fine if you are caught in an avalanche because you are carrying rescue equipment.

AVALANCHE RESCUE. Avalanche rescues are not fool-proof, so the best defense is to avoid getting caught in the first place. However, you increase your chances of survival by being prepared. **All** winter backcountry travellers should carry an avalanche rescue transceiver (beacon), avalanche probe, and a shovel. These items are worthless if you don't know how to use them. Have a rescue plan, because time is critical. A person buried under snow is like a drowning victim. You only have so much time to save them before it'a too late. **Do not go for help, because you are the help.**

IF CAUGHT IN AN AVALANCHE. Yell — so that other members of your party know where to watch for you, then close your mouth so you don't inhale snow. If possible, try to discard gear such as skis or poles because they can pull you down into the snow. Fight with all your strength to stop yourself, or work your way to the side of the avalanche, or stay on top by "swimming." When the snow starts to slow down, try to thrust some part of your body above the snow surface and create an airspace in front of your face with your arm. Stay calm and try not to panic as this will conserve precious oxygen.

IF YOU ARE A RESCUER. Keep a sharp eye on a victim being carried downslope to establish a Last Seen Area (LSA). Make sure there is no additional avalanche hazard before you enter the area. (*Note:* A slope which has just avalanched is extremely unlikely to slide again, but — are there are other paths which might run into the same area? If the avalanche was human-triggered, you are probably safe and can enter the debris path.) Now you can conduct a thorough initial search, looking for clues. Leave all clues in place. They may be helpful in establishing the victim's line of travel. Probe around the clues and other likely spots. If you are wearing rescue transceivers, conduct a beacon search at the time of the intial search. (You should have practiced many times before.) If the victim is not located by any of these methods, you will need to systematically probe the most likely location. Search quickly, but thoroughly. You are the victim's best chance for survival. When you dig out a victim, free their mouth and chest of snow as soon as possible. Be alert for problems in their airway, for signs of hypothermia, and other injuries.

## FROSTBITE & HYPOTHERMIA

Cold alone has its hazards, but add wind or water, and conditions may become critical to human survival. Wind makes the temperature feel colder than is indicated by a thermometer. In winter, when the wind picks up, it pierces the thickest clothing. Hands and feet can't stay warm. Exposed skin experiences a burning pain in a matter of minutes. Movement is necessary to keep from shivering.

**Hypothermia** is a loss of body heat due to the combined effects of temperature and wind. Our bodies are continually generating heat in order to maintain a constant body temperature. This heat is radiated into the environment. On a warm still day we experience little discomfort, but as the temperature drops, so does our ability to stay warm. If the wind picks up, the air flowing by takes the warm air with it. Standing outside on a winter's day with the temperature at zero is uncomfortable, but tolerable. If the wind picks up to 10 mph, rapid heat loss occurs; this "windchill" would be equivalent to 21 degrees below zero. If not properly dressed, the risk of hypothermia increases. It can take as little as one hour, or as long as six hours for the first signs to occur.

First signs of hypothermia are a sensation of chilliness and shivering, followed by lack of coordination and stumbling, mild confusion and apathy. As the body temperature drops, muscular uncoordination increases, with frequent stumbling and inability to use hands; speech becomes slow. Once body temperature drops below 90° shivering stops and victims are unable to walk or stand; they become incoherent and irrational. Treatment should begin at first signs of hypothermia by removing wet clothing and replacing with dry; windbreakers and rainjackets are especially effective. **Victims cannot supply their own heat**. Provide the victim with warm liquids if a mild case, or place in sleeping bag with a second body as heat source. Hypothermia victims are highly susceptible to frostbite.

**Frostbite** occurs only when temperatures are below freezing, and impairs circulation causing fluids in cells to freeze. The combination of wind and temperature can hasten frostbite. Faces, especially the nose, cheeks, and ears, are most susceptible to wind and cold. Feet and hands are susceptible after prolonged exposure to cold. Signs of frostbite are a feeling of cold or pain, or pale area on skin. Skin becomes whiter as freezing progresses and feeling is lost. With severe frostbite the tissues become hard. Once an injured area has begun to thaw it will become very painful and red with small blebs, or blisters, which form into large blisters. In severe cases the skin will appear ashen gray and may later turn black and wrinkled. Rapid rewarming is the recommended treatment, but NOT until victim has reached a place where entire body can be kept warm and there is no chance of refreezing.

**Some Simple Precautions to Avoid Hypothermia and Frostbite.**
When heading out into the Park, or anywhere in Alaska, BE PRE-
PARED for getting wet and cold even in summer. Prevent heat loss
when resting, or in windy conditions, with rain or wind pants and
jacket with a warm layer for summer, wind protection and insulating
layers with adequate hand and foot gear for winter. Keep hydrated by
drinking plenty of fluids, especially in winter, and eat to provide
energy for warmth. Under heavy physical exertion remove layers to
comfortably ventilate perspiration, do not allow clothes to become
soaked. When resting, protect yourself from heat loss. Make sure
boots are not tight, constricting circulation. If detected early on, treat
( if possible), and head for home.

Table 3. Windchill Compared to Ambient Temperatures.

| WIND Speed | Ambient Air Temperature (° F) | | | | | | | | | | | | |
|---|---|---|---|---|---|---|---|---|---|---|---|---|---|
| Calm | 40 | 30 | 20 | 10 | 5 | 0 | -5 | -10 | -15 | -20 | -25 | -35 | -40 |
| 5 | 35 | 25 | 15 | 5 | 0 | -5 | -10 | -15 | -20 | -25 | -30 | -40 | -45 |
| 10 | 30 | 15 | 5 | -10 | -15 | -20 | -25 | -35 | -40 | -45 | -50 | -65 | -70 |
| 15 | 25 | 10 | -5 | -20 | -25 | -30 | -40 | -45 | -50 | -60 | -65 | -80 | -85 |
| 20 | 20 | 5 | -10 | -25 | -30 | -35 | -45 | -50 | -60 | -65 | -75 | -85 | -95 |
| 25 | 15 | 0 | -15 | -30 | -35 | -45 | -50 | -60 | -65 | -75 | -80 | -95 | -105 |
| 30 | 10 | 0 | -20 | -30 | -40 | -50 | -55 | -65 | -70 | -80 | -85 | -100 | -110 |
| 35 | 10 | -5 | -20 | -35 | -40 | -50 | -60 | -65 | -75 | -80 | -90 | -105 | -115 |
| 40* | 10 | -6 | -21 | -37 | -42 | -53 | -63 | -69 | -75 | -85 | -96 | -106 | -116 |

Little Danger
Increasing Danger     (Flesh May Freeze in 1 minute)
Great Danger     (Flesh May freeze in 30 seconds)

DANGER OF FREEZING EXPOSED FLESH
EVEN WHEN PROPERLY CLOTHED

*Winds above 40 mph  have little additional effect.

# TEN ESSENTIALS

This is a modified list of classic items prepared by the Seattle Mountaineers. These items will meet most of the needs confronting someone in the Alaskan out-of-doors, whether on a day hike or a long excursion. Keep these items together so they're ready to toss in a pack at a moment's notice.

1. EXTRA CLOTHING - Always bring a rainjacket and pants, and extra warmth such as a sweater or bunting jacket, and socks packed in plastic bag.

2. FOOD - Carry more food than you plan to eat, and take water. Expending energy hiking requires more food and water than you would consume at home.

3. FIRST AID KIT - To fix people and things: Moleskin, bandaids, aspirin, extra matches or butane lighter, elastic bandage, adhesive tape, safety pins, wire, needle and thread, stick-on ripstop repair tape, paper and pencil, pamphlet on first aid (in case you forget).

4. KNIFE - An amazingly versatile piece of equipment, especially if it's the Swiss Army type.

5. MATCHES - Waterproof/windproof matches or lighter should be carried even if it's just to burn your toilet paper.

6. FIRESTARTER - Commercial paste or container of wood shavings.

7. MAP - especially if you plan to stray away from popular trails and valleys.

8. SIGNAL - A whistle or mirror or bright colored cloth to attract attention in an emergency.

9. INSECT REPELLANT - A pleasant hike can be turned into a stress-test without it.

10. TOILET PAPER - Remember to burn it, bury it, or carry it out.

# CHAPTER TWENTY

# PARK FACILITIES

**Potter Section House** - Mile 115 of Seward Highway
Headquarters - Chugach State Park
(907) 345-5014 or 688-0908

This state historic site features a restored roadhouse and outbuildings of a 1920's section camp of the Alaska Railroad. Potter Section House is reportedly named for New Yorker, Allen B. Potter, who joined the gold rush to Turnagain Arm in 1896 at the age of 47. He worked the Seward-Anchorage section of the Iditarod Trail until his death in 1910 in a house fire in Seward.

Potter Section House & Chugach State Park Headquarters (Al Meiners)

Facing page: Kanchee Campground at head of Eklutna Lake, The Mitre looms up in the background (Steve Johnson)

**Potter Section House** (continued)

Features & Services:

- Railroad museum - open daily June through August; operates on a reduced schedule the rest of the year.
- Information and brochures on the park are available at park Headquarters in the basement
- Old Snowblower train permanently on exhibit.
- Trailhead for Turnagain Trail (formerly Old Johnson Trail) is across the road from Potter Station House
- Toilets are Handicapped-accessible.

**Eagle River Visitor Center** - Mile 12 of Eagle River Road

Eagle River, Alaska. (907) 694-2108

**Southbound** take Eagle River Exit (Mile 12.6 of Glenn Highway) cross over highway, turn right at light, and go 12 miles to the end of the road to the Visitor Center.

**Northbound** take Hiland Road Exit (Mile 10 of Glenn Highway), bear right and go 2.5 miles to light at intersection with Eagle River Road. Turn right and drive 10.6 miles to Eagle River Visitor Center.

Visitor Center has displays on plant and animal life, as well as a spotting scope to look for wildlife on the valley walls. For information on hours of operation, call the Visitor Center or Park Headquarters.

- Water available in summer at Visitor Center
- Restrooms inside Visitor Center
- Payphone outside Visitor Center
- Two nature trails -Rodak and Albert trails leave from Eagle River Visitor Center

**Rodak Trail** - An easy two-thirds (.6 ) of a mile-long gravel, self-guided interpretive walk.

**Albert Nature Trail** - An easy 3.2 mile round trip hike through boreal forest to Eagle River. Handicapped accessible.

- Historic **Iditarod Trail** (See Chapter 8) was used by gold seekers and mail teams traveling the winter trail between Seward and the Interior Gold fields of Iditarod and Nome. On this 26-mile segment of the Iditarod trail, you follow the route up Eagle River valley to Raven Creek, where it goes up and over Crow Pass to the historic town of Girdwood.

Travel on the Iditarod Trail is for non-motorized use only. Snow machine use is restricted to the frozen surface of Eagle River. Proceed with caution and watch for overflow and pressure ridges.

## CAMPGROUNDS

Visitors may purchase annual state park campground pass at state park offices or from state park rangers.

### Bird Creek

Bird Creek Campground

- Mile 100 on Seward Highway - campground is just off the road in mixed coniferous woodlands overlooking Turnagain Arm.
- Open summer only (May 1 to September 30) - stay limit 7 days.
- 22 campsites plus overflow area.
- Picnic tables, fire pits, water, and toilets are available.
- Bring your own firewood.

Bird Creek Campground Host (Jenny Zimmerman)

## Eagle River

### Eagle River Campground

- Mile 11.5 on Glenn Highway -Take Hiland Road Exit, turn left and follow signs down the Frontage Road to campground.
- Summer only (May 1 to September 30) - stay limit 4 days.
- 38 campsites with 6 overflow units in mixed deciduous-conifer woodlands.
- Electricity, picnic tables, fire pits, water and flush toilets are available.
- Bring your own firewood.

## Eklutna Lake

### Eklutna Lake Campground and Ranger Station (907) 688-0908

- Take Thunderbird Falls Exit at Mile 26 on Glenn Highway, drive 2.5 miles to turn-off, and follow park signs 10 miles to Eklutna Lake. Road is plowed in winter.
- Open summer only (May 1 to September 30).
- 50 campsites plus handicapped and overflow sites.
- Water, latrines, picnic tables and fire pits.
- Bring your own firewood.
- Camping fees are posted & camping is allowed for 15 consecutive nights
- Group picnic shelter in day-use area
- Large group picnic and camping area may be reserved by calling Chugach State Park Headquarters at the Potter Section House
- Groups of 20 or more must have a permit.
- Three remote backcountry campgrounds accessible by foot, bicycle, horseback, ATV, or snowmachine (ATV/snowmachine use is Sunday through Wednesday **only**.)
- Each campsite has toilets, picnic table and fire ring .
- Mile 8.8 - Eklutna Alex Campground at head of Eklutna Lake
- Mile 11 - Kanchee (means "porcupine" in Athapaskan) Campground at confluence of East Fork and Eklutna rivers
- Mile12 - Cottonwood Campground just off Eklutna River near Eklutna Glacier. No motorized vehicles are allowed here.
- 27 miles of maintained trails around Eklutna Lake area (See Chapter 19).

# PICNIC AREAS

## McHugh Creek Wayside
- Mile 112 on Seward Highway
- Open 9 am to 9 pm daily; camping is not allowed at picnic area, or within a half mile of highway.
- 30 picnic sites with tables and charcoal fire grates. Water is available.
- Scenic overlook trail and toilets are handicapped-accessible.

## Upper Huffman - Susitna View Trailhead
- Take O'Malley Road to Hillside Drive, continue south until Park sign points way to Upper Huffman, turn left, and continue to T in road, take left to end of road.
- 8 picnic tables and toilet as well as trails leading to views of the mountains.

## Eagle River
- At Eagle River Campground - Hiland Road Exit off the Glenn Highway; at stop sign drive straight across Highland Road .x of a mile to the campground.
- 12 picnic sites with fire grates.
- Water, flush toilets, and electricity are available.

## Eklutna Lake
- Use Thunderbird Falls Exit at Mile 26 of Glenn Highway, watch for Eklutna Lake sign, turn right and drive 10 more miles to Chugach State Park.
- 32 picnic sites, picnic shelter for large groups, fire pits, toilets, and water are available.

| SPECIES | SP | S | F | W | COMMENTS |
|---|---|---|---|---|---|
| __Red-throated Loon* | R | R | R | | |
| __Arctic Loon* | C | C | C | | |
| __Common Loon* | U | U | U | | |
| __Pied-billed Grebe | | AC | | | |
| __Horned Grebe* | C | C | C | AC | |
| __Red-necked Grebe* | C | C | C | | |
| __Forked-tailed Storm-petrel | | | CA | | |
| __Leach's Storm-petrel | | | AC | | |
| __Great Blue Heron | R | | R | CA | |
| __Tundra Swan | C | | C | | |
| __Trumpeter Swan* | U | R | U | | |
| __Greater White-fronted Goose | U | | U | | |
| __Snow Goose | C | | | | |
| __Brant | CA | | | | |
| __Canada Goose* | A | C | A | R | |
| __Green-winged Teal* | C | C | C | AC | |
| __Mallard* | A | A | A | C | |
| __Northern Pintail* | A | C | A | CA | |
| __Blue-winged Teal | R | R | R | | |
| __Cinnamon Teal | AC | | | | |
| __Northern Shoveler* | C | C | C | | |
| __Gadwall | R | R | R | AC | |
| __Eurasian Widgeon | R | | | | |
| __American Widgeon* | C | C | C | CA | |
| __Canvasback* | U | U | U | | |
| __Redhead | U | CA | CA | | |
| __Ringed-necked Duck* | R | R | R | AC | |
| __Greater Scaup* | C | C | C | CA | |
| __Lesser Scaup | U | U | U | AC | |
| __Common Eider | | | CA | | |
| __Steller's Eider | AC | | AC | | |
| __Harlequin Duck* | R | R | R | R | |
| __Oldsquaw* | U | R | R | | |
| __Black Scoter | R | R | R | | |
| __White-winged Scoter | R | R | U | | |
| __Common Goldeneye* | C | U | C | U | |
| __Barrow's Goldeneye* | U | R | U | R | |
| __Bufflehead | U | | U | | |
| __Hooded Merganser | AC | | CA | | |
| __Common Merganser | U | R | U | U | |
| __Red-breasted Merganser | U | R | R | | |
| __Osprey* | R | CA | R | | |
| __Bald Eagle* | U | U | U | R | |
| __Northern Harrier* | C | U | C | | |
| __Sharp-shinned Hawk* | U | U | U | R | |
| __Northern Goshawk* | U | U | U | U | |
| __Red-tailed Hawk* | U | R | U | | |
| __Rough-legged Hawk | U | | R | | |
| __Golden Eagle* | U | U | U | | |

| SPECIES | OCCURRENCE | | | | COMMENTS |
|---|---|---|---|---|---|
| | SP | S | F | W | |
| __American Kestrel | R | | CA | | |
| __Merlin* | U | CA | U | R | |
| __Peregrine Falcon | | | R | CA | |
| __Gyrfalcon* | R | R | R | R | |
| | | | | | |
| __Spruce Grouse* | C | C | C | C | |
| __Willow Ptarmigan* | U | U | U | U | |
| __Rock Ptarmigan* | R | R | R | R | |
| __White-tailed Ptarmigan* | U | U | U | R | |
| | | | | | |
| __American Coot | CA | CA | CA | | |
| | | | | | |
| __Sandhill Crane* | C | R | C | | |
| | | | | | |
| __Black-bellied Plover | R | R | R | | |
| __Lesser Golden-plover | U | | U | | |
| __Semipalmated Plover* | C | C | C | | |
| __Killdeer* | R | R | R | | |
| | | | | | |
| __Greater Yellowlegs* | C | C | C | | |
| __Lesser Yellowlegs* | C | C | C | | |
| __Solitary Sandpiper* | U | U | U | | |
| __Wandering Tattler* | U | U | U | | |
| __Spotted Sandpiper* | C | C | C | | |
| __Terek Sandpiper | AC | CA | | | |
| __Upland Sandpiper | AC | | CA | | |
| __Whimbrel | U | R | U | | |
| __Hudsonian Godwit* | U | U | U | | |
| __Bar-tailed Godwit | CA | | | | |
| __Marbled Godwit | AC | | | | |
| __Ruddy Turnstone | U | R | R | | |
| __Black Turnstone | U | R | R | | |
| __Surfbird* | U | U | U | | |
| __Red Knot | | CA | CA | | |
| __Sanderling | CA | | CA | | |
| __Semipalmated Sandpiper | R | U | R | | |
| __Western Sandpiper | U | A | U | | |
| __Rufous-necked Stint | AC | CA | | | |
| __Least Sandpiper* | A | A | C | | |
| __Baird's Sandpiper | R | R | R | | |
| __Pectoral Sandpiper | C | AC | U | | |
| __Dunlin | R | | | | |
| __Short-billed Dowitcher* | A | A | A | | |
| __Long-billed Dowitcher | U | CA | R | | |
| __Common Snipe | C | C | C | AC | |
| __Wilson's Phalarope | AC | | | | |
| __Red-necked Phalarope* | C | C | C | | |
| | | | | | |
| __Parasitic Jaeger | | R | R | | |
| __Long-tailed Jaeger | | R | | | |
| __Franklin's Gull | AC | | | | |
| __Com.Black-headed Gull | | AC | | | |
| __Bonaparte's Gull* | C | C | C | | |
| __Mew Gull* | A | A | A | CA | |
| __Californian Gull | | | R | | |

| SPECIES | OCCURRENCE | | | | COMMENTS |
|---|---|---|---|---|---|
| | SP | S | F | W | |
| __Herring Gull* | A | C | C | R | |
| __Thayer's Gull | R | | U | | |
| __Slaty-backed Gull | | | R | | |
| __Glaucous-winged Gull* | A | A | A | U | |
| __Glaucous Gull | R | R | U | R | |
| __ Black-legged Kittiwake | | | AC | | |
| __Ivory Gull | AC | | | | |
| __Glaucous-winged x Herring (hybrid) | A | A | A | R | |
| __Arctic Tern* | C | C | C | | |
| __Common Murre | | | AC | AC | |
| __Rock Dove* | C | C | C | C | |
| __Mourning Dove | | CA | | | |
| __Great Horned Owl* | U | U | U | U | |
| __Snowy Owl | | | R | R | |
| __Northern Hawk-owl* | R | R | R | R | |
| __Great Gray Owl | R | R | R | R | |
| __Short-eared Owl* | U | U | R | AC | |
| __Boreal Owl* | U | U | U | U | |
| __Northern Saw-whet Owl* | U | U | U | U | |
| __Anna's Hummingbird | | | AC | | |
| __Rufous Hummingbird | | R | CA | | |
| __Belted Kingfisher* | U | U | U | R | |
| __Downy Woodpecker* | U | U | U | U | |
| __Hairy Woodpecker* | U | U | U | U | |
| __Three-toed Woodpecker* | U | U | U | U | |
| __Black-backed Woodpecker* | R | R | R | R | |
| __Northern Flicker* | U | U | U | | |
| __Olive-sided Flycatcher* | R | U | | | |
| __Western Wood-Pewee | U | U | U | | |
| __Alder Flycatcher* | C | C | U | | |
| __Least Flycatcher | | AC | | | |
| __Say's Phoebe* | | R | U | R | |
| __Eastern Kingbird | | AC | | | |
| __Horned Lark* | U | U | U | | |
| __Purple Martin | AC | | | | |
| __Tree Swallow* | A | A | A | | |
| __Violet-green Swallow* | C | C | C | | |
| __Bank Swallow* | C | C | C | | |
| __Cliff Swallow* | U | U | U | | |
| __Barn Swallow | | R | R | | |
| __Gray Jay* | U | U | U | U | |
| __Steller's Jay* | R | R | U | R | |
| __Black-billed Magpie* | C | C | C | A | |
| __Norhtwestern Crow | | AC | CA | | |

| SPECIES | OCCURRENCE | | | | COMMENTS |
|---|---|---|---|---|---|
| | SP | S | F | W | |
| __Common Raven* | C | C | C | A | |
| __Black-capped Chickadee* | C | C | C | C | |
| __Boreal Chickadee* | C | C | C | C | |
| __Red-breasted Nuthatch* | R | R | R | R | |
| __Brown Creeper* | U | U | U | U | |
| __American Dipper* | U | U | U | C | |
| __Golden-crowned Kinglet* | U | U | U | U | |
| __Ruby-crowned Kinglet* | A | A | A | CA | |
| __Northern Wheatear* | AC | R | | | |
| __Townsend's Solitaire* | R | U | R | CA | |
| __Gray-cheeked Thrush | U | U | U | | |
| __Swainson's Thrush* | C | C | C | | |
| __Hermit Thrush* | U | U | U | | |
| __American Robin* | C | C | C | R | |
| __Varied Thrush* | C | C | C | | |
| __White Wagtail | AC | | | | |
| __Water Pipit* | | A | C | A | |
| __Bohemian Waxwing* | U | U | A | U | |
| __Northern Shrike* | U | U | U | U | |
| __Brown Shrike | | | AC | | |
| __European Starling | R | AC | R | R | |
| __Warbling Vireo | CA | AC | | | |
| __Red-eyed Vireo | | AC | | | |
| __Orange-crowned Warbler* | A | A | A | | |
| __Yellow Warbler* | U | U | U | | |
| __Yellow-rumped Warbler* | A | A | A | CA | |
| __Townsend's Warbler* | U | U | U | | |
| __Blackpoll Warbler* | U | U | U | | |
| __Northern Waterthrush* | U | U | U | | |
| __MacGillivray's Warbler | | | | AC | |
| __Wilson's Warbler* | C | C | C | | |
| __American Tree Sparrow* | U | R | U | R | |
| __Chipping Sparrow | AC | CA | | | |
| __Savannah Sparrow* | A | A | A | | |
| __Fox Sparrow* | C | C | C | CA | |
| __Song Sparrow* | | U | U | U | |
| __Lincoln's Sparrow* | C | C | U | | |
| __Swamp Sparrow | | AC | | | |
| __Golden-crowned Sparrow* | C | C | C | CA | |
| __White-crowned Sparrow* | A | A | A | R | |
| __Dark-eyed Junco* | A | A | A | U | |
| __Lapland Longspur* | A | | U | | |
| __Snow Bunting* | U | U | U | R | |
| __Red-winged Blackbird* | R | R | R | | |

256 APPENDIX A

| SPECIES | OCCURRENCE | | | | COMMENTS |
|---|---|---|---|---|---|
| | SP | S | F | W | |
| _Yellow-headed Blackbird | | AC | | | |
| _Rusty Blackbird* | C | C | C | R | |
| _Brown-headed Cowbird | | R | R | | |
| _Brambling | | | AC | AC | |
| _Rosy Finch* | | U | | CA | |
| _Pine Grosbeak* | U | U | U | U | |
| _White-winged Crossbill* | U | U | U | U | |
| _Common Redpoll* | C | C | C | A | |
| _Hoary Redpoll | R | | | R | |
| _Pine Siskin* | U | U | U | U | |
| _Eurasian Bullfinch | | | | AC | |

**LEGEND**

**A  Abundant:** species occurs repeatedly in proper habitats, with available habitat heavily used, and/or the area regularly hosts great numbers of the species.

**C  Common:** species occurs in all or nearly all proper habitats, but some suitable areas are sparsely occuppied, or not at all; or area may host large numbers.

**U  Uncommon:** species occurs regularly, but utilizes part of suitable habitat, or is found in small numbers; not observed regularly even in preferred habitat.

**R  Rare:** species occurs in region, but in very small numbers.

**CA  Casual:** species has been recorded only a few times; irregular observations over the years.

**AC  Accidental:** species far from normal range; usually occurs singly; further observations unlikely.

**SP  Spring:** 1 March to 15 June
**S  Summer:** 16 June to 15 August
**F  Fall:** 16 August to 30 November
**W  Winter:** 1 December to 28 February

* Breeder

Checklist courtesy of the Anchorage Audubon Society, Inc.

# 258 INDEX OF SCIENTIFIC NAMES